D1020770

DEFENCE AND DISSENT IN CONTEMPORARY. FRANCE

DEFENCE AND DISSENT

IN

CONTEMPORARY FRANCE

EDITED BY

JOLYON HOWORTH AND **PATRICIA CHILTON**

CROOM HELM
London & Sydney
ST. MARTINS PRESS
New York

© 1984 J. Howorth and P. Chilton
Croom Helm Ltd, Provident House, Burrell Row,
Beckenham, Kent BR3 1AT
Croom Helm Australia Pty Ltd, First Floor, 139 Kings Street,
Sydney, NSW 2001, Australia

British Library Cataloguing in Publication Data

Defence and dissent in contemporary France.
   1. Antinuclear movement−France−History
   2. France−Military policy
   I. Howorth, Jolyon II. Chilton, Patricia
   355'.0335'44   UA700

   ISBN 0-7099-1280-3

Library of Congress Cataloging in Publication Data
Main entry under title:
Defence and dissent in contemporary France.

   Bibliography: p.
   Includes index.
   1. France−Military policy−Addresses, essays,
lectures. 2. France−National security−Addresses,
essays, lectures. 3. Antinuclear movement−France−
Addresses, essays, lectures. I. Howorth, Jolyon.
II. Chilton, Patricia.
UA700.D42 1984   355'.0335'44   84-40043
ISBN 0-312-19100-6

Printed and bound in Great Britain

Contents

Contributors

Claude Bourdet has been active in French political life since the 1930s and has written extensively on French and European politics. Among other things, he has been instrumental in the founding of *Combat*, *le Nouvel Observateur*, the Parti Socialiste Unifié and, more recently, CODENE.

Philip G. Cerny is a Lecturer in Politics at the University of York.

Tony Chafer is Senior Lecturer in French Studies at Portsmouth Polytechnic.

Patricia Chilton was formerly a Lecturer in French Studies at the University of Aston in Birmingham.

Vladimir Claude Fišera is Professor of Contemporary European Studies at Portsmouth Polytechnic.

David Hanley is a Lecturer in French Studies at the University of Reading.

Jolyon Howorth is Senior Lecturer in French Studies at the University of Aston in Birmingham.

Christian Mellon is a Jesuit priest and Lecturer at the Catholic Institute in Paris. He is editor of *Alternatives non-violentes*, co-founder of the *Mouvement pour une Alternative Non-violente*, and a leading member of CODENE.

Admiral Antoine Sanguinetti has served in the French Navy since 1939. Prematurely 'retired' in 1976, he has recently been reinstated with full honours, though he continues to speak and write critically on French defence matters. He is also a member of the Socialist Party's Defence Commission.

E. P. Thompson is well known as a historian and writer. He is a founder member and principal theorist of the European Nuclear Disarmament movement, for which he has campaigned actively since 1980.

Neville Waites is a Lecturer in French Studies at the University of Reading.

The editors wish to thank Cyrrhian Macrae for her help in the typing of the manuscript.

INTRODUCTION: DEFENCE, DISSENT AND FRENCH POLITICAL CULTURE

Jolyon Howorth and Patricia Chilton

> La France fut faite à coups d'épée. Nos pères entrèrent dans l'Histoire avec le glaive de Brennus. Ce sont les armes romaines qui leur portèrent la civilisation. Grâce à la hache de Clovis, la patrie reprit conscience d'elle-même après la chute de l'Empire. La fleur de lys, symbole d'unité nationale, n'est que l'image d'un javelot à trois lances.[1]

> Charles de Gaulle, *La France et son Armée*, Paris, Plon, 1939, p.1.

With these words, de Gaulle gave expression to an aspect of popular culture which is deeply rooted in the French national psyche. In order to understand the role of military structures and defence strategy in the life of a nation, one cannot avoid an assessment of the place of the armed forces and of military tradition in that nation's historical culture. For centuries, France was the foremost military power on the continent of Europe. The French nation and the French state were, as de Gaulle put it, 'forged by the sword'. Defence issues have played a fundamental role in French history and to a very large extent her political and cultural values are deeply imbued with references to her martial past. In the pages that follow, we have used the word 'defence' to cover those structures, forces, individuals, groups and ideas which have held official sway over France's defence policy.

It is important to stress, however, that, unlike her neighbour to the east or her Mediterranean cousins to the south, France has never allowed the military to *replace* the state, has never quite subordinated civil life to military order. A solid strand of popular control ('dissent') constitutes the complementary weft to the central, statist warp of France's national fabric. This is as true in matters military and in defence policy as it is in other areas. Yet dissent does not necessarily imply antimilitarism. Where 'militarism' would be an inappropriate word to designate those features of French life we have referred to under the cover of the word 'defence', 'antimilitarism' would be an

1

inadequate one to cover the opposition to those features. Antimilitarism in its strict sense has constituted only a small part of the forces of popular control exercised upon the military. We have therefore chosen the word 'dissent' to cover the broad span of individuals, organisations, forces and ideas which have striven to question, to control or to present alternatives to the military structures or defence policies of France.

Two seemingly antagonistic constituencies, the established military structures and the popular masses, have, for two centuries, related to and reacted upon one another in a remarkably complementary fashion. Although, in general, the army has busied itself with preparing for defence, and the popular masses have concentrated on the organisation of political democracy, these roles have occasionally been reversed. On the one hand, the army leaders who most perfectly symbolise France's military traditions — Napoleon I and Charles de Gaulle — also proved to be the statesmen who bestowed upon the nation the lasting structures of her juridical, administrative and constitutional order, based, as it is, on a tense synthesis between authority/hierarchy and democracy/popular control. On the other hand, the people, the 'masses', who symbolise historically the intervention of democracy on the stage of politics, and who have kept a constant vigil over the excesses of political and military power, have, on several occasions, when the regular army proved deficient, replaced the permanent military structures and taken the defence of the fatherland into their own hands.

Defence

The military traditions of contemporary France owe as much to left-wing as to right-wing forces and actors and traditions. Long before Napoleon 'exported' the message of the Revolution as far afield as Lisbon and Moscow, the citizen masses had risen up in arms to defend the nation from foreign invasion. The *levée en masse* (1791) may not have been as enthusiastically supported or as widespread as history has hitherto been wont to claim,[2] but French popular culture is convinced (and rightly so) that the defence of *la patrie* was attributable, first and foremost, to the barefoot volunteers who drove back the Duke of Brunswick's army at Valmy.[3] Even Napoleon's 'second coming' (between Elba and Waterloo) is perceived in French popular culture as a national uprising, a cross-class crusade against foreign occupation and diplomatic humiliation.[4]

Napoleon's military exploits were, of course, co-opted by the traditional, 'right-wing' military caste as an integral part of France's glorious past, symbolised by the history of her army. That military caste remained, throughout the nineteenth and most of the twentieth century, firmly confined, not only in popular perception, but also in reality, to the officer corps which made up the permanent kernel of the French army.[5]

On the other hand, the spirit of armed resistance and military independence has been a genuine heritage of the left. The popular masses have taken up arms both to cast down unpopular monarchs (1792, 1830, 1848) and to resist foreign invasion and occupation (1791, 1871 and 1940-44). The *Republic* is intimately associated, in popular culture, with the right to bear arms: 'Only *citizens* have the right to bear arms in Paris', proclaimed the National Convention in 1793, echoed by the Paris Commune of 1871.[6] And the Third Republic (1870-1940), by making military service a national obligation for all, was merely translating into institutional form an ideology of nationhood which was also a powerful cultural force in forging national unity.

Thus, both right and left in France have their deeply-rooted military traditions and culture. The dichotomy between these traditions was most poignantly emphasised between 1940 and 1945. On the one hand, there was the permanent army, represented in its outmoded, traditional and most introverted values by Marshal Pétain, and in its modernistic, innovative and expansive values by General de Gaulle. On the other hand, the Resistance, symbolising and perpetuating the eternal left-wing traditions of the armed citizenry. Both the latter forces participated in the Liberation of France and both have since laid claim to the fruits of national recovery which are today most powerfully symbolised by the nuclear strike force.

To some extent, of course, these historical developments can be explained by the fact that each nation has the history of its geography. Britain, as an island, has never had to face the internal political problems posed by the existence of a powerful land army. France, on the other hand, with its exposed position at the extremity of the European land mass, situated as it is at the crossroads of several expansive and aggressive national units (British, German, Italian, Spanish) has long been obliged to keep a steady eye to its land defences. This permanent anxiety over defence explains the omnipresence of warriors in French politics.

One does not have to go back to Vercingetorix or Charlemagne, to Joan of Arc or even Louis XIV. Never has the role of the military been so great as in the two centuries since Napoleon Bonaparte stepped in, in 1799, to impose order on a Revolution which had begun to lose its way. Every single regime since Napoleon has fallen victim to armed struggle. The most durable regime, the Third Republic, began life as it was to end it: with German soldiers parading on the Champs Elysées. Its first head of state was a marshal (MacMahon): its last head of state was another (Pétain).

The ill-fated Fourth Republic (1944-58) also began life as it was to end it: with a General at the helm. Ironically, between de Gaulle's two short spells of office, the Fourth Republic's civil and political leaders were to blunder from one disastrous war to another, wars they knew neither how to wage, nor (still less) to win. Indochina (1946-54) and Algeria (1954-58) were the cancer of the regime, a military running sore, which eventually proved terminal. It was rebellious soldiers in Algiers who sparked the crisis leading to the Republic's demise. It was another soldier who laid the old one to rest and gave birth to the new.

What is the significance of this constant intervention of the military in the political arena? The warrior chief has come to symbolise, in France, more than any other single force, the unity and continuity of the nation. Since the Revolution, the ideological dimension of political debate has always rendered compromise problematic, and occasionally impossible. The violence which has accompanied the polarised confrontation between the opposing forces either within the 'political class' or within the nation at large has periodically subjected the political institutions to an intolerable strain. At moments when the political process itself has seized up under these pressures and the nation has faltered in its stride, the instinct has been to call forth a saviour from among the ranks of the military, thus symbolising the eternity of the nation over the ephemerality of politics.

Perhaps it has been the strength of democratic mystique in France, perhaps the measured example of the first such saviour, Napoleon I, which has ensured that the trust confided in the military was never overly abused. Whenever the army has been tempted to overstep the mark of political interference (as, for example, during the Dreyfus Affair in the late nineteenth century, or during the Algerian War) the rule of law and the supremacy of the political process have not been long in reasserting themselves, even if, as was the case during the Algerian crisis, they did so in the person of yet another military saviour.

For, beyond the virulence of ideological polemic, French men and women can agree on one thing: the all-abiding value of the nation. They may have totally contradictory perceptions of what that value is (the Jacobin tradition or *le pays profond*) but, as the socialist revolutionary Louis-Auguste Blanqui wrote in 1870, when *la patrie* is in danger, there can only be one enemy.

In this way, France's exposed geographical position and the vulnerability of her political institutions, added to her long military traditions and the depth of her belief in her universal political role have, when the occasion called for it, allowed the warrior chief to epitomise national unity, the closing of ranks. The present Republic —the Fifth (1958-) — owes its very existence, its constitution and its ethos to such a warrior chief. Where politicians gave the Fourth Republic war, the warrior gave the Fifth Republic peace. In 1962 de Gaulle put an end to the Algerian War and brought silence to French arms for the first time in a quarter of a century. He also presided over the transformation of France's military identity. The French independent nuclear 'deterrent', as Philip Cerny shows, was not only the symbol of the state in the technological world of late-twentieth-century advanced capitalism; it was also to become the means whereby the old dichotomy between the permanent army and the armed citizens, between right-wing and left-wing notions of defence could be superseded. What need was there for foot-soldiers in the age of the atom? The nation whose defences had for so long relied on demo-graphic efforts (producing numbers of infantrymen) was now to gamble on demographic targeting (pointing nuclear missiles at urban centres). But with the bomb came the very real problem of how to use it, which is where geography enters the picture once again.

France, the Atlantic Alliance and Nuclear Strategy

France's traditional enemies have been her closest geographical neighbours, Britain and Germany; her traditional ally has been that other great land mass at the antipodes of the European continent, Russia. The atomic age changed all that, for not only did it usher in weapons of mass destruction, but it also coincided with a radical restructuring of the political geography of the world. No longer was the European continent torn between the rival claims of Germany and France. No longer was the rest of the world a prey to the imperialist appetites of the European powers. 1945 was the year which finally raised the curtain on the age of Soviet-American world condominium, a joint hegemony which many thinkers and writers had been predicting for over a hundred years.[7] Totally overshadowing the continent of Europe, the US and the USSR also extended their ideological rivalry to every corner of the globe. What role was there, in such a new setting, for a small nation like France?

Her administrative and geographical frontiers remained the same, but her political, economic and cultural frontiers rapidly spread in all directions. Now she was said to be part of the 'free world', an association of capitalist states which stretched from the shores of the Pacific to the banks of the Elbe, stopping abruptly before an 'Iron Curtain' rung down across Europe by the stern fortunes of war. Her traditional adversary, Germany, was divided in two, the western part becoming her closest ally. Her traditional ally, Russia, was recast, along with her former friends in eastern Europe, in the new role of mortal foe. She was asked to espouse a new cause: 'Atlanticism'.

Yet France's historical and ideological link with her new protector, the USA, had always been tenuous. The British could persuade themselves that linguistic and cultural affinities constituted the bases of a genuine 'special relationship', which allowed the old and sinking imperial power to continue to bask in the reflected sunlight of the new and buoyant one ('Greeks in the Roman Empire'). The French, however, could harbour no such illusions. Cultural affinities with the great power to the West were virtually non-existent. Political sympathies engendered during the final year of combat in the Great War had rapidly evaporated at Versailles. And during the Second World War, France had received no favoured treatment from the United States, which clearly considered her a spent force and even envisaged dismemberment as part of the post-war settlement.[8] France, in US eyes, had lost not only her place as a world power, but also her right to a seat in the great councils which carved out the pattern of the post-war world (Teheran, Yalta and Potsdam). Her economy was in no position to escape subordination to the rule of the dollar. For de Gaulle and the traditional nationalist constituency of the French right, 'Atlanticism' was a situation and an ideology to be resisted at all cost. As for the French left, the revolutionary tradition whose mantle had been assumed in 1920 by the Communist Party militated vigorously against accepting the internationalist lead of Washington and Wall Street. To the right's rejection of American political and cultural hegemony, the left added rejection of capitalist economic hegemony. There is, to this extent, no 'natural' Atlanticist constituency stemming directly from French political culture.

It was only in the 'unnatural' ideological conditions of the Cold War that Atlanticism found a substantial audience in France. As early as 1917, a section of French social-democracy, having found itself in an ideological impasse through support for the French war effort and rejection of Leninism, had looked to Woodrow Wilson as the prophet of post-imperial social-democratic moderation. In the chilly climate of 1947, they were joined by most 'centrists' in looking once again to America, as the middle ground between national liberalism and communism disappeared rapidly before their eyes. Obliged to seek justification for their status as masters of the Fourth Republic, especially in the teeth of the rival claims of Gaullists and Communists, the 'third force', already dependent on Washington for economic and military security, gradually came to accept the *ideological* message of Atlanticism.

This involved an extrapolation from and an extension of the military solidarity expressed in NATO into the political project of constructing an economic, cultural and political community extending well beyond the confines of the North Atlantic. That project was indeed drafted by NATO in a very detailed report whose findings were unanimously adopted in a little-known resolution voted by all member countries in December 1956.[9] The desire to create such a 'world liberal community' has always haunted the centrists and it underscores the defence options of the CDS referred to by David Hanley. To some extent the right-wing of the socialist family in France has also been constantly tempted by such a vision.

Given this complex geo-political background, and given the fact that it was the 'third-force' politicians who took France into NATO in 1949 in the face of opposition from left and right, the coming of the French nuclear weapon posed the very real dilemma of what to do with it.

In the mid-1950s, when the notion of developing a nuclear arsenal was first contemplated, official military circles in France tended to espouse the strategic thinking of NATO at the time. This attitude saw nuclear weapons in similar terms to conventional ones: utilisable not only for strategic bombing but also in classic and tank warfare. Very few senior officers questioned this approach. Those who did were soon to rise to prominence as the fathers of 'Gaullist' *independent* nuclear strategy. Generals Charles Ailleret and Paul Gérardot and Colonel Pierre-Marie Gallois all argued, in seminal papers published in the mid-1950s, that since there was no possible defence against nuclear missiles, the coming of the atom bomb had totally transformed the rules of the military game and provided the basis for a 'deterrence strategy' founded on 'demographic targeting' of enemy cities.[10] These early notions were the first attempts to theorise a strategy of nuclear defence for a small country like France, but there was no real effort made to elaborate on them until the early 1960s, after de Gaulle had taken the *political* decision to create a genuinely independent French nuclear arsenal and to resist the military constraints of Atlanticism.

In this sense, the development of French nuclear strategy was essentially reactive rather than *sui generis*. The catalyst was the American decision (duly adopted by NATO) to abandon the strategy of 'massive retaliation' in favour of that of 'flexible response'. Coincidentally, the year, 1962, synchronised with French disentanglement from Algeria. By then, Soviet progress in the development of thermonuclear warheads and their intercontinental delivery systems (not to mention satellite technology) had effectively put an end to US monopoly of the nuclear threat. In Washington, it was no longer judged either wise or credible to threaten the Soviet Union with nuclear holocaust if she dared move a muscle in central Europe, for the price might just be the incineration of American cities. Boston could not be offered up as a hostage to secure the peace of mind of Bonn. From that moment onwards, Europe and its defences have, at various levels of theory and practice, been 'decoupled' from the defence of the USA. The Atlantic Alliance has remained, and American supremacy has been institutionalised, but the key question of the precise role of the US in the defence of Europe has remained a grey area. It was as a reaction to this grey area that French nuclear strategy came into its own.

'Flexible response' really implied two new notions. First, that the 'nuclear umbrella' which had covered the whole of Europe since 1945, was being withdrawn. Second, that in its place had come the very real prospect of armed conflict between the superpowers on European territory. Whether that conflict remained at the level of conventional weaponry, or whether, in accordance with the theory of flexible response, it gradually escalated via tactical, 'miniaturised' nuclear exchanges to all-out nuclear war (without necessarily being extended to the 'sanctuarised' territory of the superpowers), the result for Europe would be the same: utter devastation and ruin. French nuclear theorists therefore sought to demolish at a theoretical level or to short-circuit at a tactical level the new American doctrine.

General Gallois launched a major theoretical onslaught on Robert McNamara's 'counterforce' proposals; General Noiret drew the military consequences for the French army of the new battle-fighting scenario; and General Ailleret offered a more global critique of flexible response in the specific context of the European theatre. The conclusions of all three studies were the same. Flexible response would be likely to 'completely destroy Europe over a 3,000 km stretch from the Atlantic to the Soviet frontier'. The logic of 'deterrence' led inevitably back to the original scenario of 'massive retaliation', or, in the rather more precise formulation of General Gallois, 'proportional deterrence', which allowed a small country like France to inflict on a superpower damage of an economic, industrial and 'demographic' nature so extensive that the risk would not be worth taking. This strategy has subsequently been named *'du faible au fort'*.

At the same time as Gallois, Ailleret and others were attacking the theory of flexible response, another military strategist, General André Beaufre, was attempting to 'short-circuit' its decoupling implications. Beaufre, as Neville Waites explains, saw the role of small countries like France, possessed of nuclear weapons, as being to raise the level of nuclear uncertainty by increasing the number of decision-making centres (what he called 'multilateral deterrence'). Under this scenario, should the Soviet Union 'call the NATO bluff' and discover that the American umbrella had indeed been withdrawn, the French would then threaten a nuclear attack on Moscow and/or other Soviet cities as a way of forcing the Americans back into the fray.

For a brief period, this attempt to pressurise the US —either by way of preventing them from gambling on a war in Europe, or by way of forcing them back into the nuclear defence of Europe — was taken to its logical conclusion by General Ailleret who developed the theory of *défense tous azimuts*, or 'omnidirectional targeting'. The advent of this theory coincided with de Gaulle's withdrawal, in 1966, from the integrated military structures of NATO, with his increasing overtures towards the old ally in Eastern Europe, and with his virulent denunciation of American policy in Indochina. It represents the nadir of Atlanticism in France and, for many, prefigured French withdrawal from the Atlantic Alliance itself. According to the strategy of *défense tous azimuts*, France would programme her strategic nuclear weapons for targeting anywhere in the world, not simply against the Soviet Union. Although de Gaulle himself was in favour of this notion — and indeed is said to have been its real inventor — several of his ministers regarded it as financially and/or politically non viable.

But *tous azimuts* was not to last. Formulated in 1967, it was immediately flawed in 1968 with the Soviet invasion of Czechoslovakia and dealt a fatal blow with the death in a plane crash (in suspicious circumstances which have recently been re-examined) of its foremost spokesperson, General Ailleret.[11] De Gaulle himself passed into history the following year (1969) and from that moment, French nuclear strategy began, as Antoine Sanguinetti argues, once more to align itself with that of NATO. From the moment Georges Pompidou arrived in the Elysée in 1969, plans began to materialise for the adoption, by France, of the battle-fighting, tactical nuclear weapons she had so forcefully denounced in her attacks on the doctrine of flexible response.

However, so great was the prestige and heritage of Gaullism, and so deeply-rooted were the seeds of 'anti-Atlanticism' in France, that it was necessary to devise a strategic rationale for the deployment and use of these weapons which would appear to distinguish them from similar weapons in the NATO arsenal. This was to be the task of Ailleret's successor as Chief of the General Staff, General Michel Fourquet. It was he who put his name behind the theory of the 'test of enemy intentions'. Although France still rejected utterly the battle-fighting implications of flexible response, it was clear that massive retaliation alone offered very limited options with which to respond to enemy movements in Europe (which was one reason why flexible response had been adopted in the first place). Massive retaliation alone implied all-or-nothing (*tout ou rien*), the choice between nuclear holocaust or surrender. Furthermore, this approach seemed to confine to the rubbish-heap of history the French army, the backbone of her military past. The writings of Generals Noiret and Ailleret (who were both *army* officers) had stressed that the French army should be stationed in the western part of the Federal Republic and should not be used in the first engagement between NATO and the Warsaw Pact, but should be held in reserve for 'the battle of France'. But clearly the French army on its own would stand little chance of resisting a Red Army which had just defeated the American and German divisions on the NATO front line. So the theory was devised of the 'test of intentions'. The scenario would be a victorious Soviet advance towards the Rhine. How would France respond? It would obviously be premature to launch a strategic nuclear strike on Moscow (there would, as yet, have been no engagement between France and the Soviet Union). Such a strike would almost certainly be suicidal. Therefore another option was required in order to establish whether or not the Soviets intended to actually *cross* the Rhine. That option involved firing a tactical nuclear 'ultimatum' shot (using either short-range Pluton missiles or Mirage IV bombers) behind the Soviet lines (in effect somewhere inside West Germany). Such a shot was presented as a final warning for the enemy to stop in its tracks immediately, or else risk incurring France's strategic nuclear fire. Much was to be made of the distinction between this *political* use of tactical nuclear weapons (under the personal direction of the President of the Republic) and the *military* uses of tactical weapons (at the discretion of the generals) implicit in flexible response. The former, closely tied in to the strategic arsenal, were presented as aimed at battle-*prevention* whereas the latter were clearly intended for battle-*fighting*.

However, when Valéry Giscard d'Estaing took over the Presidency in 1974, Atlanticism found its way back into the Elysée. By 1976, French nuclear strategy had become indistinguishable from that of NATO. The 'test of intentions' was discreetly dropped, and the tactical nuclear weapons were openly described as battle-fighting weapons. The prospect was now raised of the French army being moved eastwards to participate in the initial 'forward battle' in central Europe. The wheel, it seemed, had come full circle. It was at least in part because of this new development that the socialists and communists decided, in 1977, to abandon their opposition to nuclear weapons and to take up the mantle of Gaullism. Since the election of François Mitterrand in 1981, nuclear strategy has reverted, at least in its public theoretical presentation, to the original Gaullist precepts, even though, as can be seen from Patricia Chilton's account, these have long since been overtaken by technological developments. Can these now be contained?

Most of the theories of nuclear strategy which have been formulated in France these past twenty years were initially sketched out in the Army Ministry's *Centre de Prospective et d'Evaluation*. The man whose name is most closely associated with that *Centre* is General Lucien Poirier, who is widely regarded in France as a new Clausewitz. The publication, in 1982, of his *Essais de Stratégie théorique* was hailed as the major defence publishing event of the decade and the reader wishing to follow the fine print, the sophisticated nuances between the various strategies we have been rehearsing can do little better than to go direct to Poirier.[12] It should be stressed, however, that there has probably been no entirely 'innocent' nuclear strategy devised in France in the entire thirty years of reflection on these matters. Most of the theories to which the names of the then Chiefs of Staff were attached were in fact elaborated by junior officers working in the *Centre de prospective*. For the most part, they were responding to clear-cut political directives from the Elysée. At the same time, inter-service rivalry resulted in pressure-group pleading for specific weapons systems. Air-force General Gallois' penchant for aeroplanes or missiles is not unconnected with the fact that he has for many years been the principal consultant of aircraft magnate Marcel Dassault. General Noiret, who first proposed equipping the army with tactical nuclear weapons, was an army officer. It is strange to reflect that there have been no naval officers among the leading nuclear strategists: the more so in that the nuclear submarine is now universally seen as the heart of the French nuclear arsenal. To some extent, this is no doubt due to the disinterested pleading and strategic finesse of Poirier, an army general who resisted the temptation to put his own service first, and who early saw the strategic significance of submarines.

The cardinal feature of all these nuclear strategies, however, has been the emphasis placed on the political independence which the technical credibility of France's nuclear arsenal confers on her as a nation. The bomb has come to appear, in popular political culture, as one potential answer to France's perennial problems. Nuclear weapons avoid overdependence on allies, without excluding the value of alliance membership. They can be seen as a form of geographical fortification, an atomic Maginot line, which 'sanctuarises' French territory at very little cost. The weapons have always been publicly presented as 'war-preventing', and that, for a nation which has suffered constant defeats since 1815, also means 'defeat-preventing'. Taken in combination with the political powers of the Presidency under the Fifth Republic, nuclear weapons appear to solve the age-old problem of needing to bring in a military 'strong-man' to bail out the ailing political structures. For the national legitimacy once symbolised by the soldier-hero is now embodied in the political chief who holds the nuclear code.[13] Finally, perhaps most importantly of all, they allow France once again to walk the world stage with head held high and to take her seat at the awesome table of nuclear diplomacy.

Such are the perceived advantages of the French nuclear force. But each 'advantage' has an obverse side to it. Sooner or later, the paradox, even the contradiction between France's membership of NATO and her non-membership of its integrated military structure has to be resolved. It will be necessary to know whether the defence of France begins at her geographical frontiers or at her 'political' frontiers. In connection with this, the more the notion of the independent nuclear Maginot line is subject to scrutiny, the more it appears that this 'sanctuarisation' may be as fragile and irrelevant as the original Maginot line proved to be. Is it really credible that a French President would knowingly precipitate the utter incineration of every French city and the slow radioactive suffocation of her towns and villages, the eradication of two thousand years of civilisation, by pushing the button? Is it wise, indeed, to confer on one individual such awful real and symbolic power? Finally, are the political and diplomatic benefits of having a seat at the nuclear table as tangible as is often suggested? In

May 1983, President Mitterrand attended the economic summit at Williamsburg having proclaimed high and low that President Reagan's economic policies were ruining the European economies (in particular that of France) and that membership of the Alliance meant economic as well as military solidarity. He demanded a 'new Bretton Woods'. He returned from Williamsburg having accomplished nothing on the economic front, and having been pressured into signing a highly 'Atlanticist' joint communiqué on the defence of the free world. French people are increasingly asking where the 'independence' nuclear weapons are supposed to confer is to be located. If the bomb is now at the heart of French political culture, support for it is liable to undergo unpredictable and highly erratic oscillations. Dissent, as Christian Mellon, Tony Chafer and Vladimir Fišera show, is on the move again.

Dissent

It seems surprising to many observers that there should be so little dissent in France on the nuclear weapons issue. While other countries throughout the Western Alliance and beyond have, since the late 1970s, had their nuclear policies and strategies challenged at a bewildering variety of levels, from the established political parties to new and unexpected forms of direct action, from disputes among military strategists to demonstrations of widespread popular concern, the French people have unswervingly supported first a right-wing, then a left-wing government in the continuance of a nuclear deterrence policy which has fascinated the political actors in France, and apparently numbed the contestatory reflexes of the French population. Some of the reasons for this comparative lack of dissent, whether political, moral, intellectual, ideological or popular, stem from a peculiarly French perception of the bomb itself; others have more to do with the political culture of a country in which dissent on matters of defence has historically more often meant bearing arms than opposing them, and which has had little experience of successful pressure-group activity outside the sphere of armed resistance or the channels of the established political parties.

Among the established political parties, the existence of the French Communist Party (PCF) requires special mention as both a distinctive channel for, and an obstacle to dissent in many areas. The nuclear weapons issue makes an instructive case study in this regard. Communism in France is far from being a minority political force.

Though its electoral support and parliamentary representation have declined since its post-war peak (in 1981 the PCF had 44 seats and 16% of the vote, as opposed to 166 seats and 28.6% of the vote in October 1946), it is still a major political party with a solid base of popular support throughout France. Neither is it the creature of the Kremlin it is generally assumed to be in the other western democracies. The communist following is staunchly French, proud of its wartime resistance record, and relatively unconcerned by the vicissitudes of party cadres' relationships with Moscow. Nevertheless there are problems in the mediation of dissent in France which are exacerbated by the existence of such a strong national Communist Party. Christian Mellon points to the Communist Party's appropriation of dissent on the nuclear weapons issue, leading to a failure either to further the cause of disarmament or to provoke debate on the question. In the first place, it tends to marginalise the peace movement by making it unacceptable for non-communists to associate themselves with it; secondly, the party line, with its official ambiguity on nuclear weapons (see David Hanley), is too top-down and too involved in international diplomacy to allow the accurate reflection of any popular dissent; and thirdly, this structure neutralises the genuine dissent of party members or of those who avail themselves of the party's mobilisational capacity in the absence of other means of expression. Hence the dilemma of minority movements in France seeking to enlarge their constituency, but afraid that cooperation with like-minded communist militants might ultimately detract from their efforts to sustain broad-based interest.

The activities of pressure groups in modern France, while spectacular in certain instances, like the students' revolt of 1968, have been notoriously inadequate in fostering a climate of sustained and broad-based collaboration between individuals with no pretension to belong to the political class. Some American-style experiments have been conducted in consumer protection groups, residents' associations and so on, but in general these have either been short-lived, become bureaucratised, or served as springboards for local personalities to get into national politics. Interest groups when they become organised tend to split along ideological lines, establishing grounds for exclusion rather than exploring common ground. This has happened to the students both before and since the brief 1968 interlude, and is the dominant feature of trade unions and professional associations at every level. Fragmentation and party-politicisation are the pattern of French pressure-group behaviour. Those pressure groups which do function effectively are usually highly localised, like the Breton farmers or the southern winegrowers, and it is interesting to note the relative success of the Larzac campaign in this connection. The low level of participation in civic affairs, the weakness of associative life, the limitations of local government are all well-documented features of French political life in its broader sense. Particularly relevant to comparisons between nuclear disarmament movements in France and Britain is the fact that local government in France has no responsibility for civil defence, this being a matter for the *Préfecture* and the *Gendarmerie*, which makes it relatively safe from contact with the local population. Not only is the anglo-saxon concept of grass-roots politics, in which fund-raising and door-knocking confer policy-making rights, largely ignored in France, but there is a strong spirit of conformism among the political class proper, which makes it difficult for ideas which do not fit one or other of the political orthodoxies to penetrate. Vladimir Fišera and Tony Chafer both illustrate the problems of expressing dissent through the traditional political structures in France.

The very nature of dissent has changed since the invention of the atomic bomb, and the image of the armed citizen opposing the state has run its course. Nevertheless, there is a distinctive history of pacifist and alternative defence traditions in France which deserves closer examination.

In the nineteenth century, dissent mainly took the form of opposition to the structures of the army. There was, until the very end of the century, no widespread opposition to defence as such. It must be remembered that 'nationalism' in France remained for the greater part of the century an ideology of the left, associated with Jacobinism and the spirit of 1792. With the coming of the Third Republic in 1870, France finally began to implement the 'egalitarian' principles of generalised conscription which her republican ideologues had been calling for ever since the standing army had been re-formed in 1815.[14]

However, towards the end of the century, a more far-reaching and systematic current of dissent came into existence. It had several discrete underlying causes and took on two quite different forms: the virulent antimilitarism of the anarcho-syndicalist labour movement (CGT); and the more studied proposals of the nascent Socialist Party for reconciliation of the army and the nation. In the short run, the weakness of these two movements was manifest. The CGT's critique of military structures was too exclusively motivated by its vision of the army-as-strike-breaker to allow of any serious attempt to rethink the general question of national defence. Furthermore, the French workers, culturally saturated since defeat in 1871 with nationalist propaganda in favour of *la revanche*, were unable to move beyond a purely theoretical belief in internationalism. As for the Socialist Party, it was torn between its perceived role as the custodian of Jacobin nationalism and its new, theoretical role as the French branch of international socialism. The minority, professing revolutionary internationalism, considered national defence to be as irrelevant as antimilitarist activity. The majority, under Jaurès, extolling the cultural value of the nation, advocated the merits of a restructured army of citizens' militias, incapable of attack and invincible in defence.

War came before any of these theories could move beyond a very embryonic stage. August 1914 saw an immediate and quasi-total closing of ranks around the national war effort. It was not until 1917, with widespread mutinies in the trenches and the success of Leninism in Russia, that dissent once again came into its own, albeit with a completely different configuration of forces and actors. It was towards the infant Communist Party that the majority of those who, prior to 1914, had voiced the syndicalist form of dissent were attracted. Under the watchful eye of the Third International, their instinctive refusal was given its badly-needed theoretical base. The anti-strike activities of the army were linked to the class dimension of its foreign, imperialist activities. Proletarian internationalism was placed at the heart of a campaign to undermine the strength and credibility of the existing structures of national defence. At the same time, the element of 'pure' pacifism in the old syndicalist dissent was eradicated in favour of a sense of the virtue and necessity of armed resistance and revolutionary warfare.

However, after 1935, when Stalin, conscious of the real threat of fascism, signed a military pact with France, this revolutionary internationalism was able to coexist with a commitment to French national defence in the perspective of an international class war against fascism. In this way, the PCF inherited and solved the pre-1914 SFIO's dilemma of how to reconcile Jacobinism with international socialism. At the same time the communists' refusal of pacifism and their rediscovery of the French nation allowed them to emerge, during World War Two, as the 'natural' focus of popular armed resistance to the Nazi occupier and his Vichyite collaborators.

The socialists, on the other hand, were quite lost in the inter-war world. 'Socialist internationalism' appeared to have been co-opted by the Comintern and ceased to have any serious ideological implications for the SFIO. Traumatised by the bloodletting of the Great War, the socialists were no longer convinced of the merits of 'national defence'; still less were they certain of the structural forms which it ought to assume. The Jaurésian vision became very much of a minority phenomenon within the party. The 'pacifist' majority, after a bitter propaganda battle in the 1920s, eventually went to a combination of pure pacifists and revolutionary internationalists. The former, represented by the party's general secretary, Paul Faure, regarded war as the ultimate evil, to be avoided at all cost. They put their entire faith in collective security through international bodies such as the League of Nations. The revolutionary internationalists espoused a class-based ideology close to that of the PCF and roundly condemned any talk of national defence under a bourgeois government. After the rise of Hitler, one wing, under Jean Zyromski, espoused the PCF attitude towards marrying internationalism with national defence, while the other wing, under Marceau Pivert, continued to reject any defence preparations at all prior to the revolution. The utter confusion which reigned among the socialists prevented them from adopting any coherent line on defence prior to 1939.[15]

Dissent on defence and military issues was thus a dominant feature of the entire French left in the inter-war years. All that was to change totally yet again with the new political geography inaugurated in 1945. The overall result of the new situation has been to marginalise and even to ghettoise dissent, while the former dissenting parties have come to be identified with the cause of defence.

The PCF found an easy solution to its ongoing dilemma of reconciling socialist internationalism with Jacobin nationalism. It simply channelled all its dissent into anti-American protest movements. While, as Christian Mellon shows, the communist dominated *Mouvement de la Paix* (MDP), born in 1948, mobilised the masses in favour of a vague, universal PEACE, and against American hegemonic or anti-Soviet tendencies, the PCF, under the Fourth Republic, generally *supported* French military policy and, under the Fifth Republic, confined its opposition to de Gaulle's *force de frappe*, an opposition which grew weaker with the years. As for the Socialist Party, it abandoned any pretence at dissent. Traumatised this time by the failure of its 1930s pacifism, acutely conscious that the world had changed, it reconnected with its previous penchant for collective security by embracing Atlanticism and NATO. After 1958, it too used the *force de frappe* as a political football only so long as it remained unable to conceive of a way of reconciling the bomb with Jaurès.

Dissent, as Claude Bourdet explains, thus passed into other hands. Essentially, it passed into the hands of those who refused the politics of superpower hegemony and military blocs. In effect, this meant the Gaullists and the 'non-aligned disarmers'. Since Gaullism was concerned solely with the re-establishment of French *grandeur*, its dissent was purely formal, opposed not to French military strategy as such, but merely to its domination by the USA. It nevertheless gradually attracted to it a majority of French men and women. The non-aligned disarmers offered a more radical and complex package, combining the rejection of superpower hegemony in favour of a 'third way' in Europe with the rejection of the nuclear society as a centralised, hierarchical, bureaucratic leviathan, and coming eventually through its concern for human rights to equate disarmament and freedom, peace and civil liberties, an equation which spoke to the problems of a divided Europe. This movement, marginalised in the French political spectrum, formed the basis of the present independent peace movement in France.

At the same time, it is true that the pacifist tradition in the strict sense of a refusal of all forms of armed conflict or defence is scarcely represented in France. Quakerism has been imported on a small scale, and conscientious objection has become bound up with a more broad-based opposition to the interference of the state in the individual's personal choices through the imposition of compulsory military service. 'Non-violent' movements, as Christian Mellon shows, have recently been instrumental in the development of an embryonic French peace movement, but the constituency of pure pacifists in France has always been extremely limited.[16]

Paradoxically, the word 'pacifist' is widely used in France to designate any group or individual concerned with arms reduction, non-nuclear defence, or a critique of present deterrence strategy, defence spending or military organisation, so that the outsider might be forgiven for assuming that pacifism played a more significant part than it does in French political life. In fact, it is universally applied as a term of abuse. Internationally, the American Freeze movement, the German Green Party and the British Campaign for Nuclear Disarmament are all dismissed as 'pacifist', while the odium attaching to the term is such that few within France would wish to claim it. The term therefore bears little relation to the aims and principles of those to whom it is applied, whether it be the efforts of a high-ranking officer like Antoine Sanguinetti to bring his military judgement to bear on the defence strategies of his government, or the long struggle of a resistance leader like Claude Bourdet to question the international alliances forced upon France through her nuclear diplomacy. It bears telling witness, however, to the obsessive fear of pacifism which pervades the French media and political discourse.

The remark by a recent observer[17] that Charles de Gaulle had 'exorcised pacifism' in France is only partly true. Its spectre still haunts the French subconscious and is closely connected with the experience of 1940. For French 'pacifism' of a certain kind is extremely strong and deep-rooted, as the still very recent and perfectly 'rational' capitulation of 1940 showed, not just at the level of a political and military class which was prepared to negotiate sovereignty in order to preserve its traditional custodial role, but also at the level of ordinary working people who walked away from their rifles and collaborated with a foreign administration, because, after all, despite their chauvinist reputation, staying alive seemed more important than national identity. Anti-pacifism may be seen as a fear the French still have of themselves, of their own rationality and sense of self-preservation in the face of such irrational behaviour as war, and in this context the nuclear deterrent is as much as anything an insurance policy against their re-committing the crime of 1940.

Yet the very concept of deterrence in France, embodied as it is in the less threatening and less aggressive term *dissuasion*, with its implications of rational argument, can be interpreted as a covert form of 'pacifism'. Though *dissuasion* and *pacifisme* are consciously opposed in current French usage, *dissuasion* has pacifist connotations which are not purely semantic, but emerge from the elaborated strategies of the military theorists themselves. The official line on France's contemporary military strength amounts to a recognition of its inadequacy to combat the superior forces of the major powers in war-fighting, whether at the level of conventional warfare, tactical nuclear warfare, or all out nuclear war. Since any trial of strength would inevitably mean defeat for France, whatever damage she succeeded in inflicting on the enemy, *dissuasion* implies the primacy of war-*avoidance* rather than a serious threat.

No clearer statement to this effect has yet been made publicly in France than the controversial attack by Michel Pinton,[18] secretary-general of ex-president Giscard d'Estaing's UDF party, on the 'pseudo-gaullism' of current nuclear policy, which exposes France's demographic targeting for the 'collective suicide' it is *if* it were ever carried out, and argues that it can therefore only be interpreted as defeatism. As it could never conceivably be in France's interest to use the deterrent, the strategy based on it would lead in any likely scenario to capitulation and 'negotiation with the enemy' before the first shot was fired. This then is the paradox. *Dissuasion* is identified with *pacifisme*, and the only use of the bomb is that it relieves the French meanwhile of the obligation to defend their country. This analysis was naturally rejected by both Gaullists and socialists, and even by the bulk of Giscardian atlanticists, but it tells us a good deal about perceptions of the bomb in France, and helps explain why the French seem so impervious to the notion that nuclear weapons might be dangerous.

The French doctrine of *dissuasion* certainly spells out more clearly than the strategic doctrines of the other nuclear powers, with their concepts of flexible response and limited nuclear war, that its aim is war-*prevention*. This is no mere afterthought, and has long been the perception of most French people. What has come to be widely perceived elsewhere as a nuclear time-bomb is still largely symbolic to the French, a powerful abstraction which ensures non-war, as well as non-defeat, rather than a weapon which might be used in conflict.

In such a climate, where pacifism is on the one hand reviled and culpabilised, and on the other hand enshrined in the country's strategic doctrine, it is difficult for a nuclear disarmament lobby to find a niche. Even the issue of bloc dissolution, raised from their different perspectives by Antoine Sanguinetti and Edward Thompson, with its traditional appeal in France, appears covered in the popular view by the very existence of French nuclear weapons. De Gaulle himself had the image of a dissenter on the international scene, by virtue of his independent nuclear stand against the superpowers. The search for independence on the world stage, and its various compromises, are charted throughout the postwar period by Neville Waites, Philip Cerny and Jolyon Howorth.

But there is another feature of the French perception of the bomb which is at least as striking as the belief in its political symbolism: a refusal to contemplate the physical facts. Claude Bourdet, Antoine Sanguinetti and Christian Mellon all offer insights into the formal and informal control of information in France. There are certainly few descriptions of real or projected effects of nuclear explosions available in print, whether in specialist literature or in the popular press. Even such accounts as are to be found in the 'peace' literature in France are more often than not technical, anaesthetised, unimaginative and difficult to make sense of, so that it is impossible not to conclude that the taboo is at least partly self-imposed.

It matches the refusal in the popular understanding of *dissuasion* theory to go beyond the non-war stage to the possible implementation of the deterrent, and the ensuing automatic devastation of French territory. There is a failure of imagination visible at all levels which has to some extent affected the credibility of the French defence posture in many quarters. It has also had serious consequences for disarmament initiatives. As long as the bomb spelled *dissuasion*, non-battle, and therefore non-defeat, then it was rational to choose nuclear defence in preference to dissent.

But that belief is increasingly being questioned, as the debate on the present French defence plan shows, and the nuclear option, even to those who accepted the gamble of the strategic deterrent, no longer seems so logical given the profusion and ambiguity of tactical nuclear weapons in current defence planning. Particularly if the myth of the independent deterrent continues to crack under the strain of super-power technological development and France is seen to be relying increasingly on NATO for the implementation of its defence policy, the way will be open for the contributions of dissenting voices in matters of defence.

Two specifically French orientations for alternative defence stand out: a return to the Jaurésian notion of popular, territorial resistance; or an integrated, European, non-nuclear defence free of American control. The two are by no means contradictory. They are, with national modifications from country to country, the same as the options being studied by dissenters throughout the continent of Europe. France is perhaps at last coming home to roost.

Notes

1. 'France was forged by the sword. Our forefathers entered the stage of History through the blade of Brennus, and were civilised by the force of Roman arms. After the fall of Rome, it was Clovis's axe which gave these lands a new sense of identity. The fleur de lys, long the symbol of national unity, is but the image of a three-headed javelin.'

2. In a paper presented to the Annual Conference of the French Historical Studies Society in New York in March 1982, 'Problems of military recruitment in village society, 1792-1814', Alan Forrest convincingly demonstrated that the attempts to raise a citizen army to drive back the counter-revolutionary invaders, far from generating universal popular enthusiasm throughout France, were in fact often met with sullen refusal, active disobedience and even, on occasion, wholescale flight of all able-bodied men in a village, at the sight of the recruiting officers.

3. The battle of Valmy (20 September 1792) constituted the first ever victory in modern times of a 'citizens army' over a 'regular army'. Goethe, who watched the battle, commented: 'From this day and in this place dates a new era in the history of the world'.

4. See René Kaes, 'Mémoire historique et usage de l'histoire chez les ouvriers français', *Le Mouvement Social* 61, (1967), p.17.

5. Jacques Nobécourt, *Une Histoire politique de l'armée* (Paris, Seuil, 1967), pp.47-49.

6. On the notion that political enfranchisement necessarily involved the *right* to bear arms, see Jacques Rougerie, *Paris Libre* (Paris, Seuil, 1971), pp.88-96.

7. Louis Adolphe Thiers had noted in 1847: 'Old Europe's time has run out. There are only two peoples left. Over there, there's Russia, still barbarous but great and (Poland apart) respectable. Ageing Europe will sooner or later have to reckon with this youth, for Russia is youth. The other youth is America, an adolescent and inebriated democracy which will know no obstacle. The future of the world is there, between these two giants. They will come into conflict one day and then we shall see struggles which the past could not conceive of ...', *Cahiers de Sainte-Beuve*, 19 December 1847. Napoleon on St. Helena, Michelet, Tocqueville and many others expressed similar views at the time. See André Fontaine, *Histoire de la Guerre Froide* Vol.I, Paris, Seuil, 1983, pp.15-16.

8. Roosevelt, on one occasion during the War, suggested to Anthony Eden that a solution to the 'weak link' in the north-east of western Europe, might be the creation of a new, strong Walloon state comprising Belgium, Luxembourg, Alsace-Lorraine and a part of northern France. See A. Eden, *L'Epreuve de force* (Paris, Plon, 1965), p.298.

9. The text of the so-called 'Report of the Committee of Three' (Gaetano Martino — Italy; Halvard Lange — Norway; Lester Pearson — Canada) on non-military cooperation in NATO is reproduced in full in [NATO]: *Documents Fondamentaux* (Bruxelles, 1981), pp.78-102.

10. The best general presentation of these papers, all of which were published in the *Revue de Défense Nationale*, is in Lothar Ruehl, *La Politique militaire de la Ve République* (Paris, FNSP, 1976), Chapters 9 and 10.

11. See John Saul, *Mort d'un Général* (Paris, Seuil, 1977).

12. Lucien Poirier, *Essais de Stratégie Théorique* (Paris, FEDN, 1982).

13. As anybody who studied the transfer of power from President Giscard to President Mitterrand will have observed, the symbolic moment was marked by the two men moving alone into a private room where Giscard communicated to Mitterrand the code which controls France's nuclear firepower.

14. The French army was never, in fact, a purely volunteer corps. Throughout the nineteenth century, the main form of recruitment was the *'tirage au sort'* (drawing of lots). The main burden of this fell on the peasantry, both as the most numerous social class and because a bourgeois youth who 'drew a bad number' could normally find a peasant boy to replace him on payment of a negotiable sum of money. Workers in large towns often escaped service on account of their physical condition. The average length of service was 7 years, after which, on returning to his village and discovering that both his job and his girl were now taken, the peasant soldier would often sign on again ... permanently. The republican laws of 1872, 1873 and 1875 instituted the *principle* of universal conscription, reducing the length of service to five years. But students, priests and other 'privileged' categories could easily obtain exemption. The law of 1889 abolished these exemptions and reduced the length of service to 3 years (even though most 'bourgeois' recruits managed to get away with one year). In 1905, the length of service was reduced to 2 years and exemptions made almost impossible. The period was increased to 3 years again in 1913.

15. See, on these questions, Richard Gombin, *Les Socialistes et la Guerre* (Paris,

Mouton, 1970) and Michel Bilis, *Socialistes et Pacifistes, 1933-1939* (Paris, Syros, 1979).

16. Madeleine Meyer-Spiégler: 'Antimilitarisme et refus du service militaire dans la France contemporaine'. Doctoral thesis, 2 Vols, Paris, 1969 (FNSP).

17. Jean-Marie Colombani, 'Le Pacifisme peut-il prendre en France?', *Le Monde*, 19-20 June 1983.

18. Michel Pinton, 'Une nouvelle ligne Maginot', *Le Monde*, 16 June 1983.

PART ONE

DEFENCE POLICIES IN POST-WAR FRANCE

1 DEFENCE POLICY: THE HISTORICAL CONTEXT
Neville Waites

Defence policy is a function of foreign policy which involves perceptions of hostility or cooperation in relations with other states. Political judgements in foreign policy regarding the degree of positive threat or negative obstruction are articulated with appropriate responses chosen from a power spectrum ranging from diplomatic notes to the use of military force. Defence policy is geared to providing the quantity and quality of military force that might be needed to fulfil the purposes of foreign policy. The intention here is to examine the distinctive features of French defence policies during the last hundred years in the context of foreign policy problems which have a decisive influence on the role of France within the changing world system.

From Independence to Dependence 1870-1944

The French nation was the most populous in Europe outside Russia until the mid-nineteenth century and it was often possible for French governments to issue threats or counter-threats independently in the knowledge that they were capable of mobilising a larger army than any single opposing state. Since that time the French population has been overtaken by those of many states, notably Germany, Great Britain, and the USA, so that by the nineteen-eighties France accounted for little more than one per cent of the world population. Awareness of this relative decline was heightened to a sense of extreme vulnerability by the rapid development of destructive power generated by military technology, and France oscillated in less than a century from confident independence to depressed subordination to other states.[1]

The last truly independent French action was the disastrous declaration of war on Prussia in 1870. It took fifty years and a lot of blood to recover territory lost in that war. Ever since 1870 France has had to act within an international system that exercises considerable constraining and disposing force, and consequently she has always pursued alliance politics and military cooperation in one form or another.[2] French attempts to arrest or even reverse their growing dependence on other states were most clearly exemplified by Gaullist pursuit of *grandeur* and independence, but this was part of a long tradition of national reassertion in foreign and defence policies.

Between 1870 and World War I French national reassertion took three forms. Firstly, defence policy adjusted to demographic weakness by introducing a fully effective system of universal military conscription that could be expanded to three years at a time of crisis such as 1913 or contracted to one year at a time of détente such as 1928; this system has been maintained with remarkable consistency up to the present time. Secondly *grandeur* was pursued through a vast expansion of the empire in North and West Africa and in the Far East. And this in turn helped defence policy by providing extra military conscripts from a total pool sometimes euphemistically estimated as one hundred million Frenchmen. Thirdly, a counter-threat to potential enemies was created in the form of a mutual assistance pact with tsarist Russia, reinforced by military protocols, so that France could hope to control the balance of power in continental Europe by enlisting the support of the most populous state and forcing potential opponents to face the danger of a war on two fronts. These three developments in French power enabled her to survive the battles of the Marne in 1914 and Verdun in 1916; but subsequent developments were to transform her international position, and consequently her defence policy requirements, by creating new problems that were to be of fundamental importance to French governments up to the present time.[3]

In 1917 the exit of Russia from the war as a result of revolution, and the entry of the United States of America into the war as an associated power in support of France and her allies, suddenly converted France from the pursuit of security by means of a continental alliance strategy to a role dependent on the elements of an Atlantic alliance. Although this brought military victory in 1918 the subsequent peace terms did not fully satisfy French war aims because territorial and economic interests that had corresponded with those of Russia were not shared to anything like the same extent by Britain and the United States. This change in French relationships with other powers was accentuated by the emergence at the same time of American predominance in the world economic and financial system.

France tried to adjust to the requirements of her new western orientation after World War I by appealing to principles of international law as a means to enlist British and American support for her defence of the Versailles peace settlement of 1919. The League of Nations at Geneva and the International Court of Justice at the Hague were the first experiments with international machinery to prevent disputes developing into armed conflict. France unsuccessfully tried to ensure automatic and reliable international action by proposing that the League should have an army to deal with an aggressor as defined by the terms of the 1924 Geneva Protocol. But other states were not prepared to pool their sovereignty in such a universal system of collective security, particularly in view of an American refusal to ratify the Versailles treaty or to join the League of Nations. Governments of the right in France tried to use national power to reinforce international law, but they gave fundamental priority to keeping good relations with the western powers. The military occupation of the Ruhr in 1923 was principally designed to induce Britain and the United States to find a solution to the reparations problem.[4] Moreover, French alliances with the new states of Eastern Europe were never backed up with such firm military protocols and privileged access to French financial markets as had characterised the pre-1914 alliance with Russia. By not tying themselves too closely to the east the French hoped to convince the western powers that their policy was neither expansionist nor provocative towards Germany. Governments of the left in France placed more emphasis on a defensive policy geared to international arms control in the hope that this would attract British and American backing for collective security and international arbitration of disputes. But their formula for security-arbitration-disarmament, in that order, reflected a French conception of balance of power principles that drew little sympathy from the western powers. Subsequent French military weakness, together with inadequate allied support in 1940, discredited disarmament initiatives so far as France was concerned for many years thereafter.

Faced with the constraints of the new international system, French defence policy in the inter-war period sought to overcome three basic problems with heavy investment in military technology, particularly during the years of relative economic prosperity in the late nineteen-twenties.[5] A comparable scale of investment was pursued with more success under the Fifth Republic. The first problem was demographic weakness exacerbated by heavy casualties in World War I. The second problem was that the richest industrial and agricultural regions were near the eastern frontiers and were vulnerable as German power began to revive during the nineteen-twenties. The third problem was that men and resources from metropolitan France and the empire would need to be mobilised and moved rapidly to help defend the frontiers against invasion, and it was hoped that reinforcements from western allies would arrive shortly afterwards. The proposed solution to the first two problems was to sanctuarise French territory with a system of reinforced concrete fortresses and a curtain of continuous gunfire maintained by limited manpower in complete safety. The Maginot

Line was one of the marvels of its time, yet it was never intended to guarantee security by itself. It was linked to the fortresses of Belgium who later became neutral in 1936. It provided a shield from behind which a counter-attack could be launched; but economies during the depression years left France without a counter-attacking capability and even prevented further works to extend or reinforce the Maginot Line itself. The solution to the third problem was more successful and involved building a large navy of submarines and medium-sized warships to keep open the Mediterranean supply-lines between France and North Africa. The French built a formidable navy which fulfilled this purpose until it was largely destroyed by the British in July 1940 after the Armistice. Unfortunately, the incomplete defences on the eastern frontier crumbled too soon so that French forces were outnumbered and outmanoeuvred without the large-scale support from western allies that had been hoped for.

France went into World War II with a foreign policy excessively dependent on western allies, and with a defence policy excessively dependent on the inflexible Maginot Line. These dangers had already been apparent to some perceptive Frenchmen by 1934 when Hitler had begun to accelerate German rearmament. To strengthen foreign policy Louis Barthou, prompted by Edouard Herriot, created a new bridge to the east in the form of a mutual assistance pact with the Soviet Union. But it failed to give France that degree of control over the continental balance of power achieved with the alliance with Russia in 1890, essentially because it was not made effective by military protocols, perhaps to avoid upsetting western opinion with provocative old-world alliances and perhaps to avoid upsetting French opinion by close involvement with communism. Moreover, Barthou was assassinated before the Franco-Soviet Pact was signed in 1935, and it soon became a diplomatic dead letter as his successors reverted to a purely western policy orientation. To strengthen defence policy Charles de Gaulle produced a book in 1934 arguing for the creation of a fully motorised striking force, a *force de frappe*, capable of rapid offensive action in support of allies or of counter-offensive action to resist invasion. Unfortunately, de Gaulle's call for expenditure on a highly-equipped new force came during the depths of the economic depression at a time when French governments were intent on limiting their budgets in accordance with deflationary economic policies. Having built the Maginot Line they hoped to rest on their laurels for a time rather than to contemplate building a mobile force that might even make frontier defences irrelevant. Nevertheless, some mobile tank units were built shortly before 1940, but too few and too late. The main reason why de Gaulle's book met with opposition in 1934 was his choice of title: *Vers l'armée de métier*; its emphasis on the need for highly trained professionals to man the proposed striking force was not only expensive but threatened to undermine the conscription system which was fundamental to the traditional republican consensus on defence policy. If his title had been *La Force de Frappe*, and he had fitted his ideas into a conscript system, perhaps of variable duration, then his proposals might have evoked a positive response resulting in a considerable strengthening of French military capabilities.[6]

One new venture of military importance to France that was supported energetically in the nineteen-thirties was atomic research. But the research of Frédéric Joliot-Curie had not quite reached the point where a conclusive test could have proved the possibilities of an atomic chain reaction, in spite of being given every facility by the far-sighted Minister for Armaments, Raoul Dautry, when it was disrupted by the German invasion in 1940. Some members of the French research team took their know-how to Britain and from there to Canada and the United States, thus contributing in a small way to the eventual production of an atomic bomb by 1945. But Frédéric Joliot-Curie remained in France and later joined a Communist branch of the Resistance; this led the Americans to refuse to share with post-war France the fruits of atomic research in the way they were prepared to do with the British. Thus it was that a scientist of the French left gave an impetus to atomic research yet in such circumstances that the research could only be contemplated through an independent national commitment. After the war, Joliot-Curie tried to insist that the research programme be confined to peaceful uses of atomic energy, but he was removed from his post in 1950 due to his communist affiliations, and by 1954 the research involved specifically military aims.[7]

The disastrous defeat in 1940 gave France the bitter experience of total dependence for the first time in her history. The experience took two forms. For the Vichy regime it involved over four years of military occupation and economic exploitation by Germany, and the threat that German victory in the war might result in a shrunken France stripped of her empire and her richest eastern and northern provinces. For the Free French and the Resistance it involved subservience to British and American authorities without any guarantees as to the timing of liberation or the nature and size of post-war France. In 1943 President Roosevelt seriously considered detaching northern and eastern French territory to make a new state that might be called Lotharingia; and for much of 1944 the Americans wanted to treat

France as an occupied territory rather than as a liberated ally.[8] Frenchmen therefore shared a lasting determination to recover independence to the greatest extent compatible with the need for military and economic cooperation with their allies. French troops depended on American equipment and support, and France's economy would have to be rebuilt in the context of American predominance which had been achieved by massive wartime industrial expansion and financial leadership under the 1944 Bretton Woods agreement to make the dollar a reserve currency according to a gold exchange standard. Nevertheless, the defeat of Germany gave encouragement to the aspirations of liberated France in its quest for strategic independence.

Post-World War II Problems and Policies

In the autumn of 1944, de Gaulle's provisional government saw a golden opportunity to recover some freedom from the constraints of France's western orientation imposed by the international system after 1917 by seeking to achieve control over the continental European balance of power. The Soviet Union, with the Red Army in Berlin, had achieved many of the aims pursued by tsarist Russia before 1917 and de Gaulle went to Moscow in December 1944 to sign a Franco-Russian mutual aid and assistance pact committing them to take measures to eliminate any future German threat. De Gaulle interpreted this to mean dividing up Germany in a way that would establish French control on the Rhine, while in the east the Polish border would be on the Oder-Neisse line so that any future understanding between Poland and Germany would be precluded.[9] At the same time de Gaulle sought to enlist British support for French objectives, arguing that Britain and France had common interests in a European balance of power, a guarantee of peace on the Rhine, the independence of states on the Vistula, on the Danube and in the Balkans, the continued support of peoples in the world to whom they had brought civilisation, a system of international relations not confined to Russo-American quarrels and a conception of humanity transcending the progressive mechanisation of society.[10]

The overriding difficulty for France in taking up her First World War aims again in 1944 was that she was not nearly such an attractive ally as in 1917. Stalin was contemptuous towards the French war effort and regarded her as a broken reed. The victory in the west had been won essentially by British and American efforts, and Churchill was not prepared to underwrite French objectives without American concurrence in view of Roosevelt's suspicions of de Gaulle's ambition. It is true that the British saw it as in their interest to help reconstruct France as a strong power on the continent and in the empire; Churchill succeeded with his proposal that France should participate in occupying and governing Germany and should be a member of the United Nations security council. But the crucial decisions to divide Europe into zones of influence at the Yalta conference in February 1945 were taken in the absence of France. Whatever status France was accorded as a valued client of the other powers, she was left in no doubt about her intended role as a satellite state. Tensions and challenges arising from the subsequent development of the Cold War and colonial wars were to reinforce the French satellite role in spite of efforts by Fourth Republic governments to achieve some strategic independence on the basis of economic reconstruction which in itself, however, required external support in the form of American Marshall Aid.

From one point of view, the massive involvement of the western powers in Germany provided a degree of security greater than France had ever known. And even if this generated friction with the Soviet Union, at least the front line would be well to the east of the Rhine. But any French aspiration to act as an arbiter in Europe was thwarted by the breakdown of the 1947 Moscow conference and the need to shift attention from security against Germany, which motivated the Franco-British Dunkirk treaty of 1947, to security against the Soviet Union. In 1948 France, Britain and the Benelux countries signed the Brussels treaty which was a mutual assistance pact applicable against an attack from any power; and its anti-Soviet character was underlined when it was joined by Italy and the German Federal Republic in 1954. A communist coup in Czechoslovakia in 1948 intensified the sense of danger in Western Europe and French leaders were foremost among those who pressed the Americans to join in creating an Atlantic Alliance in 1949. It lacked the automaticity of the Brussels treaty in that each signatory would respond to aggression against a fellow member by taking immediately 'such action as it judged to be necessary including the use of armed force'. This enabled the U.S. Senate to reserve the ultimate decision on the appropriate response to aggression. But European anxieties were allayed by setting up an integrated military force in the North Atlantic Treaty Organisation under an American commander. This device surmounted American constitutional problems and permitted automatic military action in practice.[11] Compared with the American commitment of 350,000 troops to Western Europe under the NATO system the French contribution was to be very slight owing to involvement in colonial wars in Indo-China and later in Algeria. Thus it was that France enjoyed greater security in NATO than for more than a century but under such conditions that she was more dependent on others to defend her than ever before. The Americans were likely to be successful in their policy of 'containment' towards the Soviet Union because at that time Washington had an atomic bomb while Moscow did not.

Battered during World War II and subordinated during the peace process, it was not surprising that in France a sense of demographic weakness and cultural vulnerability should be uppermost in the minds of the founders of the Fourth Republic. An ambitious *code de la famille* helped to stimulate population growth at home, while determined administrators and soldiers were sent overseas to restore and defend the empire as a means to resuscitate French status as a major power. But the postwar world was inimical to a reassertion of imperial ambitions. Both the United States and the Soviet Union favoured decolonisation to bring reform and modernisation, though for different reasons. Moreover, the involvement of colonial peoples in World War II had been justified by appeal to the principles of democracy, ethnic and religious equality, and self-determination. But if this led them logically to the conviction that they should be free from foreign domination, such an aspiration was rejected by de Gaulle at the Brazzaville conference in 1944 and by Fourth Republic leaders in their conception of the *Union française* which conceded ethnic equality and common citizenship but in order to promote the traditional French principle of assimilation rather than as a step towards autonomy or independence. What appeared to be improvement of a valid tradition to French minds was seen by others as a frustrating logical contradiction.

Immediately after 1945 a French expeditionary force was sent to Indo-China to restore French rule and could be justified to even the French left in terms of protecting Indo-China against Japanese and Chinese imperialism. Opposition from liberation movements, such as that led by Ho Chi Minh, was treated as conspiracy sponsored by the Chinese, the Americans or the Russians and was repressed accordingly. The onset of Cold War resulted in the communists being dismissed from government in France and the war in Indo-China being regarded as a part of the world-wide struggle against communism, particularly when the Far East was transformed by the Chinese revolution and the Korean war. This development not only justified French concentration of their military power in Indo-China but also enabled them to persuade the United States to increase financial aid to the point where they bore most of the cost of the war. This external subsidy, and the policy of using only professional troops, account to a large extent for the remarkable willingness of French people to support a distant colonial war for eight years. As for the determination of French governments, that was indicated by their proposal that the United States should bring the atomic threat into play to save French troops from the disastrous defeat at Dien Bien Phu. The American refusal played a significant part in the French decision to develop a military programme of atomic energy, though the process of decision-making spanned several years and was influenced as much by incremental actions of civil and military members of the bureaucracy as by the decisive intervention of political leaders such as Pleven, Mendès-France, Edgar Faure and Gaillard.[12]

The brief respite from colonial war won by Mendès-France with his honourable peace in Indo-China, agreed at the Geneva conference in 1954, was followed later the same year by the outbreak of war in Algeria. Geographical proximity made it possible for Frenchmen to believe that as well as fighting to contain the spread of world communism, they were also fighting to defend the political and territorial security of the Western Alliance, for Algeria was north of the Tropic of Cancer and therefore within the security line defined by NATO in 1949. Seeing the rebellion in Algeria as part of a plan for communist encirclement of western defences, France undertook a counter-revolutionary war, thereby justifying their inflexible political and military strategy at home and abroad. Moreover, Algeria was part of France, ruled from the Ministry of the Interior and sending deputies to the National Assembly just like Alsace, Brittany or other metropolitan provinces. Thus it was impossible to recognise the claims of Algerian nationalism. Left, centre and right in France agreed that the security of the nation was threatened in Algeria. Only the extreme-left Trotskyists were prepared to consider independence for Algeria during the early years of the war.[13] This high level of consensus that 'the Mediterranean and no longer the Rhine, is the axis of our security and therefore of our foreign policy', as Minister of the Interior François Mitterrand put it in 1957, helps to explain why French people could support yet another eight years of colonial war. In Algeria nearly half a million troops, including conscripts, were required by 1957. And over a quarter of the French budget was committed to the war, because this time there was no American subsidy.

American refusal to take part in the struggle to preserve colonial power in the Arab world became clear during the Suez crisis in 1956.

This involved an Anglo-French invasion of Egypt in November. The French were convinced that Egypt was supplying arms to the Algerian rebels, and it was known to the secret service that rebel documents were deposited in Cairo. Although France was able to enlist British and Israeli forces in a combined operation against Egypt, the British insisted on confining action to the Suez canal instead of entering Cairo; and when American disapproval took the form of pressure on the pound the British called a halt to the invasion before any of the objectives had been achieved and without adequate consultation with the French. This enterprise not only increased the French sense of impotent frustration with their allies; it was also the occasion when a Soviet threat to use nuclear weapons on London and Paris, although met with an American counter-threat, strengthened the French conviction that only an independent military organisation with a nuclear dimension could provide the security they needed. Now that the dynamic effects of postwar reconstruction were helping France to achieve a consistent economic growth rate of five per cent per annum, it had become possible to finance ambitious civil and military projects ranging from the Caravelle airliner to a nuclear test by 1960. These motivations and assets were to be taken up by de Gaulle from 1958.[14] The pursuit of not only security but also *grandeur* had driven Fourth Republic governments to defend the integrity of the empire at the cost of engagement in two long and unsuccessful military conflicts that had important repercussions on the character of French military organisation and its relationship with allied forces.

Defence and Military Systems Since World War II

After World War II, French armed forces were given two roles: firstly, to defend Western Europe in the context of the Atlantic Alliance, and secondly, to protect the French empire. Although theoretically these roles were originally intended to be equally important and inter-related, in practice the imperial role took priority, involving the vast majority of French troops, apart from the conscripts. They too were involved in Algeria from 1954, so that the bulk of French military resources was diverted overseas and was in no position to operate with allied forces in Europe. French governments sought to rationalise their small contribution to NATO in Europe by arguing that it would in any case be impossible to withstand a Warsaw Pact offensive for long and that the American nuclear weapons would have to be invoked. The doctrine of massive retaliation was therefore regarded as a reliable deterrent to aggression, and its effect was to allow France to divert her troops to defend the empire. During the Algerian war almost all French troops were even removed from the centre of the NATO front line in Germany.

These developments made a mockery of official military doctrine, not merely through imbalance between roles that were supposed to be of equal importance but even more because the continuing theoretical attachment to the post-1870 principle of the nation-in-arms was being undermined. In Indo-China professionals were operating independently from conscripts, and in Algeria conscripts were sent overseas for long periods of service. For French Socialists, who still paid lip-service to the ideas that Jaurès had set out in his 1911 book, *L'Armée nouvelle*, the hypocrisy and self-contradiction was particularly poignant in that whereas he had advocated training a militia for six months to defend national frontiers when mobilised from civilian life at home, socialist ministers extended conscription to eighteen months and sent men overseas to spend many months in barracks defending the *Union française*. A further irony was that if ever there had been a valid case for the profitability of the French empire, the socialists were now disproving it by making the empire a drain on the money and manpower of the metropolis.

It has been argued convincingly that the colonial wars brought France a spin-off advantage in the form of increased scope for independent action. From this point of view 'national socialists' like Max Lejeune and Robert Lacoste, who wanted to keep French influence over the Maghreb and West Africa as outlets for exports in return for oil, gas and minerals that would give tremendous impetus to the French economy, and thereby allow France to recover her former status as a world power, were essentially precursors of de Gaulle. In this sense, an important military point is that the insistence on sending troops overseas served as a pretext for Fourth Republic governments to avoid fulfilling the defence commitments in Europe sought by the Americans and to avoid the integration of French forces in NATO. By retaining direction over most of their troops they made an important affirmation of their independence, and therefore one could argue that de Gaulle's exit from the integrated military command of NATO in 1966 was largely a *de jure* clarification of a *de facto* situation created under the Fourth Republic, though of course the effects of removing allied bases and headquarters from France in 1966 were quite new.[15]

Nevertheless there were some serious military disadvantages derived from the experience of sixteen years of colonial warfare, quite apart from the failures of the actual campaigns. Firstly, military expenditure between 1945 and 1960 amounted to well over a quarter of all public spending and represented nearly eight per cent of French GNP. This illustrates the relatively high cost of using conventional forces of a largely professional character. Secondly, the military budget was very unstable and unpredictable, varying from 5.4 per cent of GNP in 1950 to 11.8 per cent in 1952 and back to 6.3 per cent in 1955. This was due to short-term variations in commitment to the Atlantic Alliance in Europe and in the scale of operations in Indo-China and Algeria. This experience of instability handicapped military planning and would have interfered intolerably with civil planning if the French budget had not been subsidised by Marshall Aid until 1954. The third disadvantage for the military was that, by minimising commitments to NATO in Europe while maximising involvement of troops in colonial wars, the Fourth Republic governments prevented the modernisation of their armed forces. While other NATO allies maintained approximate technological parity, French forces became alienated from modern technology. Their needs for colonial warfare were large numbers of men equipped with traditional conventional weapons. Rather than technical military sophistication, the men needed the varied skills of the policeman, the civil engineer, the builder and the civil servant. Rather than heavy tanks or fast jets, the weapons needed were hand guns, jeeps and helicopters. Moreover, colonial wars occupied the army while the navy and air force had more marginal roles and were therefore starved of the investment in advanced technological equipment being used by their counterparts in NATO. This was one reason why France was allocated the menial role of providing footsoldiers in NATO while more prestigious roles went to other allies, thus fomenting the kind of resentment that led France to leave the NATO command in 1966.[16] The essential point regarding the damage to French interests is that throughout the period of the Fourth Republic there was a failure to invest in advanced military technology to compensate for relative demographic weakness and especially for a scarcity of skilled labour, even to the extent that had been achieved in the nineteen-twenties. It was this failure that de Gaulle was most concerned to correct after 1958 with his programme of modernisation for the army, navy and air force.

It should be recognised that the Fourth Republic governments did invest in nuclear military technology, though this was still in the experimental stage and came too late to have any wider dynamic effects on military modernisation until the Fifth Republic. Apart from stimulus to a French nuclear programme arising from Soviet development of nuclear weapons from 1953, which was likely to increase

American reluctance to invoke their ultimate weapon on behalf of France as already seen in Indo-China in 1954, it was perhaps the French refusal to integrate their forces in Europe that proved to be decisive in their development of a nuclear weapon because it resulted in the creation of a West German army. The French proposal for a European Defence Community in 1950 was finally killed by France herself in 1954 because of fear that any gain in security from having German troops integrated in a European army would be outweighed by the disadvantage of having French troops similarly integrated. Apart from French need for a national army in the colonies, the fact that West Germany was on the front line with the Warsaw Pact would mean that any international force in Germany would be most likely to serve German interests while being beyond the control of other governments. The breakdown of the EDC plan cleared the way for allied governments to permit West Germany to rearm, but within NATO. In view of natural West German advantages over France in terms of population and industrial assets, this was an added incentive to France to acquire superiority through nuclear weapons which were forbidden to West Germany by agreement between the allied victors of World War II.

Nevertheless, Fourth Republic governments had no intention of developing an independent arsenal of nuclear weapons to rival those of the superpowers. Their ambition was limited to creating merely a 'trigger' that would bring the American deterrent into play in the event of confrontation between France and the Soviet Union. This was a credible prospect in the nineteen-fifties when the United States could strike the Soviet Union without risk of retaliation. But some French leaders were dubious about developing such a French nuclear weapon because it might reflect lack of confidence in American massive retaliation and thereby create the insecurity it was designed to overcome.[17] This fear of destabilisation in the Western Alliance due to proliferation of nuclear weapons was a major consideration in recurrent Socialist Party proposals to give up the French nuclear programme under the Fifth Republic.

De Gaulle took the opposite view, regarding as inevitable and perhaps even welcoming some destabilisation of the Western Alliance likely to occur in the late nineteen-sixties when the strategic balance would change with the Soviet capability of reaching the United States with nuclear missiles. The decline in the automaticity of American security guarantees to western Europe was reflected already in Defence Secretary McNamara's promotion of a flexible and graduated response strategy which carried the implication that part of western

Europe might be regarded as an expendable battleground. By 1970 American leaders were openly admitting that New York or Chicago would not necessarily be risked for the defence of Bonn, Paris or London. De Gaulle responded to this situation with a philosophy of independent deterrence by which any attack on France would be met with massive retaliation from the French *force de frappe*. This doctrine was developed to its logical conclusion by 1967 with the adoption of a defence strategy of *tous azimuts*, geared to creating a multi-directional defence system to counter a threat from any quarter, even from the United States. But political and economic instability in 1968 not only led to the resignation of de Gaulle the following year; it also raised doubts as to whether France had the ability to build a viable multi-directional nuclear force. Defence expenditure had been intended to increase substantially but in fact it stagnated, sinking from 4.3 per cent of GNP in 1968 to 2.9 per cent by 1975.[18] Moreover, de Gaulle's expectation that the bipolar international system would crumble, allowing NATO and the Warsaw Pact to disintegrate, was not borne out by events.

Firstly, the Brezhnev doctrine, asserting Soviet rights to control the security of fellow socialist states, was applied when Warsaw Pact forces invaded Czechoslovakia in August 1968. This demonstrated the military effectiveness of the Soviet bloc as a potential threat to western security and helped to encourage an improvement in Franco-American relations. French strategy reverted from 1968 to a specifically anti-Soviet posture in liaison with NATO. During Pompidou's presidency from 1969 to 1974 French troops in Germany even received American training in the use of battlefield tactical nuclear weapons. Economies in defence spending could be justified by adopting a role defined by 1974 in terms of engagement in battle in the framework of allied forces rather than on an independent mission. But an expansion of the military budget was undertaken in 1976, raising it from 17 per cent of government expenditure back to the 1968 level of 20 per cent by 1982. This was to pay mainly for modernisation of conventional forces for roles in Europe, Africa and the Indian Ocean in response to rearmament and increased activity in those regions by the Soviet Union and her allies. It also reflected French uncertainty about US determination and capability to defend allied interests after the traumatic end to the Vietnam war. For much of his presidency from 1974 to 1981 Giscard d'Estaing was deeply disturbed by the inconsistency and caprice that characterised American foreign policy, especially under President Carter.

Secondly, the bipolar international system codified by the Yalta agreements of 1945 was further reinforced in 1976 in a form that not only offended Gaullist principles but also presented a particularly alarming threat to the French left. In April that year, American doctrines defined by Sonnenfeld and Kissinger recognised Soviet rights to determine the security needs of eastern Europe while asserting corresponding American rights in western Europe which would include a refusal to allow communist participation in allied governments. It was clear that European dependence on the United States involved the danger of interference to prevent the accession to power of any movement of the left committed to a Socialist-Communist alliance. This was the very strategy adopted by the French left in 1972. The evidence of American interference in Portugal in 1974, in the Italian elections of 1975, and in securing the agreement of French, British and West German leaders at a Puerto Rico conference in January 1976 to apply financial and economic sanctions against any involvement of communists in government in Italy, could only be seen as an implicit threat to the left in France. This was perhaps one of the reasons why the communists, and then the socialists changed their policy in 1977 from opposition to support for the French nuclear force. The communist insistence, in particular, on an independent, multi-directional deterrent was intended to provide security against American as well as Soviet interference. In the event the left split over various issues and lost the 1978 legislative elections. The danger of American interference in French politics had been avoided for the time being; but it was soon to return quite unexpectedly.

The victory of Mitterrand in the 1981 presidential election was a surprise to most observers and the character of his government was uncertain until after the legislative elections in June. Presidential power, consolidated by the sweeping victory of the Socialist Party, enabled Mitterrand to bring Communists into the French government and to present the United States with a *fait accompli* that challenged directly the Kissinger doctrine. This was coupled with a further challenge on economic policy where Mitterrand chose a Keynesian approach that contradicted current American monetarist principles. American leaders warned that their relations with France could not have the same tone or content so long as communists were in the government. This reaction may well have influenced Mitterrand in his efforts to reassure Washington that he intended to remain a staunch member of the Atlantic Alliance and that he supported the 1979 NATO decision to install Cruise and Pershing missiles in western Europe (though not in France) unless the Soviet Union agreed to balanced arms reduction. He insisted, moreover, that the Russians should remove their forces from Afghanistan, refusing to meet Soviet leaders until they complied. But apart from considerations of political tactics or diplomatic reassurance, there was no doubt that Mitterrand believed firmly in balance of power approaches to international relations and perceived a Soviet advantage in the arms race that might represent a real military threat to France and her allies.[19] His hope was that the superpowers could agree to arms control, but pending such agreement his intention was clearly to encourage American rearmament to counter any possible Soviet advantage while at the same time promoting French rearmament in order to maintain a credible independent deterrent. Thus French defence policy from 1981 made them the staunchest (non-integrated) member of the Atlantic Alliance. This commitment on the part of the French government of the left enabled the NATO Council to hold its annual meeting in Paris in June 1983 for the first time since the rupture of 1966.

Mitterrand's administration increased spending on the strategic nuclear force to provide for a seventh nuclear submarine by 1995. The costs incurred would not be offset to any great extent by the decision to retain conscription for periods varying from one year to three years which delayed a move towards the idea of a six-month trained militia expounded by Jaurès. In other respects the military programme inherited from the Giscardian era was pursued with little change. But an important innovation in the 1984-1988 military *loi-programme* was the creation of a highly-equipped rapid action force capable of operating beyond French frontiers either in Europe or overseas.[20] This provided the kind of conventional *force de frappe* that de Gaulle advocated in 1934 to complement the Maginot Line, but in the nineteen-eighties it was intended to complement the *forces de dissuasion* by giving France further alternatives to the stark choice between suicide and surrender.

There are three fundamental questions still left unresolved by the Mitterrand administration. Firstly, whether the sophisticated array of weapons acquired by France on land, sea and air could be maintained and modernised at effective levels of credibility with the limited resources of a middle-sized power, however ambitious, particularly during a period of prolonged economic depression. Secondly, the continued research and development of tactical nuclear weapons such as Hades and the neutron bomb, even if the latter has not yet been given the go-ahead for production, raised the question posed most vociferously by Gaullists and communists as to whether involvement in a forward battle alongside NATO troops as part of a graduated response strategy might undermine the concept of French *sanctuari-*

sation and the deterrent effect of the strategic nuclear force. Thirdly, there was the question of what position France should take on arms control. Since Giscard d'Estaing decided in 1977 to engage in disarmament talks via the Conference on Security and Cooperation in Europe (CSCE), the French dilemma had been whether to admit the possibility of control over their conventional and nuclear weapons, thereby sacrificing independence, or to face accusations of obstructionism if superpower talks broke down over the advantage to the United States of the existence of uncontrolled allied nuclear forces such as that of France.[21] Although the original French aim had been to build a minimum deterrent force, by the 1980s the very success of their efforts had put them in the embarrassing position of having a strategic nuclear force approaching ten per cent of the Soviet level. In isolation this might not have been a cause for concern. But if added to a comparable British force, and aligned apparently to American forces, it represented a threat that Soviet negotiators insisted should be taken into account; and even West German opinion was that France and Britain should accept nuclear arms control to help promote agreement in the START negotiations at Geneva between the superpowers.

So long as a Cold War atmosphere persisted the pressure on France to sacrifice military independence was limited. But if the START talks at Geneva or the CSCE meeting in Madrid overcame their state of deadlock then France would have to translate verbal support for disarmament expressed repeatedly since 1977 into action at last. The overriding French concern was to find a way to promote détente and to avoid an arms race in which it was beyond her power to compete, while at the same time avoiding the kind of military weakness and overdependence on allies that resulted in the traumatic experience of defeat and enemy occupation in 1940.

Notes

1. For a discussion of French concern about demographic weakness see T. Zeldin, *France 1848-1945* (Oxford, Clarendon Press, 1977) vol. 2, chapter 19; Zeldin is mistaken, however, in treating this as a concern limited to the right when it was fully shared by the centre and left in France.

2. A fuller discussion of the French role in the international system can be found in N. H. Waites, 'French Foreign Policy: external influences on the quest for independence', in *The Review of International Studies*, 1983, No. 4.

3. For analysis of French policy in World War I see D. Stevenson, *French War Aims*

Against Germany 1914-1919 (Oxford University Press, 1982).

4. This interpretation is based on J. Bariéty, *Les Relations franco-allemandes après la Première Guerre Mondiale, 1918-1925* (Paris, Ed Pedone, 1977); the tremendous influence of reparations and war debts on French policy in the 1920s is discussed in D. Artaud, *La Question des dettes interalliées et la reconstruction de l'Europe 1917-1929* (Lille, Université de Lille III, 1978) 2 vols.

5. An appreciation of French attempts to solve security problems, while taking account of their failure, is in R. J. Young, *In Command of France: French Foreign Policy and Military Planning 1933-1940* (Harvard University Press, 1978).

6. An analysis of de Gaulle's thought in the context of 1930s military organisation is in R. D. Challener, *The French Theory of the Nation in Arms 1866-1939* (New York, Columbia University Press, 1955).

7. An account of French atomic research by a participant is in B. Goldschmidt, *Les Rivalités atomiques 1939-1966* (Paris, Fayard, 1967) pp. 49-56; see also W. L. Kohl, *French Nuclear Diplomacy* (Princeton University Press, 1971) pp. 16-29.

8. At the Aston University Conference on French defence policy in November 1982 Admiral Sanguinetti referred to this wartime treatment of France by the United States as an example of the dangers arising from excessive dependence on allies.

9. Further details are in A. Grosser, *The Western Alliance* (Macmillan, 1980) pp. 38-9.

10. Charles de Gaulle, *Mémoires de Guerre* (Paris, Plon, 1959) vol. 3, p. 52.

11. The important difference in the degree of automaticity between the Brussels Treaty and the Atlantic Alliance, both of which are still binding on France, was emphasised by A. Grosser in *Le Monde,* 20 November 1975; for a well-documented analysis of the development of the Atlantic Alliance see P. Mélandri, *L'Alliance atlantique* (Paris, Gallimard, 1979).

12. A good account of the development of French nuclear weapons and the influence of colonial wars on them, is in W. Mendl, *Deterrence and Persuasion* (Faber, 1970) pp. 95-109.

13. The political consensus on keeping Algeria is discussed in A. Grosser, *La IVe République et sa politique extérieure* (Paris, Colin, 1961) pp. 384-9; the lasting importance of North Africa in French cultural *rayonnement* is indicated in quite recent French school geography textbooks which include a section on North Africa as part of their analysis of France.

14. The most recent penetrating analysis of French economic growth is in J.-P. Rioux, *La France de la Quatrième République* (Paris, Seuil, 1983) vol. 2, 1952-8, pp. 167-202.

15. This is the argument of P. Buffotot, *Le Parti socialiste et la défense, ou la recherche de la fonction patriotique* (Institut de Politique Internationale et Européenne, Université de Paris X, Paris-Nanterre, 1981) pp. 7-11.

16. These criticisms are based on M. L. Martin, *Warriors to Managers: the French*

Military Establishment since 1945 (University of North Carolina Press, 1981) pp. 34-8.

17. The theory of the French 'trigger' for the American arsenal is expressed most clearly in A. Beaufre, *Introduction à la stratégie* (Paris, Colin, 1963); see also M. L. Martin, *Warriors to Managers*, p. 38, and P. Buffotot, *Le Parti socialiste et la défense*, pp. 9-11.

18. M. L. Martin, *Warriors to Managers*, p. 54.

19. At the Aston University Conference on French defence policy in November 1982 Claude Bourdet reported that Socialist Party visitors to the Elysée who were critical of French support for American nuclear policy were frequently assured by President Mitterrand that if they could see the secret service data available to him it would convince them of the reality of the Soviet threat.

20. For details of the 1984-8 military *loi-programme* see an interview with Defence Minister Charles Hernu in *Le Monde*, 22 April 1983, pp. 1 and 7.

21. This dilemma is discussed in an article by J. Klein, 'Continuité et ouverture dans la politique française en matière de désarmement', in *Politique étrangère*, 1979, No.2, pp. 213-47.

2 GAULLISM, NUCLEAR WEAPONS AND THE STATE
Philip G Cerny

When France exploded its first atomic bomb at Reganne in the Sahara Desert on 13 February 1960, it unleashed a political chain reaction the significance of which went far beyond the military utility of nuclear weaponry and an independent French deterrent. In spite of the problematic and ambiguous strategic and security value of the *Force nucléaire stratégique* (FNS), not to mention the unresolved role of the later generation of tactical nuclear weapons added to the French arsenal in the 1970s, the development of an independent nuclear capability by France had profound consequences for the organisation of the French state, for French political culture and for the wider influence of France on the world stage. These three elements have made a crucial contribution to the resolution, in the Fifth Republic, of the central problematic of French politics since the Revolution of 1789 — the emergence of a national consensus on the political 'rules of the game', the bridging of the gap between the *pays légal* and the *pays réel* in a stable advanced capitalist state.

The Ambiguities of the Independent Deterrent

France as a great power has always had problems adjusting to the conditions of the last 100 years or so in foreign and defence policy. Three disastrous German invasions between 1870 and 1940, victories in two world wars dependent upon the intervention of the United States, and a foreign policy vacillating between weakness and dependence, on the one hand, and rancorous implacability, on the other —from the *revanchisme* of the late nineteenth century, through the complexities of the interwar period, to the failure in 1946 to persuade either the United States or the Soviet Union to approve a tough and unified occupation policy in Germany — all went along with a defence policy which never quite overcame the eighteenth-century revolutionary doctrine of the 'nation-in-arms' and the doctrinaire rigidity of which in 1914 (overdependence on lightly-armed infantry) and 1940 (overdependence on fixed positional defence) left the otherwise

46

'introverted'[1] France at the mercy of more powerful and aggressive neighbours.

France had particular difficulty in the twentieth century in adapting to the changing international environment in a number of ways which highlight the links between internal political and economic conditions and foreign and defence policy. Her economy, for long, critical periods, grew rather less quickly than those of her major international competitors such as Britain, Germany, the United States and Japan, especially in the later years of the nineteenth century, when rapid industrialisation was shaping the economic infrastructure of the twentieth-century world, and between the world wars, when France's huge losses and slow recovery led to periods of stagnation and actual decline before an upturn in the later 1930s — just in time for the shattering blow of the German invasion. In a world which was rapidly coming to be dominated by an international division of labour between a developed capitalist 'core' and a comparatively underdeveloped 'periphery', France, with a highly protected domestic economy and an inefficient, mercantilist empire (which had never provided the outlet for or impetus to capitalist development in France which the British Empire had done or which its nineteenth-century foundation had envisaged) lost the relative economic strength to play a Great Power role, whether in terms of external influence or of maintaining an effective defence policy.

Also connected with this relative economic stagnation was the growing difficulty of the French state in dealing with internal social and economic crisis and change, much of which reflected wider transnational developments, from the emergence of communism and fascism as political forces to the economic and social policies necessary to deal with the Great Depression, the dislocation of the peasantry, the growth of an urban industrial working class, and changes in the tempo and content of the life of the various middle classes and 'influentials' (*notables*) upon which the fragile equilibrium of Third Republic political life depended. Closely linked with the crisis of the political economy, then, was the instability of the political state — the increasing tendency for governments to fall at critical times, and for the rigid political practices of parliamentarism to dominate the rituals of the political class. Indeed, a central symptom of this *immobilisme* was the creeping sclerosis of military organisation and doctrine, symbolised in the career through two world wars of the ageing Marshal Pétain, once the prophet of military modernisation become in 1940 the personification of defeatism and collaboration.

In this context, the foreign and defence policies of the Fourth

Republic, which were the backdrop for Gaullist policy from 1958 onwards, demonstrated both the possibilities for, and the limitations upon, any attempt to define a French role in the postwar world. De Gaulle's ambitions — as leader of the Free French and President of the Provisional Government during and immediately after the Second World War — to turn French weaknesses into strengths through national intransigence, diplomatic pragmatism and the force of character of his personal leadership floundered in 1945 and led to his resignation in January 1946. His successors were left constrained by both superior external forces and the legacies of internal political stalemate, exacerbated by two new elements in the equation — the development of the Cold War, in terms of both East-West economic and political rivalry and the hierarchical economic and political integration of both blocs, on the one hand, and the narrowed scope for internal political coalition-building, with the growing challenge of 'anti-system' opposition parties of both right and left (the Gaullists and the Communists), on the other.[2]

The desire of successive French governments to define a constructive yet independent international policy posture suffered at all levels. In terms of economic development, the Fourth Republic represented both the innovative successes of the economic planning processes set up after the war, on the one hand, and the damaging 'stop-go' policies of unstable governments, on the other. The most positive initiatives, the various proposals for European integration, were primarily the responsibility of the Christian Democratic *Mouvement Républicain Populaire* — the pivotal grouping in the governmental coalition-building process and the party which controlled the Foreign Ministry from 1947 to 1953 — and appeared partly as a panacea to counteract the growing weakness of both domestic and foreign policy-making. Fear of German economic and military revival, along with jealousy of continuing British power due to her 'special relationship' with the United States, were major elements in both the proposals for, and the internal opposition to, the European Coal and Steel Community, the abortive European Defence Community and the European Economic Community — as was the desire to transcend the weaknesses of domestic economic and social policy-making.

American protection, primarily through the North Atlantic Treaty Organisation, was sought in the name of tying American military power to European security, but the fact that France could not achieve equal status to Britain within the Alliance, along with French opposition to the growing ties between the United States and a renascent West Germany, meant that French participation in the

Alliance was ambivalent and often grudging.[3] Deep French military and economic involvement in colonial wars in, first, Indochina and, later, Algeria faced American hostility in principle — American anticolonial traditions meshing with a feeling that France was not pulling her weight in the continental defence of Western Europe — yet often support in practice, as France donned the mantle of anti-communism in Indochina following the outbreak of the Korean conflict in 1950. (However, the United States distrusted the French war effort even here and sought to replace French influence herself after the Geneva Conference of 1954.) Change, weakness and resentment flowed into a vicious circle — the old post-1870 syndrome — and nowhere was this more significant for later developments than in the dimly-perceived but inexorable French acquisition of an independent nuclear capability.[4]

A number of factors contributed to the determination of key groups and policy-makers within France to forge ahead with the nuclear programme: the easing out of the French from the wartime atomic programme by the Americans (and the British); the strict application of the McMahon Act after 1946; American suspicions of French Cold War reliability, given the importance of the French Communist Party and the fact that France's first High Commissioner for Atomic Energy was a Communist (the Fuchs spy scandal in Britain was fresh in the memory); and the election in 1952 of the Eisenhower Administration in the United States, with its 'New Look' defence policy based on massive nuclear retaliation and the comparative running down of its land forces abroad after the Korean cease-fire — a policy which also prescribed the conventional rearmament of Western Europe, including Germany, to act as the 'shield' for the American nuclear 'sword'.[5] (The 'New Look' was to provide the model for French defence policy under all governments from 1958 to the present day.) A *de facto* alliance of left-wing neutralists (who wanted to avoid the rigidity of the Cold War bloc system) and right-wing quasi-militarists (who wanted to make France great and independent again), along with both the military and civilian bureaucracies (with their respective internal-organisational emphases on weaponry and on scientific-technological development), and taking in governments, parties and factions of all hues (who wanted to strengthen the autonomy and political effectiveness of the state — and of their positions in it —both at home and abroad) implicitly applauded French progress in the nuclear field.

By 1958, all other avenues of French assertion had turned into dead ends. The humiliating withdrawal from Indochina, the escalation of an unwinnable colonial war in Algeria, the erosion of French influence within NATO and France's increasingly inferior status in the Alliance *vis-à-vis* Britain (especially after the amendments to the McMahon Act in 1954 and 1958, which included Britain in the sharing of nuclear secrets but not France), the economic revival of a West Germany indebted to the United States, and the failure of the European Defence Community (and the watering down of the supranational ideal) —all combined with the instability of governments and the difficulties in economic policy of dealing with inflation and increasing demands for protectionism (despite — or because of —the Rome Treaty) to further restrict France's freedom of action. The gap between continuing aspirations and increasing operational limitations was growing. Only the nuclear programme remained — a political, economic, technological and military panacea for French ills.

Into this ambiguous context was thrust in May 1958, as the direct result of the collapse of civilian control over the military in Algeria, that one-time political 'has-been', General Charles de Gaulle. De Gaulle's role during the Fourth Republic had been one of blaming all of France's political, economic and military weaknesses on the form of the state. His consistent line had been to stress the links between political instability, economic weaknesses, and the sort of fatal vacillation in foreign and defence policy which had led to the defeat in 1940 and the collapse of the regime in 1958.[6] He immediately set about reforming the constitution to provide greater possibilities for strong yet democratic leadership,[7] establishing a political party which would have a 'majority vocation'[8] and which would transcend the 'perpetual political effervescence'[9] of French life,[10] and inculcating a new language of foreign policy leadership and national identity focused upon a high profile foreign policy of 'grandeur'.[11] Giving unity, continuity, manipulability and salience to this project — bringing together a range of loose threads while simultaneously highlighting the global significance of the Gaullist approach — was a determination to bring nuclear weapons 'out of the closet' and make them the focal point of a reorganisation of defence policy and of the defence establishment too. Thus the increasing ambiguities over the twentieth century of the role of the French state at home and the role of France in the world came to be bound up in a crucial and blatant way with the development of an independent nuclear deterrent.

As we shall see, Gaullist policy too was not free from ambiguity at a number of levels — ambiguities which reflected both the background discussed above and the wide variety of functions which the deterrent was designed to perform. It is a measure of de Gaulle's consummate skill as a *bricoleur* of political culture that the FNS became a condensation symbol for the political stabilisation of the state, the economic and technological modernisation of French society, the maintenance of a strong and effective defence alongside an efficient and cost-conscious approach to defence expenditure, and an independent and relatively autonomous role for France on the world stage. In learning the lessons of the 'New Look' for the smaller power with limited capabilities, de Gaulle was able to establish the minimum political and military credibility necessary for the FNS to gain domestic and international (especially American, Soviet and Chinese) recognition of its potential role in conflict situations — despite early domestic opposition to the expenditure involved, reluctance within the armed forces to undergo the necessary organisational changes (especially during the process of disengagement from Algeria in 1960-1962), the shift of the United States to a new and contrasting strategic doctrine of 'flexible response' from 1962 onwards, opposition from many non-nuclear European allies including Germany, doubts about the purely military effectiveness of the FNS itself, the strong Atlanticist orientations of the French right, centre and much of the non-communist left, and the deeply-rooted pacifist traditions of other elements of the non-communist as well as the communist left. Yet by the end of his period of office in 1969, the independent nuclear deterrent had become the touchstone of consensus politics in the Fifth Republic, and it was not long before the Socialist Party took the concept and its baggage on board in the mid-1970s while in the late 1970s even the Communist Party firmly supported it. Differences of strategic and tactical emphasis have certainly come to the fore, but they are divergences *within* the consensus, reflecting ambiguities inherent in the early stages of development in the 1960s between, for example, different types of weapons system or different levels of Alliance cooperation on deployment, and not a questioning of the principle of the independent deterrent itself.

In considering the nature and impact of the Gaullist legacy, the emphasis in this chapter will be on the functions of nuclear weapons within the wider context of Gaullism and its relationship to the critical transitional phase of the consolidation of the Fifth Republic. We will focus on, firstly, the significance of the nuclear programme for the organisational and economic functioning of the state apparatus, with particular reference to the historical transition of the French state to advanced capitalism. Then we will turn to the political and ideological role of the independent deterrent for the political state, in terms of both the legitimation of the state and the political control of the state and the executive branch in particular; and finally we will look at the international role of the state, with particular attention to the role of France in the Atlantic Alliance and to the wider question of French influence and the hierarchical structure of the international system.

Nuclear Weapons and the State Apparatus

The most immediate task faced by General de Gaulle when he became Prime Minister in June 1958, and later the first President of the Fifth Republic in January 1959, was to restore a state apparatus which was not only weakened from within but also stalemated in effective policy-making. In the former case, the colonial bureaucracy and sections of the armed forces had been in clandestine and open revolt against attempts by the central authorities in Paris to even consider making concessions to colonial independence movements, especially Algeria; they had strong support from within the political institutions, even from within the Gaullist party, and it was as the direct result of an Army revolt in Algiers, abetted by the administration there, that de Gaulle was himself returned to power. Despite these pressures, he was convinced from the beginning that the crucial prerequisite of political stability and effectiveness was responsible political control of the bureaucracy and clear civilian control of the military. Nuclear weapons were to play a crucial role in that reorganisation.

In the latter case, not only had the economic planning process set up after the Second World War been declining in effectiveness, but the instability of short-term and medium-term economic policy, along with the reluctance of major sectors of French finance and industry to open themselves to international competition with the Treaty of Rome soon due to come into effect, had also raised the question of France's capability to continue the economic reconstruction and growth process begun in the late 1940s; here too, the prior opposition of de Gaulle and his supporters to European integration and to the signing of the Treaty of Rome seemed to herald an ambiguous conservatism, possibly even a return to protectionism. De Gaulle and his most important advisers, however, most notably Jacques Rueff and Georges Pompidou, had come to believe that the only road to the effective modernisation and future economic strength of France was through the combination of a state-led and state-supported policy of industrial modernisation at home and an opening of the French economy, not only to the winds of international competition, but also to the wider opportunities of European and world export markets. Here, too, nuclear weapons and, in fact, the whole military modernisation programme, like the 'New Look' in the United States in the mid-1950s, involved the identification of the defence industry as the lead sector of state capitalist intervention.[12]

The military provided the greatest threat. Whereas the Third Republic's collapse can be attributed to immediate external causes (the German invasion) aided by indirect internal causes (instability, immobilism) the Fourth was brought down by immediate internal causes (political stalemate and an army revolt) aided by indirect external causes (Third World revolutionary nationalism and the bankruptcy of French colonialism[13]). The outbreak of the Algerian Revolution in 1954 virtually coincided with the French defeat in Indochina after a long and costly war; bitter recriminations in both the army and the colonial bureaucracy seriously affected Algeria. The officer corps determined to read Mao Tse-tung and General Giap and to develop effective counter-guerrilla strategy and tactics which would prevent any further defeat. An alliance between the relatively large settler population (10 per cent of the total), the colonial bureaucracy and the army was reflected in a broad spectrum of political support in Paris; acts of insubordination under the Fourth Republic had become *faits accomplis*, with the Paris governments powerless to react; and metropolitan politicians and bureaucrats sent into the field became powerful lobbyists for *Algérie française* at home. These were the factors which brought de Gaulle himself to power after the Algiers *coup d'état* of 13 May 1958.

De Gaulle gradually evolved a multifaceted political strategy to deal with these constraints — including the purge of hardliners from the Gaullist Party (UNR), adoption of a policy of self-determination for Algeria (from September 1959), a crackdown on direct opposition through his use of intransigence to bolster presidential authority (particularly after the 'Generals' Putsch' of April 1961), a crackdown on the settler 'Secret Army' terrorists (OAS) through an irregular anti-terrorist squad (the *barbouzes*),[14] and the use of referenda to line up public opinion on the side of negotiations, including the 1962 Evian Agreements. But the key to breaking the vicious circle was the reorganisation of the army, made possible by the advent of nuclear weapons. Two other features of the wider position of the French military reinforced this process. Firstly, there were strains within the Atlantic Alliance, in which France aspired to a higher status of political consultation equivalent to that of Britain with her 'special relationship' with the United States; however, French colonial wars had made her a virtual non-participant in the military side of NATO, which was essentially limited to Europe. There was pressure from the other allies, and from some groups within the armed forces and the politicians at home, for a greater contribution to European theatre operations; given already strained finances, however, this was not entertained at a political level. Secondly, an articulate group of younger officers, associated with the early (and mainly unpublicised) stages of the nuclear development programme from 1952 onwards — most notably Colonel Charles Ailleret — had begun to develop a powerful lobby for nuclear weapons, a lobby which benefited from inter-service rivalry (with a greater role for the Air Force, as was characteristic also of American defence reorganisation in the late 1940s and 1950s) and which was aligned with the developing although publicly muted political-bureaucratic consensus on nuclear policy in 1954-1958.

The reorganisation of the armed forces involved a complex political and bureaucratic process along all of these lines, eventually converging in 1961-1962. Chronologically the first step was the attempt to convince the Americans and British to reorganise NATO. After a vain meeting with the Secretary of State John Foster Dulles in July 1958 in which he sought exemption for France from the restrictions of the McMahon Act, de Gaulle sent a memorandum to Eisenhower and the British Prime Minister, Macmillan, in September 1958, containing specific reorganisation proposals — mainly for the establishment of a formal three-power political consultation mechanism for the determination of the Alliance's overall political and military strategy, and formal extension of the Alliance's political strategy to cover situations outside Europe where the vital interests of allies were at stake. This therefore involved the recognition of France as a world power with global interests, the formal recognition of a hierarchy *within* the Alliance on the basis of nuclear (or, in France's case, potential nuclear) capability, and the broadening of the Alliance itself to include a wider form of political cooperation rather than limiting it to military matters. Thus de Gaulle was offering the United States greater French participation in the Alliance in Europe on a nuclear basis in return for greater political influence on a world-wide scale. The outright rejection of the memorandum determined him to go it alone and to reorient military policy along independent lines.

The second element was the taming and disengagement of the Algerian-based army, its return to France and its internal reorganisation. After de Gaulle's accession to power, temporary concessions had been made to the army; its strength in Algeria had been further increased and its counter-insurgency operation had been stepped up (including the use of search-and-destroy missions, torture, etc., which, when publicised in France, fed a growing student-based anti-war movement) to the point where its leaders believed by 1960 that they could win the war, albeit with a few new modifications such as raids on supply bases in Tunisia. But during the same period the foundations were being laid for profound changes. Measures begun as early as January 1959 effectively reduced military influence on the higher levels of defence policy and centralised decision-making power in the hands of de Gaulle and his subordinates, increasing political control not only over policy but also over the operational command structure, culminating in the reorganisation of July 1962 and the setting up of the *Secrétariat général de la défense nationale* under Air Force General Michel Fourquet. Ailleret was himself appointed Chief of the General Staff, the highest-ranking military officer, in April 1962 (at the same time that the Evian Agreements between the French Government and the Algerian National Liberation Front were ratified by a large majority in a referendum), and the nuclear delivery force was put under the direct command of the President in January 1964.[15]

At the same time, the army's Algerian role was being undermined. De Gaulle's well-known speech at the Ecole Militaire on 3 November 1959 had not only stressed the principle of a national and non-integrated defence and announced that French policy would hence-forth centre on an atomic *force de frappe* ('whether we make it ourselves or buy it'), but also stressed the need to modernise the officer corps and, more importantly, to base future defence strategy and organisation on metropolitan France. French alternation between a continental role (*vis-à-vis* Germany) and an overseas role was an old theme in French foreign policy.[16] De Gaulle's priorities became clearer as France's African colonies acceded to independence, mainly in the course of 1960, as de Gaulle pursued negotiations with the FLNA and spoke of his decision upon coming to power to follow a 'new road', which 'no longer leads to an Algeria governed by metropolitan France, but to an Algerian Algeria' which 'will have its own government, its own institutions and its own laws',[17] and as France distanced herself from NATO and the government reduced the influence of the most pro-*Algérie française* and pro-NATO senior officers (who were often the same individuals).[18] 1961 was a key year. A referendum in January on the principle of self-determination for Algeria was approved by three-quarters of the voters; the Generals' Putsch in April, led by some of the senior officers just referred to, was rapidly put down; and, after a false start in April, negotiations with the FLNA began their bumpy ride in May.

The application of Article 16 of the Constitution — full

emergency powers exercised directly by the President — from the April *coup* until September enabled de Gaulle to purge the officer corps through new military courts. Major strategic changes were announced in a speech by de Gaulle to a gathering in Strasbourg of eighty generals and admirals and two thousand other officers on 23 November, setting out the new organisation of the armed forces into the nuclear force, the mobile 'intervention forces' — originally with a limited overseas role, but primarily meant to complement nuclear forces on the ground — and the conscript-based home forces, the 'operational territorial defence'.[19] On 1 January 1962, the official *Ordre aux Armées* called on the army to wind up its activities in Algeria and prepare for a permanent return to Europe and to those 'great warrior actions that could be imposed on the nation and on its allies'.[20] The Evian Agreements were concluded in March and approved by 90 per cent of the voters in a referendum on 8 April; a referendum in Algeria on 1 July resulted in a vote for independence, duly recognised on 3 July. And, in line with the financial priority given to the nuclear force, swingeing cuts in conventional forces were imposed — 43 per cent between January 1962 and January 1967[21] — and the nuclear force developed rapidly despite attendant crises in Franco-British and Franco-American relations,[22] leading to eventual *rapprochement* after the French withdrawal from the NATO military organisation in 1966.[23] Thus the new nuclear role for the French armed forces reintegrated them into the state, removed the most serious element of potential instability in the Fifth Republic, and consolidated presidential authority.

The question of economic policy was more indirectly related to nuclear weapons, but no less significantly so. The package of devaluation and austerity measures taken in 1958 — the Pinay-Rueff plan — did not mark the limits of economic policy in the broadest sense. The aim of restructuring French capital in such a way that it would become sufficiently competitive and growth-oriented to respond to the challenges of a more open European and world economy became the task of the state itself. As we have mentioned earlier, long-term structural problems in the French economy had impeded economic growth in the first half of the twentieth century,[24] although changes begun under the Vichy Regime, the Provisional Government and the Fourth Republic[25] helped to lay the groundwork for structural adaptation and growth under the Fifth Republic.[26] But one constant in the understanding of the nature of industrial development in France is the historical role of the state; as Zysman argues, 'from the beginning, the state was an instrument of centralising power created apart from the society ... [It] often seems to reach out to capture private allies for its own purposes, and certainly in many economic affairs the initiative lies with the state.' Its strength, which had earlier been marshalled to protect and insulate the politically sensitive economy, especially under the Third Republic, lay in 'the centralisation of the state bureaucracy, its at least partial insulation from outside interference by pressure groups or parliament, and its instruments for channelling industrial investment'.[27] The Fifth Republic in the 1960s sought to harness this potential to the ambitious task of rapid modernisation of the French economy so that French capital could compete on world markets with those of Britain, Germany, Japan and even the United States.

Obviously such a task is problematic. The difficulties of large bureaucracies in operating efficiently in the marketplace are well known, and the internal rigidities of French bureaucratic culture have been closely examined.[28] Nonetheless, as Zysman argues, 'mechanisms do exist to coordinate the decisions of the highest echelons of the state bureaucracy, and if those decisions can be implemented, then the unified weight of a centralised state can be massed for particular purposes.'[29] Indeed, he writes a bit further on, 'the easiest thing to coordinate in such a centralised system is the allocation of capital, either for private investment or for public infrastructure development. This is so because such decisions do not require the reorganisation or agreement of the lower level bureaucracies.'[30] It is a matter of controversy whether the mobilisation of the state's policy resources by de Gaulle was merely the function of a desire to improve France's international power base, as many authors have argued,[31] or whether he saw France's international role primarily as a means to stabilise and strengthen the state at home,[32] but in either case the results in the economic policy field were the same. The core of the strategy lay in reorganising industrial sectors identified as critical, where two symptoms were seen to converge: they were seen to be of long-term structural significance in the world market setting, partly because of their importance to other industries necessary for international competitiveness as well as for their own market potential; and French firms were seen not only to possess a poor potential — they were too small, inefficiently structured in terms of production, unadventurously managed — but also to lack the potential investment capital to adjust. Zysman studies oil and steel, which in his view adapted well (in the conditions of the 1960s), and electronics, where he judges the state's approach to be structurally unsound, leading to failure.[33] One might add nuclear energy and armaments, among others. Scientific and technological modernisation were key elements in the strategy.[34]

The development of the French nuclear deterrent, in fact, played an important if complex and mixed role in the process of state capitalist development.[35] For example, the combination of French determination to become independent in nuclear forces, and American reluctance to assist, led to a broad French effort to become more independent of the United States not only in nuclear technology and related areas of defence technology, but in government-supported scientific research and the development of production in advanced technology sectors in general. Government aid and guarantees were channelled to private companies, not only to the armament and aircraft industries, but also into advanced sectors of the economy such as electronics, molecular chemistry, engineering and nuclear research.[36] As Gilpin points out in his study, 'nearly 80 per cent of the total French R and D effort is being devoted to four industrial sectors — aeronautics, energy, electronics and chemicals'. Of these funds, 89 per cent went to aerospace industries (which were 73 per cent state-financed), nuclear energy (81 per cent state-financed) and electronics (36.5 per cent state-financed). In fact, ten firms received three-quarters of state funds to the 'competitive sector' despite weaknesses in these fields.[37] The French government had not failed to notice the fact that, as Kolodziej points out, 'three quarters of the research and development effort in the United States, both public and private, was financed by the federal government ... The most capitalistic nation in the world, concluded the French, rested on a socialised science.'[38]

Of course, such arguments were not new. Analyses of the development of nuclear capacity in the Fourth Republic had asserted the interlocking nature of industrial and military development.[39] But according to Gilpin, the Fifth Republic developed a more coordinated approach:

> The budget envelope, the programmes of concerted action, and the *conjoncture scientifique* of the CNRS [the National Centre for Scientific Research] were innovations intended to expand and channel the national scientific effort along more socially 'productive' lines. Of greatest long-term significance, however, has been the attempt of the Fifth Republic to utilise scientific research in the pursuit of its two major but interrelated political goals: the social and economic modernisation of France; and the development of capabilities in advanced military weaponry (especially nuclear weapons) and space technology.[40]

The results of French programmes were never spectacular, and, particularly in the weapons field, much time was lost in duplicating developments already at a highly advanced level in the United States but unavailable to the French for political reasons (although American cooperation was not totally non-existent and what there was of it was very useful in the early years).[41] Similar comments can be made over the space programme.[42] The economic effectiveness 'spill-over' from military to industrial uses of the results of research and development has been questioned,[43] although the history of the integrated circuit in the United States provides an interesting example. The economic cost of the programme has been criticised as channelling resources away from domestically significant sectors,[44] although French and German military spending overall did not significantly differ in terms of proportions of their respective GNPs.[45] Nonetheless, the 5- to 8-year technology gap with the USA which was estimated for 1959 was halved by 1963 in so far as the missile programme was concerned.[46] But costs mounted, and the technological development needed for real credibility was slow, despite the fact that on average over a quarter of the entire defence budget went into nuclear weapons in 1965-1971, and about half of French spending on heavy military equipment went on the nuclear programme.[47]

The internal impact, however, was not negligible. One benefit was symbolic. Gilpin stresses the significance of the psychological impact of the French military and space programmes, which represent the French commitment 'to become a modern scientific-technological society'. As had already happened in America, these goals, 'by making great demands on French managerial and technical skills', lead to efforts which force 'society to set a higher standard of performance and expectations for itself'. The ambitious and prestigious nature of the programmes 'have indeed undermined the psychology of dependence on American science and technology which had dominated French thinking for the past several decades'.[48] The social and economic impact of the linked programmes reinforced other changes which characterised France's postwar transition from a state of uneven and arrested socio-economic development into that of an advanced industrial society:

> More concretely, the military R and D programme
> provides reformers with a much needed lever for over-
> turning the power structure and the attitudes which have
> held back the advancement of French science and tech-
> nology for a century and a half. New organisations have

been created and new fields of study have been launched, which will increase the pace of change in French science and industry. In this connection it is instructive to note that when the accelerator was constructed at Saclay in the early postwar period, France had few theoretical or experimental physicists and many argued that it was folly for France to undertake such a project. The success of Saclay in changing the attitude of Frenchmen towards modern physics and the traditional pattern of scientific institutions is being repeated by the Directorate of Research and Testing and the National Centre for Space Studies.[49]

Direct economic results are harder to assess. Zysman points out that: 'Many industrial choices made for strictly political and strategic reasons, such as computer and aircraft policy, were costly to the government and damaging to the industry.'[50] Nonetheless, *dirigisme* exercised through military and space programmes was often as successful in terms of returns for government as the planning process which has been the focus of much greater attention.[51] And it cannot be denied that French industry, especially in technologically advanced fields, did make significant leaps forward in the 1960s. The nuclear weapons programme, then, was an important part of the state's effort to transform the French economy and to adapt it to the conditions of advanced capitalism.

Thus in terms of the modernisation of the state apparatus under the Fifth Republic, the development of the French independent deterrent became a crucial linkage mechanism for the articulation of different trends, harnessing the dynamics of military reorganisation and economic and technological change to the stabilisation and authority of the regime. As de Gaulle's Foreign Minister, Maurice Couve de Murville, has observed, nuclear weapons gave France a defence capability which was politically the most effective possible, relatively inexpensive compared with the increased firepower as well as the increased status which resulted, integrally linked with the social and economic developments which the Fifth Republic felt necessary to French progress, and a reinforcement of the national basis of political legitimacy.[52] We shall now turn to the implications of the French independent nuclear deterrent for the political consolidation of the French state both at home and abroad.

Nuclear Weapons and the Political State

The role of the state in advanced capitalist democracies is a complex and ambivalent one. On the economic front, it must maintain the dynamic of production and expansion — the profitability — of private capital, especially where national capital is ill-suited to international market conditions; thus it is pushed and pulled between systematic interventionism to attain this end (e.g. planning) and the need to adapt efficiently to wider market forces (e.g. international financial flows). On the social and administrative front, it must integrate conflicting interests and groups into a policy-making and implementation process — a trade-off of participation and compliance —especially where (as in France) both participation and compliance are historically problematic; thus a tendency towards bureaucratisation and corporatism continually needs to be balanced against the potential for grievances to erupt publicly (strikes, demonstrations, political mobilisation) if the bureaucracy is too rigid and unresponsive — particularly when 'zero-sum' economic conditions undermine 'distributive'[53] or 'positive-sum' public policies. And on the front of 'pure' politics, it must maintain the stability of the system as a whole, combining both legitimacy and effective medium-term (if not long-term) control over certain key arenas of power, whether purely-political structures (parties, parliament) or less-formal brokerage functions (tripartite government-business-labour bargaining over wage restraint, price control, industrial policy, etc.[54]); thus it is torn between electioneering and symbolic posturing, on the one hand, and decision-making and policy continuity (not necessarily congruent, of course), on the other —often reified into a 'political-business cycle'. This last feature of the advanced capitalist state is, of course, particularly problematic where the form of the state itself is a source of economic, social and political conflict.

In the Gaullist critique of the French parliamentary tradition — a critique which was not ideologically or intellectually limited to Gaullists, and which penetrated into grass-roots *anti-civisme* as well as into elite constitutional reformism (not to mention more radical anti-system opposition) —the solution to the first two of these three problem 'fronts' lay in the third. Thus the effective control of the potentially-disruptive armed forces (and the whole bureaucratic/ coercive apparatus of the state) and the modernisation of the economy (along with buying off potential protest through the welfare state and economic growth) would indeed be Pyrrhic victories if the old syndrome of governmental instability, bureaucratic *blocage* and the alienation of the masses from the *classe politique* were to lead to an eventual return to *immobilisme* and the stalemate society. Thus the overarching priority of General de Gaulle was to stabilise the state politically and to transform its structural capacity for effectively playing its role on all three fronts — taking autonomous initiatives, weighing costs and benefits and implementing effective decisions within the context of electoral competition, social bargaining and economic prosperity.[55]

The function of nuclear weapons in this process was, on the whole, more indirect than was the case in the issue-areas which we have discussed so far. Nonetheless, the development of the independent deterrent was inextricably intertwined with a range of both symbolic and tangible issues and trends in domestic and foreign policy, issues and trends which were crucial to the establishment of the stable and effective state which de Gaulle wanted. At the same time, because of these close links, the process came full circle: the successful stabilisation of the state under the Fifth Republic — and the complex intergenerational process of 'legitimation' which was initiated in its first decade[56] — has resulted in the sacralisation of the nuclear deterrent as the tangible symbol of national unity, democratic consensus, political efficacy and a significant and independent role for France on the world stage. It represents French *prouesse*,[57] the unlocking of the potential harmony of French society and culture inherent in de Gaulle's *certaine idée de la France*,[58] the creation of strength and autonomy despite the lack of material 'resource power' of the country,[59] and the focus of political life on that synthesis of French traditions, the 'Republican monarchy',[60] in which the democratic responsibility for the national interest itself resides in the office of President of the Republic and is symbolised by his finger on the nuclear button.

For de Gaulle, the original *raison d'être* of the state, and still the bottom line of its mandate from society, was defence of the territory from foreign threats. In France's case, as we have pointed out earlier, this was no hypothetical situation in the period from the late nineteenth century through the first half of the twentieth. Having written at length on military history and strategy, de Gaulle was particularly convinced that the political weaknesses of the state — and specifically the executive branch — bore the responsibility for French lack of preparedness and technical inferiority in 1870, 1914 and 1940, and, most crucially, for the decision in 1940 not to carry on the war from North Africa and instead to seek an armistice which was in effect a simple surrender. De Gaulle's political career, of course, began with his own decision to resist the armistice and to attempt to build not only the Free French forces under British tutelage but in fact an independent French government-in-exile. And his approach to constitution-building — as expressed in the Bayeux Speech in 1946 and embodied in the 1958 constitution — centred on the establishment of a strong presidency which could avoid any confusion of constitutional powers in the defence field. Only firm provision for such authority could provide, in his view, the basis for effective decision-making in other fields, because it clearly identified the executive with the national interest and imbued the presidency with both the legitimacy and the responsibility for defending that interest. [61] It is also clear that the legitimation of the Fifth Republic — which, it must be remembered, came into being as the indirect result of an illegal military *coup* — the formation of a political consensus and the foreign policy leadership of de Gaulle himself were intimately bound together.[62] There is not the space here to explore complex questions of legitimacy, ideology and culture; however, de Gaulle made it abundantly clear — and here the main text, once again, is the Ecole Militaire speech of 3 November 1959, although other symbolic instances could be cited[63] —that he regarded the link as essential.

The role of nuclear weapons was not incidental to this linkage. On the one hand, we have already pointed out the way in which public vulnerability to nuclear weapons development as a consensus-building issue already existed in the Fourth Republic, and that from a pragmatic perspective it offered a high-profile image at relatively low cost and also held the promise of reconciling the French armed forces with a new-style continental role. But de Gaulle was also a firm believer in pursuing what he saw as critical forms of technological modernisation in the defence field. In the 1930s, his one-man campaign for a highly-trained armoured strike force was in the forefront of military thinking[64] of the period, despite the fact that it had little impact on the general staff, on actual military organisation and training (although there was some progress on equipment), on strategy, or on the crucial political actors who had responsibility for defence policy. His belief in nuclear weapons was simply the contemporary analogy of the *blitzkrieg* — the imperative 'state of the art' in defence technology and strategy, and therefore the bottom line of both an effective defence (in this case, effective deterrence) and an effective independent foreign policy. In the contemporary world, moreover, nuclear weapons have taken on not merely a symbolic quality, representing real potential power, but a more dramatic quality, allowing statesmen and national actors to appear at the centre of the world stage where day-to-day events develop into complex public scenarios. Their possession was seen not only by de Gaulle but also by leaders and publics in other countries as a highly concrete symbol of the will of states to survive and to defend themselves — one which gave small countries, too, not only a greater influence than their traditional resources and capabilities might otherwise have permitted, but also the prospect of an entrée into the exclusive club of great powers.[65]

The political significance of nuclear weapons was usefully summarised in 1969 by a semi-official French study group. (1) They consecrate the French position as one of the five permanent members of the United Nations Security Council (a congruence later reinforced by the admission of the People's Republic of China). (2) They associate medium powers with the great decisions of war and peace. (3) They reinforce the important regional roles which France and Great Britain are called upon to play, leading to a more real sharing of responsibilities in the wider freedom of action; such effects are, of course, only indirect, as nuclear weapons would not be used in local affairs to support claims or interests. (4) They permit more freedom in, and give more weight to, initiatives towards the East on matters of cooperation and development. (5) However, it must be remembered that Britain and France are unique cases — with *both* global interests *and* significant regional roles — and do not reflect any universalisable rule as regards the relationship between nuclear weapons and political influence.[66] 'The effect is meant less to make France a world giant than to give her a key role in certain situations where her vital interests are involved.'[67] Thus the mere possession of such weapons was seen as having a much broader foreign policy impact almost in spite of their two main limitations, their strategic credibility and their 'non-usability'. I have dealt at some length elsewhere with the problem of the strategic and political credibility of the FNS,[68] the core of which is that the 'uncertainty' which it injects into the global and European strategic balance makes the penalties for disregarding what General Beaufre called 'the very strict rules governing the nuclear game'[69] very much greater and 'helps to re-establish in part the deterrent strength of the entire system'[70] which had grown ossified and brittle from superpower monopoly. In addition, this very uncertainty makes the recognition of *European* interests more salient and significant in the world power balance after their postwar eclipse.

Clearly, however, the wider 'diplomatic autonomy'[71] conferred by the possession of nuclear weapons had yet wider ramifications. The main direct impact was, of course, on the Atlantic Alliance and its military arm. Through the early and mid-1960s, France and the United States seemed on a collision course.[72] Even under the Eisenhower Administration, the French determination to acquire a nuclear capability had led to clashes. But American policy under the Kennedy Administration moved towards a new strategic doctrine of 'flexible response', involving a build-up at all levels, nuclear and conventional, to meet a wider variety of threats at any point on the globe — from the new Soviet capability in intercontinental missile technology of the late 1950s to national liberation movements in Latin America and South-east Asia. On the strategic nuclear level, it involved the replacement of the 'countercity' strategy of massive retaliation (a strategy adopted by the French to compensate for the small size of the FNS) with the more complex 'counterforce' strategy, which involved targeting nuclear missiles on the enemy's own nuclear forces — bringing into the equation the ever more crucial concept of a 'second-strike' capability. In the Third World, it meant the attempt to develop a 'counter-insurgency' capability, already rejected by de Gaulle both because of French experience in Indochina and Algeria and because de Gaulle believed in maintaining more flexible relationships with national-revolutionary movements, supporting, in particular, a neutralisation of South-east Asia. And in the European theatre, it meant a fine tuning of different thresholds of conventional and nuclear warfare, with escalation from one level to the next being carefully 'graduated' in order to limit and control particular conflict situations — 'crisis management' — without automatic resort to nuclear destruction. Significantly, this raised many questions about the nature of the intermediate thresholds, bringing in the critical issue of tactical or battlefield nuclear weapons to counter a Soviet invasion.

This complex and expensive American doctrine went against the emerging French strategy on a number of points: the level of the nuclear threshold, low in both the massive retaliation and French doctrines in order to deter conventional as well as nuclear attack, but higher in 'flexible response'; consequently greater emphasis by the US on the role of the European conventional 'shield', just as France was preparing to run down its colonial army; the targeting of weapons, which for the French, with a small force, meant wreaking the greatest potential social, economic and political (rather than merely military) damage through the countercity strategy, in order to deter a large force with a small force; the interlocking of American NATO forces with the US's worldwide strategy at a time when de Gaulle had been calling for greater French participation in such a strategy (through the September 1958 memorandum) but had been turned down; and, to make flexible responses militarily credible, American pressure for a greater integration of the Allied command structure in order to coordinate and fine-tune Western reaction in various set-piece 'scenarios' popular among nuclear strategists such as Henry Kissinger and Herman Kahn, just at the point when de Gaulle's entire policy was coming to revolve around the national basis of defence — the link between its legitimacy and efficacy and those of the state — and the need to reduce the level of military integration itself.[73] The specific clashes between France and the US on technology transfer, commitment of specific forces to NATO, cooperation in NATO military exercises, and the eventual withdrawal of French forces from NATO and the ejection of American forces from France in 1966, flowed from the conflict between these fundamentally opposing perspectives. De Gaulle's resolve was hardened by the October 1962 Cuban missile crisis, when US forces (and thus the key elements of the integrated NATO command structure) in Europe were put on full alert without consultation of Allies because of a crisis outside formal NATO jurisdiction — despite his political support for the American stance in the Cuban situation *per se* and his swift offer of full cooperation. The ultimate issue of French freedom, under the terms of the 1949 North Atlantic Treaty, to disagree with an American definition of a *casus belli*, became the core of the dispute, only to be resolved by the clear French measures of 1966.

But French freedom to determine its own definition of and reaction to external threat also involved differences with the United States on the broad direction in which the international system was, and should be, moving. De Gaulle's critique of bloc politics was the core of an approach in which progress towards the relaxation of Cold War tensions — *détente* — could come about only through the loosening of the two blocs themselves and the development of more, not less, freedom of action on the part of the non-superpowers on *both* sides, with tissues of cross-cutting bilateral relations at 'lower' levels restraining the superpowers themselves from both aggressive behaviour in inter-bloc relations and hegemonic behaviour in the intra-bloc relations. It involved a Europe 'from the Atlantic to the Urals' — stronger ties between Western European countries not only with the Soviet Union but also with the nations of Eastern Europe —and stronger relations too, with the Third World and China. Yet it was not a renunciation of primary alliances as such, rather a recognition not only that in a complex world different types of cross-cutting ties — diplomatic, strategic, political, economic, cultural, etc. — had a dynamic of their own and could not be forced into the rigid framework of alliance integration, but also that such overlapping ties, rather than increasing the possibilities of conflict, as the Americans believed, would in the long run reduce those possibilities by strengthening the sense of cooperation and political responsibility of individual nation-states with closer proximity to the needs and interests of their own peoples. Such a system would thus express a deeper legitimacy, linked with the legitimacy of states themselves, more closely bound up with their own societies, and consequently a greater stability, as well as a greater openness to the aspirations of Eastern European and Third World countries. This was the reflection, on the international level, of the principles which de Gaulle proclaimed for the French themselves in the Fifth Republic.

These rather abstract, symbolic aspirations were, in fact, firmly embedded in an understanding of the need for alliances and of the limits of independence in the real world.[74] Nonetheless, they found a widespread resonance not only in the world but also in French domestic politics. They came, in fact, to represent the basis for a cross-class and cross-party consensus on the legitimacy of the Fifth Republic itself. And as at the international level, where French feedom of action was symbolically condensed into her independent nuclear capability, so too at home the issue of nuclear weapons became the concrete focus of debate. Despite the fact that the Fourth Republic coalition parties had pursued an embryonic nuclear programme until 1958, it was these same parties which made the *force de frappe* the object of rhetorical attacks on de Gaulle and the subject of parliamentary motions of censure. They symbolised opposition to de Gaulle's personal power, to the running down of conventional forces, to Gaullist hegemony within the party system, to the reduced role of the National Assembly and the growing presidential supremacy of the political institutions, as well as to de Gaulle's challenge to the North Atlantic Treaty Organisation. Public opinion was always divided and unclear on the FNS itself,[75] but support for de Gaulle's foreign policy in general was strong and continuous.[76] Following the storm of the NATO withdrawal in 1966, centrist opposition to Gaullist policy eroded further, laying the basis for the emergence of a consensus on foreign policy[77] which, as we mentioned earlier, had by the late 1970s been extended to cover broad left-wing acceptance of the FNS itself. Those differences which do still exist, for example, between neo-Gaullists and Giscardians, are over the relative importance of tactical and strategic nuclear weapons and the type of cooperation envisaged with NATO implied by each.[78] Indeed, the Gaullist approach to defence policy would seem closer to the policies and style of François Mitterrand than to those of his predecesor.[79] Consensus, political leadership, constitutional authority and the legitimacy of the state itself had developed intimate links with the maintenance of the FNS, enshrining nuclear weapons in the position of a sacred cow, protected from internal dissent as well as from inclusion in the Geneva negotiations on theatre nuclear forces currently taking place.

Nuclear weapons in France have since the 1950s represented a common ground for political forces with profound divergences in other issue-areas. General de Gaulle, in his search for political stability, economic modernisation and French independence in international affairs, was able to exploit this advantage, turning the bomb into a core symbol of the change implied by the Fifth Republic. Thus it had a significance which went far beyond the military impact of the FNS itself to the whole fabric of French politics and the position of France in the world. Any progress towards nuclear disarmament in France will therefore have to reflect significant *a priori* progress towards arms reduction by both the superpowers as well as by other medium powers like Britain and China. This situation is, of course, still hypothetical.

Notes

1. On the theme of dominant 'introversionism' in the French foreign policy tradition, see Jean-Baptiste Duroselle, 'Changes in French Foreign Policy since 1945', in Stanley Hoffmann, *et al.*, *In Search of France* (Cambridge, Mass., Harvard U.P., 1963), pp. 305- 58.

2. The best source on the linkage between domestic and foreign policy in the Fourth Republic is Alfred Grosser, *La IVe République et sa politique extérieure* (Paris, Armand Colin, 1964).

3. On French alliance policy in the Fourth Republic, the best treatment is in Michael M. Harrison, *The Reluctant Ally: France and Atlantic Security* (Baltimore, Md., The Johns Hopkins U.P., 1981), pp. 6-48.

4. The standard work on French nuclear development under the Fourth Republic is Wolf Mendl, *Deterrence and Persuasion: French Nuclear Armament in the Context of National Policy, 1945-1969* (London, Faber & Faber, 1970).

5. The classic work on American defence policy in this period is Samuel P. Huntington, *The Common Defense: Strategic Programs in National Politics* (New York, Columbia U.P., 1961); cf. Michael Mandelbaum, *The Nuclear Question: The United States and Nuclear Weapons, 1946-1976* (Cambridge, Cambridge U.P., 1979), esp. pp. 41-62.

6. See Charles de Gaulle, *Vers l'Armée de métier* (Paris, Berger-Levrault, 1934) and

The Complete War Memoirs (New York, Simon and Schuster, 1967).

7. Cf. Vincent Wright, *The Government and Politics of France* (London, Hutchinson, 1978), Maurice Duverger, *La République et le régime présidentiel* (Paris, Arthème Fayard, 1961), and P.G. Cerny, *The French Presidency: The Role of the Chief Executive in the Fifth Republic*, unpublished monograph, Kenyon College, 1967.

8. Duverger's term (in French); the English translation is given as 'majority bent', in *Political Parties: Their Organization and Activity in the Modern State* (London and New York, Methuen and Wiley, 2nd edn., 1959), pp. 283-85.

9. De Gaulle's term, from the Speech at Bayeux, 16 June 1946. The definitive collection of de Gaulle's public utterances is de Gaulle, *Discours et messages,* ed. by François Goguel (Paris, Plon, 5 vols., 1970).

10. See Jean Charlot, *L'U.N.R.: Etude du pouvoir au sein d'un parti politique* (Paris, Armand Colin, 1967) and Charlot, *The Gaullist Phenomenon: The Gaullist Movement in the Fifth Republic* (London, George Allen and Unwin, 1971); cf. P.G. Cerny, 'Gaullism, Advanced Capitalism and the Fifth Republic', in D.S. Bell, ed., *Contemporary French Political Parties* (London and New York, Croom Helm and St. Martin's Press, 1982), ch.2.

11. P.G. Cerny, *The Politics of Grandeur: Ideological Aspects of de Gaulle's Foreign Policy* (Cambridge, Cambridge U.P., 1980).

12. For a treatment of the role of defence industries in the advanced capitalist state, see Seymour Melman, *The Permanent War Economy: American Capitalism in Decline* (New York, Simon and Schuster, 1974); cf. Michael Kidron, *Western Capitalism since the War* (Harmondsworth, Middx., Penguin, revised edn., 1970).

13. The *mission civilisatrice* of the settler minority led into the classic contradiction of 'assimilation' policies — that true assimilation of the indigenous minority to full social and political rights would undermine the dominance of the *colons* themselves while creating nationalist aspirations which could not be contained forever. See John Humphrey, *'Nationalism' and the Colonial Situation in Algeria under French Rule, 1830-1962*, unpublished D.Phil. dissertation, University of York, 1976.

14. See P.G. Cerny, 'France: Non-Terrorism and the Politics of Repressive Tolerance', in Juliet Lodge, ed., *Terrorism: A Challenge to the State* (Oxford and New York, Martin Robertson and St. Martin's Press, 1981), reprinted in Cerny, ed., *Social Movements and Protest in France* (London and New York, Frances Pinter and St. Martin's Press, 1982), ch. 5.

15. See Michael M. Harrison, *The Reluctant Ally: France and Atlantic Security* (Baltimore, Md., The Johns Hopkins U.P., 1981), pp. 118-20; for more detail see Bernard Chantebout, *L'Organisation de la défense nationale en France depuis la fin de la seconde guerre mondiale* (Paris, Librairie Générale de Droit et de Jurisprudence, Pichon et Durand-Auzias, 1967).

16. See Henk Wesseling, 'Constants in French Foreign Policy, 1870 - 1980', unpublished paper, Institute for Advanced Study, Princeton University, n.d..

17. Speech of 4 November 1960.

18. See Michael M. Harrison, *The Reluctant Ally: France and Atlantic Security* (Baltimore, Md, The Johns Hopkins U.P., 1981), p. 177.

19. Ibid.; also pp. 120ff.

20. Ibid., p. 116.

21. See Wilfred L. Kohl, *French Nuclear Diplomacy* (Princeton, N.J., Princeton U.P., 1971), pp. 192-200.

22. For an anti-Gaullist perspective, see John Newhouse, *De Gaulle and the Anglo-Saxons* (New York, Viking, 1970).

23. For contrasting interpretations of this rapprochement, see Michael M. Harrison, *The Reluctant Ally: France and Atlantic Security* (Baltimore, Md., The Johns Hopkins U.P., 1981) pp. 134-93, and Cerny, *Politics of Grandeur: Ideological Aspects of de Gaulle's Foreign Policy* (Cambridge, Cambridge U.P., 1980), pp. 225-44.

24. See Charles P. Kindleberger, *Economic Growth in France and Britain 1851-1950* (Cambridge, Mass., Harvard U.P., 1964), and Tom Kemp, *The French Economy 1913-1939: The History of a Decline* (London, Longman, 1972).

25. See Richard F. Kuisel, *Capitalism and the State in Modern France: Renovation and Economic Management in the Twentieth Century* (Cambridge, Cambridge U.P., 1981), chs. 5-10.

26. The classic study is J.-J. Carré, P. Dubois and E. Malinvaud, *French Economic Growth* (Stanford, Cal., Stanford U.P., 1975).

27. John Zysman, 'The French State in the International Economy', in Peter J. Katzenstein, ed., *Between Power and Plenty: Foreign Economic Policies of Advanced Industrial States* (Madison, Wisc., University of Wisconsin Press, 1978), p. 265; see also Zysman, *Political Strategies for Industrial Order: Market, State and Industry in France* (Berkeley and Los Angeles, U. of California P., 1977).

28. The classic study is Michel Crozier, *The Bureaucratic Phenomenon: An Examination of Bureaucracy in Modern Organizations and its Cultural Setting in France* (Chicago, U. of Chicago P., 1964), especially Part IV.

29. John Zysman, 'The French State in the International Economy', in Peter J. Katzentstein, ed., *Between Power and Plenty: Foreign Economic Policies of Advanced Industrial States* (Madison, Wisc., University of Wisconsin Press, 1978), p. 266.

30. Ibid., p. 267.

31. Including Zysman, ibid., pp. 274ff. Cf. Edward L. Morse, *Foreign Policy and Interdependence in Gaullist France* (Princeton, N.J., Princeton U.P., 1973); W.W. Kulski, *De Gaulle and the World: The Foreign Policy of the Fifth French Republic* (Syracuse, N.Y., Syracuse U.P., 1966); Edward A. Kolodziej, *French International Policy under de Gaulle and Pompidou* (Ithaca, N.Y., Cornell U.P., 1974); John Newhouse, *De Gaulle and the Anglo-Saxons* (New York, Viking, 1970), and various others.

32. As I have argued in *The Politics of Grandeur: Ideological Aspects of de Gaulle's*

Foreign Policy (Cambridge, Cambridge U.P., 1980). Harrison takes a nuanced intermediate position for the most part, based on a sophisticated analysis of de Gaulle's vision of the world order.

33. John Zysman, *Political Strategies for Industrial Order: Market, State and Industry in France* (Berkeley and Los Angeles, U. of California P., 1977).

34. The standard work is Robert Gilpin, *France in the Age of the Scientific State* (Princeton, N.J., Princeton U.P., 1968). He describes the interdependence of nationalism and internationalism thus: 'Contrary to the notion frequently expressed in the US and elsewhere, that French science policy is totally chauvinistic, paradoxically her policy is the most internationalist, as well as the most nationalist, science policy pursued by any European state. Though no other nation in Europe equals France, for example, in the emphasis on national efforts in space and atomic energy, the ultimate success of these undertakings is very much dependent on complementary international programmes (including Concorde, ELDO, ESRO, the International Centre for Cancer Research) ... The logic of the French position is that while international programmes can supplement national programmes they cannot replace them.' Ibid., p. 382.

35. This discussion draws heavily on *The Politics of Grandeur: Ideological Aspects of de Gaulle's Foreign Policy* (Cambridge, Cambridge U.P., 1980), pp. 198-200.

36. Edgar S. Furniss Jr., *De Gaulle and the French Army: A Crisis in Civil-Military Relations* (New York, The Twentieth Century Fund, 1964), pp. 213-16.

37. Robert Gilpin, *France in the Age of the Scientific state*, (Princeton, N.J., Princeton U.P., 1968), pp. 336-41.

38. Edward A. Kolodziej, *French International Policy under de Gaulle and Pompidou* (Ithaca, N.Y., Cornell U.P., 1974), pp. 94-5.

39. Wolf Mendl, *Deterrence and Persuasion: French Nuclear Armament in the Context of National Policy, 1945-1969* (London, Faber & Faber, 1970) p. 178.

40. Robert Gilpin, *France in the Age of the Scientific State* (Princeton, N.J., Princeton U.P., 1968) p. 217. Cf. also Marceau Long, 'L'Incidence des dépenses des Armées sur l'économie', *Revue de défense nationale*, vol. 24, no. 6 (June-July 1968), p. 987, and Maurice Schumann, 'La Politique scientifique de la France', ibid., p. 975.

41. See Judith H. Young, 'The French Strategic Missile Program', Institute for Strategic Studies, London, Adelphi Paper No. 38 (July 1967).

42. 'The French Space Programme' (London: Ambassade de France, Press and Information Service, document B/29/7/6); Général R. Aubinière, 'Réalisation et projets de la recherche spatiale française', *Revue de défense nationale*, vol. 23, no. 10 (November 1967), p. 1736; and Aubinière, 'La CNES et la politique spatiale de la France', in ibid., vol. 24, no. 10 (December 1968), p. 1791.

43. Cf. Robert Gilpin, *France in the Age of the Scientific State*, (Princeton, N.J., Princeton U.P.); Edward L. Morse, *Foreign Policy and Interdependence in Gaullist France* (Princeton, N.J., Princeton U.P., 1973) pp. 170-75; and Wilfred L. Kohl, *French Nuclear Diplomacy* (Princeton, N.J., Princeton U.P., 1971), ch. 5.

44. Edward L. Morse, *Foreign Policy and Interdependence in Gaullist France*

72 *Gaullism, Nuclear Weapons and the State*

(Princeton, N.J., Princeton U.P., 1973), ch.4, 'Welfare versus Warfare'.

45. France spent rather more on defence than West Germany in 1969, and although the absolute positions were reversed in 1970, this in fact revealed a converging trend in terms of percentages of Gross National Product: *The Military Balance 1969-1970* (London, Institute for Strategic Studies, 1970), p. 110. Zysman cites figures for 1976 (from *The Military Balance 1976-1977*) which show virtually equivalent percentages of GNP, in 'The French State', p. 277. Both of these figures were regularly significantly lower than proportions of GNP for Britain.

46. Judith H. Young, 'The French Strategic Missile Program', Institute for Strategic Studies, London, Adelphi Paper No.38 (July 1967) p. 9.

47. Edward A. Kolodziej, *French International Policy under de Gaulle and Pompidou* (Ithaca, N.Y., Cornell U.P., 1974), p. 105.

48. Robert Gilpin, *France in the Age of the Scientific State* (Princeton, N.J., Princeton U.P., 1968) pp. 299-300.

49. Ibid., pp. 300-01.

50. John Zysman, 'The French State in the International Economy' in Peter J. Katzenstein, ed., *Between Power and Plenty: Foreign Economic Policies of Advanced Industrial States* (Madison, Wisc., University of Wisconsin Press, 1978).

51. Consider the comments of Suzanne Berger, 'Lame Ducks and National Champions: Industrial Policy in the Fifth Republic', in William G. Andrews and Stanley Hoffmann, eds., *The Impact of the Fifth Republic on France* (Albany, N.Y., State University of New York Press, 1981), p. 164. Furthermore, the later progress of the French-based European space programme in competing with the United States in the commercial satellite business (although this has very recently been set back by a failure of the Ariane missile) was the direct result of these policies of the 1960s.

52. Maurice Couve de Murville, *Une politique étrangère, 1958-1969* (Paris, Plon, 1971), p. 61.

53. For the concept of 'distributive' public policy (and the contrasting notions of 'regulatory' and 'redistributive' types), see Theodore J. Lowi, 'American Business, Public Policy, Case Studies, and Political Theory', *World Politics*, vol. 16, no. 4 (July 1964), pp. 677-715.

54. See Ghita Ionescu, *Centripetal Politics* (London, Hart-Davis MacGibbon, 1975).

55. On the broad question of the 'relative autonomy' of the Gaullist state, see Pierre Birnbaum, 'The State in Contemporary France', in Richard Scase, ed., *The State in Western Europe* (London, Croom Helm, 1980), ch.2.

56. On the diachronic nature of the legitimation process, see P. G. Cerny, 'The Problem of Legitimacy in the Fifth French Republic', paper presented to the Workshop on Normative and Empirical Dimensions of Legitimacy, Joint Meetings of Workshops, European Consortium for Political Research, University of Lancaster, March - April 1981.

57. Not *machismo* — see the discussions in Cerny, *Politics of Grandeur: Ideological Aspects of de Gaulle's Foreign Policy*, pp. 27-8, and Jesse R. Pitts, 'Continuity and Change in Bourgeois France', in Hoffmann, *et al.*, *In Search of France* (Cambridge, Mass., Harvard U.P., 1963), pp. 244ff — although in the case of nuclear missiles Freudian analysts may be forgiven a more tangible symbolic analogy ...

58. René Rémond, 'De Gaulle et *une certaine idée de la France*', *L'Espoir* (journal of the Institut Charles de Gaulle), no. 43 (July 1983), and P. G. Cerny, 'Reply to René Rémond', in ibid.

59. See Johan Galtung, 'On Power in General', in Galtung, *The European Community: A Superpower in the making* (Oslo and London, Universitetsforlaget and George Allen and Unwin, 1973), pp. 33-47.

60. Maurice Duverger, *La Monarchie républicaine* (Paris, Robert Laffont, 1974).

61. See *Politics of Grandeur: Ideological Aspects of de Gaulle's Foreign Policy*, (Cambridge, Cambridge U.P., 1980), chs. 1-3.

62. Ibid., chs. 5 and 10.

63. De Gaulle's call to the army to refrain from joining the 'barricades' demonstrations in Algiers in January 1960 was televised with the President in his full military uniform, 29 January 1960.

64. See Charles de Gaulle, *Vers l'Armée de métier* (Paris, Berger-Levrault, 1934).

65. Pierre Maillard, 'La Défense Nationale de nos jours', *Revue de défense nationale*, vol.22, no.5 (May 1966), pp. 778 - 79 (Maillard was Minister Plenipotentiary and Deputy Secretary General for National Defence at the time he was writing); Pierre M. Gallois, 'Les Conséquences stratégiques et politiques des armes nouvelles', *Politique étrangère*, vol.23, no.2 (1958), p. 168; cf. W. W. Kulski, *De Gaulle and the World: The Foreign Policy of the Fifth French Republic* (Syracuse, N.Y., Syracuse U.P., 1966), pp. 121-22.

66. Groupe de travail, 'Puissances moyennes et armement nucléaire: Un groupe de travail', *Politique étrangère*, vol.34, (1969), nos. 5-6.

67. Robert J. Lieber, 'The French Nuclear Force: A Strategic and Political Evaluation', *International Affairs*, vol.42, no. 3 (July 1966), p.428.

68. P. G. Cerny, *Politics of Grandeur: Ideological Aspects of de Gaulle's Foreign Policy* (Cambridge, Cambridge U.P., 1980), pp. 194-97.

69. Quoted in Edward A. Kolodziej, 'French Strategy Emergent —General André Beaufre: A Critique', *World Politics*, vol.9, no. 3 (April 1967), p. 435.

70. André Beaufre, *NATO and Europe* (New York, Vintage, 1966), p. 85.

71. Raymond Aron, *Peace and War: A Theory of International Relations* (London, Weidenfeld and Nicolson, 1966), p. 490.

72. Michael M. Harrison, *The Reluctant Ally: France and Atlantic Security* (Baltimore, Md., The Johns Hopkins U.P., 1981), *passim*; *Politics of Grandeur*, chs.7-9.

73. For a consideration of the systemic implications of this clash, see Alastair Buchan, *The End of the Postwar Era: A New Balance of World Power* (London, Weidenfeld and Nicolson, 1974).

74. P. G. Cerny, *Politics of Grandeur: Ideological Aspects of de Gaulle's Foreign Policy* (Cambridge, Cambridge U.P., 1980), *passim.*

75. Institut Français d'Opinion Publique, *Les Français et de Gaulle*, ed. by Jean Charlot, pp. 272-74.

76. Ibid., pp. 260-61 and ff.

77. P.G. Cerny, *Politics of Grandeur: Ideological Aspects of de Gaulle's Foreign Policy* (Cambridge, Cambridge U.P., 1980), pp. 261-65.

78. Michael M. Harrison, *The Reluctant Ally: France and Atlantic Security*, ch. 5.

79. P.G. Cerny, 'Gaullism, Advanced Capitalism and the Fifth Republic', in D.S. Bell, ed., *Contemporary French Political Parties* (London and New York, Croom Helm and St. Martin's Press, 1982), ch.2. pp. 47-8.

3 THE PARTIES AND THE NUCLEAR CONSENSUS
David Hanley

Any examination of the defence policies of the four major French political parties (Gaullists, Giscardians, Communists and Socialists) necessarily begins with the fact that the French nuclear arsenal now exists. The usual questions may be raised as to its credibility (size, dependency on US technological inputs, feasibility of use outside NATO) but it is not the purpose of this chapter to ask them. What counts is the reaction of the French political class and of the wider public towards this arsenal. As late as the late 1970s, it appeared that both felt that it served some clear useful purpose, although the second half of 1983 was beginning to show some serious doubts creeping in on the part of the general public.

No single political party can credit itself with being the father of the bomb. It was the modernising radicals of the Mendès-France government of 1954-5 which first gave the go-ahead to scientists working on the project, and this initial support was sustained by other centre-left governments of the mid-fifties who saw the project through to a key stage of development. It might therefore be expected that, from the very beginning, the French deterrent enjoyed potentially wide support among the political class, if not the wider public. Gaullist governments of the sixties were merely continuing work begun by different predecessors when they made the French weapons operational and developed them to ICBM status. It may well be that they were also building upon and expanding, by sophisticated publicity, a nascent consensus among elites. Why should these latter have been largely pro-nuclear?

It seems that in their acceptance of French deterrence theory, French leaders were guided by a number of considerations, both domestic and international. Men of the Resistance generation for the most part, they could measure, by the mid-fifties, the huge change in international relations which had come about since 1945. Under the new superpower condominium which had emerged after Yalta, former first-rank powers like Britain and France seemed condemned to a minor role inside one of the big blocs. The pre-eminence of bloc leaders seemed total — and this could be plausibly ascribed to the possession of nuclear arms. Crises of decolonisation in Vietnam and Algeria, especially the disastrous Suez expedition of 1956 (see Antoine Sanguinetti's comments on this, in Chapter Six) brought home cruelly to French leaders the limitations on the action of second-rank powers. It was not that anybody seriously believed that nuclear weaponry might have kept France her colonies. Decolonisation did, however, show very clearly the political, economic and ultimately military weakness of the formerly powerful. Now it should not be thought that France, with her republican tradition, was any less attracted to a world role than, say, imperial Britain or Germany. On the contrary, republicanism in modern times (at least, since 1870) has probably felt a greater need than other systems for a visible world role, if only to counter its apparently endemic domestic weakness.

On the domestic level, such international considerations as the above could be supported by reference to powerful trends in French political culture. France's underlying republican imperialism is one such trend, but equally significant was, and still is, Germanophobia. The rise of an efficient, unified and ambitious state in a central Europe that France had long been used to dominate had inflicted on the nation of Napoleon, three times within a century, the humiliation of defeat and/or partial or total occupation. Today, to a generation for whom World War II is history, and which has never seen conflict any nearer than the Middle East, anti-German sentiments may seem hard to understand, but to the men of the fifties, some of whom were survivors of concentration camps, they were more natural. Indeed, to many leaders, the threat was posed less by Russia (traditionally France's ally, and very effectively so in 1941-45) than by Germany. It is unclear how far even the Cold War reversed such assumptions. Thus anything that might be said to enhance French security against a Germany now weak (but for how long?) could be positively endorsed.

Linked to this is the problem of anti-Americanism, or, in de Gaulle's widening of the term, feelings against 'Anglo-Saxons'. Like Germanophobia, its specific weight in French culture is hard to assess with any precision, but there is no doubt that it exists. It is a terrain on which left and right can come together — the left because America is the leading capitalist or imperialist power, the right for more emotional reasons (because the USA has supplanted France in her world role). Whatever the strength or diffusion of such feelings, it would be unwise to underestimate them in any overall consideration of an acceptance of nuclear weapons.

It is this combination of a certain generation of political leaders making their analysis of the new international system, and their reading of deep, underlying features in French culture which, in part, explain how the French deterrent ever got started. One could argue about the relative weight of such factors, and one could argue about the extent to which the deterrent carries support among the wider public as opposed to the political class. We shall return to these questions shortly. What matters here though is that once a French arsenal existed, all political forces had, willy-nilly, to take up a position on it. They did at least have a wider choice of position than their UK counterparts. For the 1963 Nassau agreement signaled the end of any ambitions that may have existed to build an independent British deterrent, as the purchase of the US Polaris system made clear. Britain thus accepted a highly Atlanticist line on defence. It was clearer than ever before that her ultimate defence was linked very specifically to that of the USA. Thus, British Labour supporters felt that they had either to endorse this Atlanticist line or, if critical, to adopt the thesis of unilateral nuclear disarmament. It would be interesting to know what many Labour supporters (and possibly some in other parties) would do if there were a British deterrent at the same level of development and independence as the French one, or if indeed a 'European deterrent' existed, based on some very detailed cooperation between France, Britain and Germany and visibly outside American control. French parties have always felt that they have a third choice — to rely on their own national deterrent. They have usually proved immune to doubts about its credibility.

The foregoing has aimed to point out the wider background to the coming of a French nuclear arsenal. Political parties must necessarily be aware of this and their pronouncements need to be seen against it. We shall now examine the attitudes of the four major parties, with a view to explaining how, within a general consensus in favour of retention of the nuclear arsenal, there can nevertheless exist an enormous variety of interpretations as to the strategic and diplomatic value of such an arsenal as well as a well-developed controversy about its military application.

Parties of the Right

The Gaullist *Rassemblement pour la République* (RPR)

Gaullism, appropriately, has a chapter to itself. Its contribution to the French deterrent was the predominant one. It will suffice here to recall rapidly the major lines of Gaullist thinking on defence, with particular reference to the present. Predicated on the belief that nation-states and national loyalties are the foundations of all politics, Gaullism adapted its nuclear doctrine to fit these assumptions. In a world dominated by two superpowers, only nuclear arms gave lesser-sized powers autonomy (just how much is a matter of very fine nuances and Gaullian discourse is enigmatic on this point). This is the theory of the 'equalising power of the atom'. Thus, the French arsenal was held to 'sanctuarise' French territory in the last resort. But there was more to it than this. Always conscious that the French deterrent alone might not enjoy full credibility, de Gaulle remained in the Atlantic Alliance (but not, of course, in its integrated military structure). As an orthodox nationalist, he was bound to mistrust his allies up to a point. In practice, this meant wondering whether the USA could actually be relied upon to defend western Europe in all circumstances.

In this connection, many people have seen the true rationale of the French deterrent as being to 'tie-in' the USA to the defence of Europe. The mere existence of a French nuclear capability would, in this view, render much less likely a trade-off between two mutually sanctuarised superpowers at the expense of their smaller neighbours (for example, the USA conceding Soviet hegemony over western Europe in exchange for some hypothetical compensation elsewhere in the world). This underlying reality was quite compatible with a discourse about French independence, which combined a discreet anti-Americanism with a refusal to belabour the Soviet Union excessively. As the RPR electoral manifesto in 1978 put it: 'allies of the USA, but also good partners of the USSR, let us be clear that we only have any value in their eyes in so far as our desire to retain our identity obliges them to consult with us.'[1]

Gaullist thinking today has retained all the hallmarks of its founder. This is evident from the neutral or even disinterested RPR reaction to the 1979 NATO decision on Cruise and Pershing.[2] It is true that, with the invasion of Afghanistan and the general hardening of détente, the party's anti-Russian sentiments have been sharpened. The SS 20 is clearly seen as a potential weapon for waging a limited war in Europe, the idea being that it can 'take out' a country without damaging its economic potential too seriously! Today's Gaullists also see the SS 20 as the logical Soviet answer to the 'decoupling' effects of 'flexible response' since it serves to further that 'decoupling' of the USA from Europe.

But what really emerges from all this is a more traditional phobia about France's being sucked into conflicts or situations beyond her control. The RPR stresses that the 'twin-track' decision was a NATO decision, hence France was not involved. While recognising the danger posed to all western Europe by the SS 20, the RPR denies that this danger implies the necessity for or the existence of a common west-European defensive space (as the Giscardians claim — see below). Rather, in the Gaullist view, the new threat increases the need for *national* self-protection. What the Gaullists really fear is that the NATO move might be a means of pressuring the USSR into across-the-board arms control negotiations. While this might seem desirable to many, it is less appealing to the RPR, because in this scenario France would find herself under very strong pressure to put her own arsenal on the negotiating table. In other words, the RPR is afraid of increased US influence and consequent loss of French autonomy.

This preoccupation with autonomy is also evident in RPR mistrust of both the neutron bomb and the notion of the 'forward battle', either of which conjures up the danger of French forces being committed automatically in the event of hostilities in Germany. Both of these possibilities are feared by the RPR because they might lead to France's involvement in a limited nuclear war. Gaullist deterrence has always been of the all-or-nothing variety, and the current policy of the RPR is to put all France's effort into the strategic nuclear arsenal, constructing up to 15 nuclear-missile-firing submarines by the year 2000. Anything which indicates to potential adversaries a willingness to get involved in a limited exchange has to be firmly scotched. This is where the distinction between Gaullists and Giscardians is at its clearest. As Dabezies remarks: 'There is a disagreement between those who remain faithful to the Gaullist doctrine of strategic nuclear deterrence, and those who favour readiness for an eventual confrontation in Europe.'[3]

With this, we are at the very heart of the dilemma and we can now complete the right-wing picture by turning to the RPR's Giscardian partners and rivals.

The Giscardian *Union pour la Démocratie Française* (UDF)

This complex of parties was formed as an electoral cartel for the 1978 parliamentary elections under the authority of the then President Valéry Giscard d'Estaing. Since the latter's defeat in May 1981, and in view of his apparent lack of a clear political future, the fissiparous tendencies of the UDF have become more noticeable; but its member parties are still tied together by the realisation that unity is strength and that the alternative is domination by so fearful a master as the Gaullist leader Jacques Chirac. The main constituent parties of the UDF are Giscard's own *Parti républicain* (PR), which was always pro-European-integration and has usually been suspected of being lukewarm towards the French deterrent; the *Parti radical*, an old and near defunct party dating back to the Third Republic, and which was always split on defence issues between pacifists and Jacobin nationalists; and the Catholic *Centre des Démocrates Sociaux* (CDS), the somewhat contracted remains of the old Christian-Democrat MRP of the Fourth Republic. This latter was always strongly anti-communist, openly European-integrationist and very uncritically Atlanticist. In particular, it was the main supporter of the abortive European Defence Community of the 1950s, which was designed to get around the delicate question of German rearmament. There are thus some distinct and even conflicting traditions involved in this alliance, but it has proved easier to find common ground on defence than might be imagined. We will concentrate in particular on the Giscardian PR and on the CDS since these days the *Parti radical* represents very little, whatever its contribution in the past may have been.

PR defence policy sticks closely to the lines laid down by Giscard during his presidency. Thus, the PR was firmly attached to détente and anti-Soviet rhetoric figured less prominently in its discourse than might be expected (given its fundamentally conservative nature).[4] This stance governs PR thinking on the delicate problem of NATO. While recognising that France dealt NATO a hard blow by leaving the military structure, it feels the Alliance to be somewhat outdated, because it merely links Europe and North America, whereas 'the camp of liberal democracy is wider'. Furthermore, the PR sees the Alliance as too narrowly military and political. The PR thus speaks of a 'community of free peoples', membership of which would be open to all states satisfying conventional criteria of pluralism. It would aim 'to harmonise the international policy of member countries in the political, economic, cultural and military fields'.[5] This is, of course, a vague notion, and deliberately so. Its function is tactical: it allows the PR, fundamentally pro-American at heart, to retain the possibility of foreign policy linkages with the USA but at the same time to avoid Gaullist and leftist charges of Atlanticism (hence the reference to NATO being outdated).

With this in mind, we may turn to purely nuclear questions. The PR officially accepts the general notion of deterrence, while adding a caveat against belief in a shared deterrent: 'this nuclear weapon can only be national: if deterrence involves holding councils and the agreement of several countries, then it is not credible.'[6] France thus remains in the Alliance, which 'guarantees a minimum of solidarity', but it is stated that the French deterrent alone is adequate, provided that it be kept up to date and conventional forces strengthened (proportionately to the growth in GDP) so as to raise the threshold of nuclear engagement. Thus far, little seems to distinguish the Giscardian programme from the Gaullist one. But there is a further element which is all-important, namely the wish to diversify the nuclear arsenal, particularly at the level of tactical weapons . Such a panoply, it is claimed, 'allows for French deterrence without the risk of "all-or-nothing" poker games'.[7] In other words, the PR believes in the doctrine of flexible response.

Two recent analysts of the Giscardian line stress this interpretation.[8] For them, Giscardian readiness to accept the euromissiles can only be understood in the context of the Giscardian view that the East-West balance must be preserved at all levels, from tactical to strategic. One cannot simply rely on the ultimate deterrent properties of one's strategic firepower. But there is a corollary to this, namely that France herself cannot match the USSR at all levels. The required balance can only be maintained by western Europe as a whole. But the latter relies on NATO. Thus French defence becomes closely keyed in to NATO. As our authors put it: 'the "European space" is the best way of re-defining Atlanticism without having to pronounce the word.'[9] Although this accusation of Atlanticism has in fact been levelled at the UDF as a whole, it seems more obviously justified if we look at the stance of the main partner in the UDF, the CDS.

The CDS is characterised by much blunter language. Belief in the Soviet threat is always stressed prominently, and is usually linked to a critique of totalitarianism. Détente was probably never taken entirely seriously by the CDS. The sheer magnitude of Warsaw Pact weaponry is held to impose alliances on France; the utility of her own deterrent is not denied as such, but the feasibility of an autonomous national deterrent, especially a multi-directional one, is denied. Indeed, this notion is held by the CDS to be dangerous:

> The dogma of 'France on her own', the idea of a nuclear 'all-or-nothing' smack of arrogance and self-delusion: they breed contradictions. They imply ultimately the neutralisation of France, and probably her becoming a satellite. The Communist Party knows what it is about when it supports the nuclear force and the doctrine surrounding it.[10]

Consequently, 'independence is limited by natural solidarities, European and Atlantic: that too is a fact'.[11]

These texts could hardly be clearer. What the CDS wants is 'organic military concertation in Europe' as the prelude to a 'truly European defence'.[12] Several factors push France in this direction — not just the Soviet threat or budgetary problems, but also the fact that a basis for European coordination already exists in the EEC. In most fields, according to the CDS, Europe is already 'gathered into a Community'. Existing EEC institutions can begin to hammer out a common defence policy, without awaiting the emergence of those federal structures to which the CDS has always aspired. Such a policy would be under-pinned by the French and British nuclear arms, but, crucially, these are seen as 'complementary to the American guarantee' rather than replacing it. If this path is not followed, says the CDS, the 'Anglo-American-Germanic world [sic] will harden its attitudes and Federal Germany may be tempted by pro-Soviet neutralism.'[13]

This vision of a fairly integrated European system of defence, organically linked to NATO, would probably have as its nearest equivalent in British politics the views which Edward Heath is said to have put to Georges Pompidou in their conversations of the early seventies. It is a classic expression of 'Atlantic Europe'. Of course, the CDS here speaks only for itself and not for the whole alliance of which it is a part (maybe the most dynamic part). In its visible fear of the USSR, its scepticism about the feasibility of autonomous French deterrence and its open preference for an integrated Europe under US hegemony, its stances might seem sharper and clearer than those of the PR. Dabezies sees such attitudes as continuing proof of 'the old masochism and servility of a part of the French bourgeoisie'.[14] Yet the policy convergences between the two groups on virtually every other issue are very strong, so much so that it is difficult to believe that many PR supporters do not share such views. Thus the CDS is saying out loud, as it were, what many Giscardians probably think in their heart of hearts. Both are clearly Atlanticist, but one group does not wish (or cannot afford, politically) to appear so in too obvious a way. Perhaps this difference is concerned with the type of audience to which they respond. We shall return to this later.

The Parties of the Left

It might be expected that anti-nuclear feeling would be the preserve of the left. So it was indeed for a long time. The two major parties, socialist and communist, have long traditions of anti-militarism and attachment to disarmament. For a while, as French nuclear capacity grew, these traditions translated into opposition to nuclear weapons akin to that of the Lab our Party. But this feeling was never unanimous and needs to be looked at with several qualifications in mind.

The *Parti Communiste Français* (PCF)

On the face of it, no party has undergone such a radical turn-around in its defence policy these past few years.[15] Before 1977, the PCF stressed above all its hostility to NATO and the Atlantic Alliance which it interpreted as a vehicle for US imperialism, underwriting the domination of western Europe, the intimidation of eastern Europe and constituting the most likely cause of war. If, after initial scepticism, the PCF slowly came to accept Gaullian notions of an autonomous defence capability, and if it approved of leaving NATO, nuclear armoury was still seen as irrelevant to such independence. Thus the Common Programme of Government (CPG) which socialists and communists signed in 1972 (for the 1973 parliamentary elections) promised that a left-wing government would abandon the nuclear arsenal, manufacture no further weapons and reconvert existing nuclear arms factories to civil nuclear purposes. In other words it was, at least on the surface, unilateralist. Although the PCF was obliged, in order to obtain the signature of the socialist partner, to commit France to continuing membership of the Atlantic Alliance, the text of the CPG hedged this promise about with numerous references to the hoped-for dissolution of blocs, which, it was alleged, might be brought nearer by vigorous French initiatives in disarmament talks. The old Rapacki plan for a nuclear-free Europe was revived and the two parties promised, if elected, to append France's signature to the non-proliferation and test-ban treaties.

As the left alliance prospered and office drew nearer, the communist line underwent metamorphosis. The PCF saw Giscardian policy generally as subordinating French interests to American ones much more so than in the Gaullian era, and this was especially true of defence. Proof of this was felt to be incontrovertible after the so-called 'Méry declaration' of 1976 in which Giscard's Chief of Staff effectively extended sanctuarisation beyond French borders, suggesting that French ground troops might be automatically committed if West Germany were invaded. This break with the 1960s Ailleret doctrine (all-or-nothing deterrence, limited strictly to French territory) was seen by the PCF as a furtive attempt to relink French defence to NATO by the expedient of committing her in advance to a battle which, in theory, she might avoid. It also weakened the notion of absolute deterrence by postulating involvement in some limited nuclear war, as did the development of the neutron bomb, to which the PCF also objected. Such arguments are, as we have seen, very similar to Gaullist critiques of Giscardian defence policy.

The PCF answer was not, however, simply to multiply its denunciations in the name of French independence. Rather, in the celebrated volte-face of May 1977, it assumed the full logic of independence.[16] Henceforth the PCF accepted both the need for a French deterrent and the need to keep it up to date. In practice this meant privileging in particular the strategic component, for which the PCF now demanded an omni-directional targeting policy.[17] To make this latter feasible, it had also logically to recommend the creation of a purely French system of reconnaissance and guidance. Finally, it demanded a collegiate system of decision-making, involving party leaders in the eventual use of such weapons.

Hostile critics saw these latter conditions as effectively undercutting PCF acceptance of deterrence — the omni-directional strategy on grounds of cost and the collegiality on grounds of credibility (how can an adversary be deterred when he knows that a riposte depends upon the outcome of a council of *notables*?). Indeed, this latter idea seems to have been played down since PCF participation in government after June 1981. Yet the fact remains that the PCF now accepts the deterrent as the foundation of an independent foreign policy for France. We need to know how this came about and what are its consequences.

PCF thinking on foreign affairs is governed by two parameters: the party's reading of domestic French politics, and its interpretation of the international scene. This latter aspect raises the key question of the party's relationship to the USSR and its ruling core, the CPSU. This is no easy matter on which to generalise. There are those who see the PCF as a willing tool of Soviet foreign policy, and others for whom it is largely autonomous, the views of the CPSU being simply one more variable which the PCF incorporates into its analyses.[18] We do not intend here to pass judgement in this complex debate. But it is generally true, as Lavau shows, that the PCF is reluctant to criticise the USSR in any structured way, preferring the one-off rebuke to detailed analysis, and that this is more the case with foreign policy than in any other area. For the PCF, world politics is a game with three players: the forces of imperialism, led by the USA; the camp of socialism, led by the USSR; and (as an ally of the latter) the 'international working class' which, being translated, means the non-ruling communist parties outside the Soviet bloc. This doubtless explains why the PCF never envisages any threat from the USSR or the Warsaw Pact and why it tends to echo Soviet arms-reduction propositions fairly uncritically. Many analysts find it rather blithe about the Warsaw Pact estimations of its own conventional and nuclear strength. The euromissile problem showed this clearly, the PCF refusing to see the SS 20 as a threat, and even initially presenting it as a reply to a US threat to develop new medium-range missiles.[19]

If the USSR plays a totally positive role in world politics, then America's role is naturally the reverse, and PCF attachment to independence bears this very much in mind. The USA aims to increase its already considerable domination of Europe (in every sphere, not just military). Cruise and Pershing are seen by the PCF as a means of increasing US leverage over its allies and should be resisted (even though none will be deployed in France). The PCF has even gone so far as to suggest that these missiles somehow give West Germany a 'finger on the nuclear trigger' — an appeal to deep-rooted fears. Anti-German feeling is also at the base of the frequently-voiced PCF hostility to any notion of integrated European defence, which the party believes could only exist under US hegemony.

Must we agree with Lavau that grudging acceptance of the deterrent has never really altered the logic of PCF thinking, and that it wants France to 'stop having a foreign policy which doesn't coincide with that of the Soviet Union'? Or is it even true that 'the PCF aims not so much to put France at the beck and call of Soviet foreign policy, but to develop, within this territory at the heart of the western system, a large "finlandised" area, which upsets Atlanticist strategies'?[20] And Lavau goes on to suggest that in time such a strategy might bring nearer the conditions for seizure of power. He himself does in fact wonder whether the PCF really thinks in these terms, but suggests that so long as the party produces no alternative discourse, then at least the question must be asked.

One might indeed wonder just how seriously this conspiratorial vision should be taken. But whether the PCF is conducting a long-term international strategy of this type, or whether it is primarily governed by its fear of US pressures in western Europe, neither hypothesis really helps to explain why it accepts the French nuclear deterrent. To explain this fully, we need to turn to domestic politics and particularly to the rise of a strong Socialist Party.

The story of the left alliance from 1972 to 1977 is too well known to need recounting here.[21] We know that the PCF expected to be the major beneficiary of such a deal and that it was ready for political compromises in order to get the alliance started. One such compromise was acceptance of the Atlantic Alliance. But it seems that this involved consequences unforeseen by the PCF (and possibly even by the socialists). For, as office came closer, it dawned on both parties that the unilateralist policies to which the CPG seemed to commit them could prove to be a severe handicap in an otherwise attractive electoral package. In other words, both communists and socialists sensed French public opinion as not being ready for a move to unilateralism and as being still very attached to Gaullian concepts of independence. Thus, when the PCF sensed that its partner was moving towards acceptance of the deterrent, it had little choice but to follow, especially if it wanted to stop the PS from forging even further ahead in terms of electoral support. This institutional factor of inter-party relationships, themselves pivoting on a reading of public opinion, will be returned to later. But it should not be underestimated in thinking about the PCF's move. In other words, it seems that the PCF switch of line was governed at least as much by domestic as by international factors and that both will play a role in its future thought on defence.

The *Parti Socialiste* (PS)

The PS has a long and complicated history on defence. Members were divided between a pacifist-antimilitarist tradition which saw war as an inevitable offshoot of capitalism (hence unjustifiable to workers), and a patriotic or Jacobin tradition which recognised the attachment of the working classes to their own national cultures and the fact that they would thus collaborate in the task of national defence. Since 1945, this polarity has been complicated by the appearance of a third factor — Atlanticism. For many years, party leaders, often in government, were so fearful of Soviet expansionism that they embraced NATO enthusiastically as a means to French security. The arrival of Gaullism set new problems for the party and, although it hammered out compromises in the end, deep divisions still remain. The very factional structure of the party helps of course to perpetuate them.[22]

Until the mid-seventies, the party line was basically that of the CPG: veiled unilateralism. The pacifist tradition, the widespread Atlanticist feelings among the party leaders, and most of all perhaps the party's complete lack of influence in a Gaullian republic which presented the deterrent as very much its own creation, all combined to build up scepticism about French nuclear weapons. Party texts usually talked more about alternative defence policies, which were traced back to the party founder, Jean Jaurès. These usually postulated a decentralised citizens' army, more or less on Swiss lines, which would involve the entire population in territorial defence. This type of theory connected well with the general philosophy of *autogestion* which the party was progressively to adopt and which pivots on decentralisation of responsibility in all areas.

But as the PS progressed through the 1970s, other voices began to sound louder, notably those of Charles Hernu, now Minister of Defence, and of the left-wing faction, *Centre d'Etudes, de Recherches et d'Education socialistes* (CERES). Both partook of the Jacobin tradition, both felt that unilateralism might not be universally popular with voters and both shared a view of international relations not all that far removed from de Gaulle's. In particular, they despised the super-power bloc system and believed that if France were to possess any autonomy other than a purely symbolic one, she must possess nuclear weapons.

It was the hard work put in by CERES and Hernu supporters which explains the fact that by 1977 the party leaders were ready to endorse the French deterrent. The party convention of January 1978 laid down the bases of subsequent orthodoxy, now clearly multilateralist. The objective of disarmament remained, but only when others were prepared to disarm. Meanwhile France's nuclear weapons would be kept in working order,[23] and France would remain in the Atlantic Alliance. The 1980 Socialist Project,[24] largely inspired by the CERES leader, Jean-Pierre Chevènement, spoke positively of modernising the French deterrent (alongside references to the old ideal of the citizen army), and Mitterrand, in his 110 propositions for the 1981 presidential campaign, spoke of building two more nuclear submarines. Thus, when the PS came to power, it was more or less committed to a Gaullian defence doctrine: reluctant adhesion to the Atlantic Alliance (Mitterrand even spoke, like de Gaulle in 1958, of renegotiating the terms of the Alliance), plus reliance on a French deterrent with land, sea and air components. The will to disarm ultimately remained, but what government does not subscribe to that?

Socialist defence policy in office is analysed in Chapter Four. Generally speaking, the government has concretised the above theoretical positions, in particular with regard to the priority attached to the strategic nuclear weapon. But at the same time, both the tactical missiles and the conventional armed forces are being modernised and updated. This has led to conflicting interpretations of French defence policy, and these are also analysed in Chapter Four. But in order fully to comprehend the source of ambiguities in PS defence thinking, it is appropriate to look at the tensions and even the contradictions within the party, as between the 'left-wing' (CERES) and the 'right-wing'

(Rocardian) factions. For if Prime Minister Mauroy speaks for the government and the collective party leadership, it is by no means certain that he also speaks for the party as a whole.

The faction grouped around Michel Rocard is usually perceived as the party's 'right wing' and it is the most likely home for unilateralists. It has a strong anti-statist ideology and great commitment to grass-roots participation and democratisation. Many of its sympathisers are active in anti-*civil*-nuclear movements (cf. the work of Alain Touraine). Added to this is the ethical and moral input stemming from committed Catholics like Patrick Viveret, editor of the faction's review, *Interventions*.

In fact, Rocardians have always had problems with defence, being far happier with economic or libertarian issues. Their international views are coloured by an increasing anti-Sovietism, which reflects not just fears about military imbalance, but also economic and political opposition to that statism of which they see the USSR as the logical conclusion. The invasion of Afghanistan and the Polish government's persecution of Solidarnosc have increased their apprehension to the point where they are ready to accept the notion of deterrence. The Rocardians - represented by Patrick Viveret and Charles Josselin - had been instrumental in 1978 in defending a nuclear 'de-escalation' resolution at the party's national convention on defence.[25] The fact that they eventually rallied to the majority line on the French nuclear arsenal was motivated not only by their desire not to 'break ranks' only weeks before the vital elections of 1978, but also by this growing 'anti-totalitarianism' within the group. It might be expected also that, given their commitment to economic and political integration in Europe, they would favour moves towards an autonomous European defence capability: indeed, their motion to the party's 1979 Congress at Metz did speak briefly of such a development. Only time will tell if the Rocardians advance further down this road, but as long as their leader (often less 'Rocardian' than his followers!) remains a loyal member of the government, it seems likely that the tendency will keep in step.

As for the CERES, it has always been quite consistent in its defence doctrine.[26] For the CERES, foreign policy has always governed domestic, even from the group's beginnings in the mid-sixties. They have always related France's potential for economic and political renewal to her defence capacity. Thus, they were the first to accept the French deterrent as a foundation for independence. Profoundly anti-American (culturally as well as politically) they have always refused NATO and their acceptance of membership of the Alliance is visibly more grudging than that of the rest of the party. They see France not as a second-rank power but conceivably playing a world role (cf. the Socialist Project). Just how seriously this is to be taken is not certain, but CERES clearly believes that as the two-bloc system slowly disintegrates and the world becomes 'multi-polar', opportunities for French influence grow apace. But so do the dangers: hence the continuing need for the deterrent. CERES is sceptical of a non-Atlantic, European defence, probably in no small measure owing to its Anglophobia and Germanophobia. It prefers to see France as an independent military power, and it is up to other states whether they choose to imitate her. CERES thus is the most Gaullian of all socialist groups, but its thinking has obviously influenced the party at large. The difference between the CERES line and the official line is now mainly one of style or degree. CERES is more explicitly nationalistic and anti-American, and perhaps more indulgent towards the Soviet Union.

As for the unilateralists, they still exist, and not all of them are in the Rocard group. At least one member of the present government admitted in 1977 to being unilateralist.[27] Many who left the CERES in the 1979 split did so on unilateralist grounds. It is hard to know the exact strength and location of the PS unilateralists: for the moment their voices are drowned in the shared orthodoxy of deterrence. Tension there certainly is within the party; but probably the need to find electorally acceptable policies in the first place, and then the need to support the party in government, where it has had a long up-hill struggle ever since taking office, explain the relative lack of public dissent over nuclear weapons. It remains to be seen whether or not this will continue.

We have thus completed this short survey of the widely differing attitudes to nuclear weapons within the general four-party consensus on retention of the deterrent. It remains to relate these differences to public opinion as perceived by the parties.

Public Opinion in the 1970s: What Sort of Consensus?

It is notoriously hard to measure public opinion on any subject. The inadequacies of survey methods, real fluctuations in attitudes over very short periods of time, the methodological and epistemological assumptions of pollsters all make generalisations hazardous.[28] With such reservations in mind, it might just be possible to try out one or two tentative hypotheses about the French and the bomb. We have taken as our base the year 1974, when Giscard became President, and official Gaullism began to take a secondary role. The notion of an independent deterrent was, however, by then, widely vulgarised.

In 1974, when questioned generally about the French *force de frappe*, the public responded more positively than negatively.[29] Thus 57% (against 33%) thought it right for France to have nuclear weapons if other nations did. 45% (against 38%) actually held that 'they gave France a means of having a policy of national independence'. On a less nationalistic/cultural level, 52% (against 34%) felt that, given the expenditure already incurred, it was too late to go back. Against these findings, one could point out that only 34% (against 52%) felt that the *force de frappe* on its own guaranteed French security. But 34% is already quite a large fraction and the question, by referring to nuclear weapons alone, omits the link between nuclear and conventional defence. As we shall see, this link is very important. Moreover, 62% of those who declared an interest in politics, and 53% of those who did not, felt it right for France to carry on testing. These figures included over 50% of both PCF and PS supporters.

The 1974 poll next asked, from a party-political viewpoint, whether nuclear weapons allowed France a policy of independence. While 66% of the right agreed that they did, only 55% of 'reformers' (basically Christian-Democrats, soon to become the CDS, but here polled separately) thought so. The figures for the PS and PCF were, respectively, 43% and 39%. 54% of PCF supporters, and 44% of socialists specifically disagreed with the proposition. When asked further whether the French deterrent guaranteed security, 66% of the left disagreed, in contrast to only 35% of the right (58% agreed) and 49% of 'reformers' (46% agreed). Again, when faced with the moral argument that possession of nuclear weapons meant envisaging the destruction of the human race, 66% of communists and 51% of socialists agreed. However, when asked whether nuclear nations were likely in future to get rid of their stockpiles, only a poor third of both left and right believed that this would happen.

How are we to interpret all this? Subject to all the caveats enunciated above, we may say crudely that the further one moves to the right, the more support the French deterrent commands. But support on the left is far from negligible. Much of this support may be on nationalistic, strategic or even fatalistic grounds, and only very detailed research could establish the specific weight of any one factor or indeed how the different factors articulate. But at any rate, committed opposition to nuclear weapons was visibly not all that strong in 1974.

By 1977, when the left parties shifted their ground, the public was even more firmly pro-nuclear. Lech claims that this is linked to growing rejection of conscription, hence a willingness to rely not on a standing army but on more sophisticated means of defence.[30] Indeed, he sees this rejection as being catalysed by public fury at the Debré-Fontanet law of 1973 which made deferments of military service for students much harder to obtain. This was resented in particular by young people as an impediment to their careers. Thus, by 1976, one found that 60% of those polled agreed that France could not defend herself without nuclear weapons. Indeed, the younger and more left-inclined the respondents were, the more they actually agreed with this proposition. Thus a corporatist reaction (defence of a clearly perceived economic interest) comes to reinforce deeper trends within the political culture. The parties of the left began to see this pressure as too strong to resist. They were, when they became pro-nuclear, according to Lech, not leading opinion but following it.[31]

The left was always bound to tread carefully if it wished to win over sections of the centre, the right or the uncommitted. CERES has long proclaimed its ambition to win over Gaullists on the basis of a common Jacobin culture. Perhaps the Rocardians, with their different style, were always best placed to win over elements of the centre, mainly Catholics potentially attracted by a discreet reformism. Neither faction could, in this case, ignore the fact that its potential clients were fairly pro-nuclear. Obviously, readings of opinion in an electoral perspective are not the only factor in determining a party's defence options. There are also all the differing analyses of domestic and international politics referred to above. Yet surely awareness that the wider public would not endorse unilateralism (and was indeed moving even further away from it) was a crucial determinant. The late Joël Le Theule, one of Giscard's Defence Ministers, once stated that public opinion in France was basically apathetic and resigned to the *status quo* on defence matters.[32] Yet it seems that opinion was, to some extent, ahead of a part of the political class (the leaderships of the left-wing parties) and that these latter followed. However, it is interesting to note that the most recent polls, analysed below,[33] suggest that the public is once again out of phase with the political class. Will the nuclear consensus, which we have seen developing throughout the 1970s, now begin to break up? Time alone will tell.

Notes

1. Rassemblement pour la République, *Propositions pour la France* (Paris, Stock, 1978), p. 216.

2. D. David & G.-P. Halleman, 'Les partis politiques français et les euromissiles', *Défense nationale*, February 1981, pp. 67-84.

3. P. Dabezies, 'French political parties and Defence policy', *Armed Forces and Society*, vol.8, no.2, Winter 1982, p. 244.

4. Parti Républicain, *Le Projet républicain* (Paris, Flammarion, 1978), p. 99.

5. Ibid., p. 99.

6. Ibid., p. 92.

7. Ibid., p. 93.

8. David & Halleman, 'Les partis politiques français et les euromissiles', pp. 70-74.

9. Ibid., p. 71. See also on this question, the UDF's own defence publications: *Une Doctrine de Défense pour la France*, (Paris, UDF, 1980) and *La Loi de Programmation militaire nécessaire à la France en 1983: propositions de l'UDF* (Paris, UDF, 1983).

10. Centre des Démocrates Sociaux, *L'Autre Solution* (Paris, CDS, 1977), p. 226.

11. Ibid., p. 227.

12. Ibid., p. 227.

13. Ibid., pp. 228-9.

14. Dabezies, 'French political parties and Defence policy', p. 243.

15. For a recent survey, see L. Whetten, *New International Communism* (Lexington, D.C, Heath), 1982.

16. *L'Humanité*, 12 May 1977.

17. The political purpose of this is to be able to allege that the deterrent can be levelled at any aggressor. The USSR is not singled out as being the only threat and the only target.

18. For views which see the PCF as very subordinate to the CPSU, see any work by A. Kriegel, e.g. her *Les Communistes français,* (Paris, Seuil, 1970) or, more recently, the three volume *Histoire intérieure du PCF* (Paris, Fayard, 1981-83) by P. Robrieux. For a study which sees the PCF as acting essentially in an autonomous fashion, see I. Wall, *French Communism in the Era of Stalin,* Greenwood Press (forthcoming in 1983).

19. David & Halleman, 'Les partis politiques français et les euromissiles', p. 75.

20. G. Lavau, *A Quoi Sert le PCF?* (Paris, Fayard, 1981), pp. 404-6. This work is one of the more sober analyses of the PCF.

21. See, in English, R.W.Johnson, *The Long March of the French Left* (Macmillan, 1980) & N. Nugent and D. Lowe, *The Left in France* (Macmillan, 1982).

22. An excellent overall account of PS defence policy is P. Buffotot, *Le Parti socialiste et la défense, ou la recherche de la fonction patriotique* (Nanterre, Institut de Politique internationale et européenne, 1982).

23. P.S., *Le Poing et la Rose*, supplément au No. 73, 'Textes de Référence', August 1978, p. 34.

24. *Projet Socialiste pour la France des Années 80* (Paris, Club socialiste du Livre, 1980).

25. See below, Chapter 4.

26. For a general account of CERES, see D. Hanley, 'Ceres, an open conspiracy?' in D. Bell & E. Shaw (eds.), *The Left in France* (Nottingham, Spokesman, 1983), pp. 97-126.

27. Raymond Courrière (now Minister in charge of Rapatriés —i.e. ex-Algerian settlers) in an interview in P.Bosc, *Les Notables en Question* (Montpellier, Presses du Languedoc, 1977).

28. On the methodological hasards, see F. Vieillescazes & J.-P. Thomas, 'Notes à propos de l'opinion publique et la défense', *Défense nationale*, August-September 1977, pp. 57-71.

29. *Sondages*, 36, nos.1-2, 1974, pp.16-18.

30. J.-M.Lech, 'L'Evolution de l'opinion des Français sur la défense', *Défense Nationale*, August-September 1977, pp. 47-56.

31. Ibid., p. 48.

32. Ibid., p. 46.

33. See below, Chapters 8 and 10.

DEFENCE AND THE MITTERRAND GOVERNMENT
 Jolyon Howorth

A Decade of Transition 1972-1981

After the creation of the new Socialist Party (PS)[1] at the Congress of Epinay in 1971, and especially after the signature of the Socialist-Communist 'Common Programme of Government' (CPG) in June 1972, it became imperative for French socialists to attend closely to matters of defence and military strategy. Most socialists had continued to believe, throughout the twentieth century, that Jean Jaurès had uttered the last word on defence policy with his monumental work *L'Armée Nouvelle*,[2] published in 1911. In that classic reappraisal of traditional socialist antimilitarism, Jaurès had sought to reconcile the republic with its army, the nation with internationalism and socialism with the requirements of national defence. Jaurès had sought to recapture for the left that tradition of national defence which had been its historical birthright ever since the *levée en masse* in 1791 and which had known its most intense manifestation during the Paris Commune of 1871. He proposed a new army of 'citizen soldiers', invincible in defence, incapable of military aggression, and fully reconciled with the nation, to which it would no longer pose any threat as a force for internal repression.[3]

The two World Wars did little to diminish the appeal for socialists and communists of the Jaurésian approach. His social critique of the professional army and his call for popular resistance militias were given new urgency and legitimacy in the tragic and confused events of 1940-1944. If the socialists in government from 1945 to 1958 shelved Jaurès' teachings and adopted more traditional 'muscular' methods in their wars against national liberation movements in Indochina and Algeria, this repression was explained away in terms of the special constraints of the situation rather than in terms of the archaism or inappropriateness of the standard socialist doctrine.

With the return of de Gaulle and the reassertion (in the person of the Head of State) of professional militarism, and especially with the advent of the nuclear arsenal, traditional socialist responses were able to surface once again. François Mitterrand, the challenger to de Gaulle in the 1965 presidential elections, was unequivocal in his denunciation of France's nuclear weapons. It is perhaps significant that Mitterrand's main objection to the *force de frappe* was connected with its lack of credibility rather than with the principle of nuclear weapons. He did not stress the professionalism and elitism inherent in that very divorce between the nation and its defences which had always been the *bête noire* of the Jaurésian tradition.[4] But despite the French socialists' worries about *la bombinette*, it was clear that they had not yet begun collectively to think about the strategic questions posed by the nuclear age. The political crises of 1968 (Paris in May and Prague in August) followed closely by the disintegration of the old SFIO and the formation of the new PS, helped perpetuate what Charles Hernu has called 'the strange intellectual paralysis' on the left when it comes to matters military.[5]

The New Socialist Party and the CPG

However, within a year of Mitterrand's emergence at the head of the new Socialist Party in 1971, defence became a major issue at the PS National Convention in Suresnes in March 1972. Various motions confronted each other in what turned out to be the first serious discussion of defence issues for decades.[6] Charles Hernu, Jacques Huntzinger and Patrice Corbin pleaded openly in favour of retaining the nuclear arsenal as the cutting edge of a new socialist diplomatic thrust in the direction of 'bloc dissolution'. The nuclear dimension of this strategy, it was argued, would prevent socialist diplomacy from becoming what Hernu disparagingly referred to as a 'lame form of neutralism'. A similar motion presented by André Riel (the pseudonym of a top civil servant in the PS and a protégé of Jean-Pierre Chevènement) saw the French independent deterrent as a potential exit route from the political constraints of the Atlantic Alliance. However, at this stage, traditional reflexes won the day and the motion put by Pierre Bérégovoy calling for the abandonment of the nuclear arsenal was passed by a sizeable majority and incorporated into the party's political programme, *Changer la Vie*, published the following month.[7]

The credibility of that programme was hardly enhanced by the fact that it was obviously rejected by the party's leading military experts. Moreover, the fact that the text called for a halt to nuclear weapons production and did not demand the scrapping of existing systems was only one contradiction in a line which many believed with good reason to be unilateralist. More significant, perhaps, for later developments, was the remark made by Mitterrand in his preface to the programme. Addressing the issue of how to nudge the world out of Yalta, he asked: 'Who can believe that France alone can recover her world position without the means of power?'[8] Already, therefore, and from three different quarters (Hernu, Chevènement, Mitterrand), the basic argument which was soon to lead the PS to its present pro-nuclear stance had been set in motion. The prime diplomatic objective of the socialists was to be 'bloc dissolution' — the extrication of Europe from the Yalta settlement. The means was to be French 'creativity' in the political, diplomatic and cultural spheres. But it was already clear that sooner or later the party would have to decide (as Hernu and others were already urging it to do) whether such pressures alone were adequate to the task. To force disengagement from Europe upon the two superpowers, and to prevent the continent from becoming the theatre for their global confrontation, the French 'independent deterrent' was destined to become an increasingly attractive agent in the mind of many a socialist.

This line was soon to be elaborated within the context of the *Commission de la Défense Nationale* (CDN) which the PS had set up shortly after the Suresnes meeting. Paradoxically, one of the first tasks of this commission was to negotiate the defence chapter of the CPG. The text signed in June 1972 by the socialists, the communists and the left radicals contained an even more categorical rejection of France's nuclear arsenal than that embodied in the socialists' own programme.[9] Charles Hernu, who, while signing the CPG with one hand, was drawing up plans for a socialist nuclear arsenal with the other, noted laconically: '[...] while our sense of unity [with the PCF] was total, our desire not to be bound by the common text was equally imperative'.[10]

Although the nuclear 'deterrent' was the first and most urgent object of socialist attention, it was directly and structurally linked to the other major military problem of the late twentieth century: what to do with the army? What was the use of a mass conscript army within a defence strategy based on the 'equalising power of the atom'? Even if 'deterrence' failed and war broke out, the structures of the land army were felt to be increasingly inappropriate to technological warfare. Modern war-fighting, it was argued in both military and political circles, required above all team work between small groups of highly trained professionals (a helicopter squadron, a command, control and communications unit, a submarine crew). If the emphasis was henceforth to be placed on quality rather than quantity, what was to become of the egalitarian principle of *le curé sac au dos*?[11] Moreover, if the armed forces were to become a professional elite, did this not resurrect the old left-wing bogey of a military establishment liable to intervene in the political process on the side of the right? Such fears were highlighted by the experience of the Allende government in Chile.

In order to cope with these two related issues, the CDN, under the guidance of Charles Hernu, began to redefine the armed forces in a variety of ways. They discarded the old Clausewitzian notion of the army as a military 'state' existing outside of and above civil society, and began to promote the new Janowitzian[12] notion of the army as a military 'function' within (and reflecting the values of) civil society. This involved two main thrusts. First, an attempt to find a new structure within which to reconcile the army and the nation. Second, an effort to enter into permanent dialogue with serving officers in order to recruit both their expertise and their political sympathies. This dialogue was to have far-reaching consequences on the development of socialist defence policy.

By the spring of 1974, these consequences had taken on two very concrete forms. First, the CDN had progressively refined its thinking on defence strategy and had prepared a series of major discussion papers, the *Fiche de Synthèse sur les Problèmes de la Défense Nationale,* the main ideas of which have informed the broad lines of socialist defence policy under the Mitterrand presidency.[13] In particular the long chapter on the mission of the armed forces attempted to redefine French military policy in terms of a triad of defence capabilities whose close integration would solve many of the dilemmas we have just been rehearsing. First, there was to be a system of 'deep territorial defence' based on the 'popular mobilisation force' which would eventually replace the conscript army. Grouped in locally-based units of 30 men (the 'basic military group' or GMB) this force would undergo regular periods of maintenance training and would act as a highly effective popular militia or resistance structure rendering military occupation by a foreign power virtually impossible. In order to pre-empt that military occupation, the main army would be structured into a 'support and intervention force' which would have a conventional defence capability based on rapid deployment, mobility and high-technology fire-power (anti-tank PGMs, missile-firing helicopter gunships etc.). Finally, in case all else failed, the strategic nuclear 'deterrent' was to be maintained and modernised.

The second concrete form adopted by the ideas set in motion in the early seventies was the launching, on 8 April 1974, of Charles Hernu's 'think-tank', the *Conventions pour l'Armée Nouvelle* (CAN),[14] an association of officers and socialist activists anxious to promote the new military thinking in an atmosphere somewhat more independent than the politically restricted confines of the official PS defence commission.

These two developments coincided with the death, in April 1974, of Georges Pompidou and the second presidential campaign of François Mitterrand. The socialist candidate trod a very cautious path during the election, refusing to state clearly his support for nuclear weapons, but at the same time leaving open the prospect of adopting a nuclear defence policy in the event of failure of the general disarmament talks he considered it the duty of a socialist government to promote. For the moment, the socialist candidate, whether for tactical or principled reasons, was unprepared to go as far as his main military advisers, even though the *Fiche de Synthèse* was universally adopted by socialist cadres as the basis of their support for the Mitterrand campaign.

Nevertheless, by the time of the *Assises du Socialisme* in October 1974,[15] several important modifications in socialist defence thinking, systematically promoted by men like Charles Hernu over the previous decade, had come to acquire more widespread acceptance within the Socialist Party:

— The need for a reinterpretation of 'defence' in a broader, more global framework, synthesising the economic, political, social, cultural and industrial dimensions of national unity.

— A rejection of traditional 'knee-jerk' socialist anti-militarism and a rediscovery of traditional socialist attempts to reconcile the army and the nation.

— A recognition that defence policy in the 1980s was going to require a radical reappraisal of its two main components: nuclear weapons and the land army.[16]

The rest was largely a matter of time. Time seemed to go into suspension during the first two years of Giscard's presidency. The first (and only) Giscardian defence white paper (*loi de programmation militaire*) was made public in 1976 and covered the period 1977 to 1982. It was accompanied by what were widely interpreted as ominous-sounding speeches from Giscard and his Chief of Staff, General Guy Méry,[17] who appeared to be shifting the emphasis of French defence away from the nuclear 'deterrent'[18] and in the direction of a revamped conventional army capable of participating in NATO's 'forward battle' in Europe.

The real intentions of Giscardian defence policy remain to this day shrouded in mystery.[19] It seems clear that Giscard had intended to bridge the gap of uncertainty which had always loomed between France's 'independence' from the integrated military structures of NATO and her commitment, under article 5 of the Treaty of Washington, to come to the assistance of her NATO allies in the event of hostilities in Europe. It is often forgotten, even by senior politicians and officers, that France has never wavered in her commitment to the defence of Europe. The problem for NATO has always been to establish exactly how this would be done.[20] As the nuclear arms race began to escalate in the mid-1970s, and as the question of the defences of Europe came to be looked at by military planners in the light of the new weapons systems being deployed, it became even more urgent for NATO planners to know exactly where France stood. As a medium power she could obviously not afford (especially in times of recession) to pay for both a modernised nuclear capability and an upgraded conventional force. Choices had to be made and priorities selected. Giscard seemed to be tipping the balance in the direction of conventional war-fighting scenarios in line with NATO's flexible response strategy.[21]

Immediately, the Gaullists, the socialists and the communists joined in a chorus of protest against what was widely seen as *de facto* 'reintegration into NATO'. The PS was spurred into action and, in November 1976, its executive committee officially endorsed the French nuclear arsenal.[22] The thin end of the wedge, which had appeared in 1972 at the very moment when agreement had been reached with the communists on phasing out the 'deterrent', had finally prised open the main gate of the socialist anti-nuclear citadel. In explaining this volte-face, the PS argued that the world situation had changed considerably since the early 1960s when they had denounced de Gaulle's nuclear pretensions. Whereas his air-borne 'bombinette' had never enjoyed any real credibility, it was now a fact that France possessed a varied and highly credible nuclear strike capability. Moreover, constant advances in Soviet weapons technology, together with the relative withdrawal of the American nuclear 'umbrella', which had been implicit in the 1960s with the adoption of 'flexible response', had combined to put Europe in a new and seemingly vulnerable situation. Increasingly, the need was felt in Europe for an independent European defence capability. Thirdly, since, for socialists, the cost of a credible conventional defence was becoming politically unthinkable, the Gaullist concept of strategic 'deterrence' based on undetectable nuclear submarines was beginning to make more and more sense. Finally, since this 'deterrent' was to be combined with a slimmed down and remodelled army which would play a full and credible part in the defences of Europe, it was felt by many socialists that such a new combination would give a left-wing government considerable clout on the international stage to pursue diplomatic initiatives on the disarmament front. None of this was at all surprising to those in the PS who had had their eyes open for the previous decade. But the new policy nevertheless had to be submitted to a special National Convention which had been summoned for the end of 1977.

Before that convention could take place, however, the PCF stepped into the breach which had been made in the ramparts of the common programme... and proceeded to widen it. At a Central Committee meeting on 11 May 1977, Jean Kanapa read out a long report proposing major changes in communist defence policy. The nuclear arsenal was now to be retained and updated. This was the most important shift in policy. But, at the same time, a whole range of apparently secondary proposals combined to render that arsenal virtually useless. First, it was suggested that France should cease to rely on NATO (i.e. US) satellites for intelligence, guidance and communications systems; rather, she should develop her own satellites (a daunting task for a medium power). Second, it was proposed that the targeting policy for the French weapons should become omni-directional (*tous azimuts*), a proposal which had found favour with hard-line Gaullists in the late 1960s, but which had really been more of a bluster tactic than a serious proposition. Some commentators mischievously noted that the main effect of the PCF proposal was to halve the number of missiles targeted on the Soviet Union. The third proposal, however, was the most serious from a strictly 'deterrent' angle since it argued in favour of the adoption by France of a 'counterforce' strategy. While on the surface laudable from a purely humane perspective, this proposal made no sense at all from a military standpoint since a small power like France does not have the resources to threaten more than a tiny fraction of Soviet weapons. The counterforce suggestion was in any case rendered absolutely meaning-less by the fourth proposal which was that France should make a 'no first use' declaration. It makes little sense to target silos which, by definition, will be empty long before they are hit. To cap it all, the PCF argued in favour of a collegiate firing committee including representa-tives from the political parties and from parliament: a virtual guarantee that, if a decision to press the button were ever agreed on, it would come too late.[23]

The immediate effect of the communist bombshell was to precipitate the disintegration of the common programme and of left-unity. There was no way in which the PS could entertain the majority of the PCF proposals in view of its own recent evolution. The details of that evolution were to be ratified at the party's special National Convention which met from 7 to 8 January 1978.

The PS National Convention on Defence, January 1978

Military matters are not normally high on the agenda of the average socialist's preoccupations and it rapidly became clear, as the date for the convention approached, that the rank and file of the party had recently been content to leave defence decisions in the hands of the 'experts'. Equally clearly, however, the 'experts' had failed to carry the party with them.[24] Two separate texts were submitted for debate, the second offered as an amendment to the first. The first, signed by all the members of the party's executive bureau, and drafted jointly by the CERES minority and by the Mitterrand majority, called for a socialist government to initiate disarmament talks immediately and, pending their outcome, to maintain the nuclear arsenal intact, with the exception of the ageing Mirage bombers, which were to be phased out. The 'amendment' accepted the temporary preservation of the submarine-launched missiles only, but proposed immediate scrapping of all the land-based systems (Mirage IV bombers, S2 ICBMs on the Plateau d'Albion and the Pluton tactical weapons). It also rejected both the principle and the 'logic' of 'deterrence' as well as any attempt to modernise the existing arsenal. In reality, the spirit of this 'amendment' was directly opposed to the spirit of the main motion and Hernu was adamant in insisting that 'it is impossible to vote for both texts. One has to choose between them.'[25]

The choice, however, was utterly confusing. Many of the most energetic opponents of Mitterrand's 'volte-face' on nuclear weapons came from the ranks of his long-term supporters. Some of his closest political associates signed the 'amendment'. Moreover, although the main motion had been drafted by Mitterrandists and by the CERES, it soon became quite obvious that each side had a very different interpretation of its significance. Indeed, the CERES had presented their own personal 'contribution', alongside the main motion, in an effort to portray the latter as being highly critical of the Atlantic Alliance, as an assertion of France's commitment to genuine independence from both blocs, virtually a call for complete withdrawal from NATO. Mitterrand, on the other hand, insisted that the main motion implied continuing ties with NATO, and he urged the delegates to reject the CERES 'contribution', which they duly did by 71% to 17.5%. Not deterred by this, the CERES presented another amendment calling for the abolition of Pluton tactical weapons, but this was voted down even by the 'anti-nuclear lobby', which was suspicious of the CERES's promotion of strategic deterrence and revolted by their anti-Atlanticism. To add to the confusion, the 'anti-nuclear lobby', which had in effect presented the original 'amendment', proved to be the most ardently 'Atlanticist' caucus at the convention, arguing that France could afford to abandon her own nuclear weapons by returning to the security of the NATO umbrella. These people (Patrick Viveret and Charles Josselin prominent among them) came to be known as 'a-nuclear' rather than 'anti-nuclear'. Many delegates, quite incapable of following the niceties of these conflicting positions, voted both the main motion (with their reason) and the 'amendment' (with their heart).

Significantly, the real debate had been about the politics of the Atlantic Alliance rather than about the French bomb. That debate persists today. The CERES case for all-out strategic 'deterrence', based exclusively on submarines, marshalled three main arguments. First, France should take 'independence' to its logical conclusion and ease herself out of NATO as diplomatically as possible. Second, her nuclear weapons would not only be the best possible defence for her as an independent nation, but they would also help protect from hostile external influence her forthcoming experiment in socialism. Third, her weapons would prevent the outbreak of nuclear war in Europe by keeping both superpowers in check. The CERES case is an absolutist one which sees the 'strategic deterrent' as the only credible weapon. There is no room in the CERES strategy for vulnerable land-based systems nor for tactical weapons, nor for 'ultimatum shots' or other battlefield games.

The proposers of the motion calling for nuclear de-escalation showed that their primary fear was that French nuclear weapons would lend added complexity to the SALT talks between the superpowers. They were not, for the most part, opposed to American nuclear 'protection', and saw very little purpose in France possessing her own 'deterrent'. They were prepared to entertain the notion of French unilateral nuclear disarmament on condition that much closer links with the Alliance be established. Their line was diametrically opposed to that of the CERES.

François Mitterrand, however, had realised that more than a decade of Gaullist foreign and defence policy had begun to acquire a certain permanency in the mind of the political class. It would have been unthinkable for him to adopt the 'de-escalation' thesis and opt for greater integration into NATO. At the same time he rejected the anti-Atlanticism of the CERES and openly criticised their absolutist approach to 'deterrence'.[26] By a process of elimination, Mitterrand therefore found himself obliged to embrace the tactical approach of de Gaulle, whom he now admitted to have 'seen things as they really were' (*'il a vu juste'*).

At the close of two very confusing days of debating, the main motion was voted by 68% of the delegates, 31% opting for the 'amendment'. A final compromise resolution, which Chevènement ridiculed as a 'papier maché synthesis', was then adopted unanimously. But that textual unanimity could not hide the fact that the PS was (and still is today) deeply divided on this issue.

From Electoral Defeat to Electoral Victory

The unanimity was, in any case, of no assistance in winning the important general elections of March 1978. In the political crisis which followed defeat at the polls, defence considerations faded totally from the scene. Even Charles Hernu's *Conventions pour l'Armée Nouvelle* went into hibernation.The premises at 50, rue de Rivoli were relinquished and the team which had worked so fervently to be ready with a socialist defence policy was left dispirited and deflated. It was not until the end of 1979 that new premises were rented and the *Conventions* began to renew their work.

By that time, NATO plans for 'modernisation' of the Alliance's intermediate-range theatre nuclear arsenal had become the focal point of world attention. In France, the debate centred on the old but increasingly urgent question of France's precise role in the defence of Europe. Centrist spokesmen like Admiral Delahousse,[27] possibly acting as a front for Giscard d'Estaing, floated once again the notion of an integrated European defence system allied to the USA. Against this oblique call for greater cooperation with NATO, came a call from two maverick Gaullists, Georges Buis and Alexandre Sanguinetti, for France to share her nuclear secrets with Germany, thereby trying to create the conditions for an autonomous *European* defence capability.[28] But from all other quarters (mainstream Gaullists, socialists and communists) came arguments in favour of the independence of the French nuclear 'deterrent'.

But if independence was an attractive political slogan, it neverthe-less required some precise strategic definition. In view of the increasingly widespread perceptions of Europe's vulnerability ('sanc-tuarisation' of the superpowers, withdrawal of the US 'guarantee', deployment of the SS 20 and adoption of the notion of 'flexible response') where, precisely, did France consider that her 'vital interests' would begin to be in danger? And where did the French nuclear arsenal fit into the various rounds of arms control talks? Again, it rapidly became apparent that the PS was deeply divided. When Jean-Pierre Cot argued, in September 1979, that French weapons should be included in the so-called 'grey-area' INF talks (SALT 3), his reasoning was publicly shot to pieces by Didier Motchane of CERES, who accused his colleague of closet-Atlanticism.[29]

It was the CERES group which took the only clear stance within the PS on the NATO 'two-track' decision of December 1979 to deploy Pershing 2 and Cruise missiles in Europe while negotiating with the Soviet Union a general reduction in the level of 'euromissiles'. Jean-Pierre Chevènement totally rejected the notion that the Soviet Union enjoyed military superiority in Europe, denounced the destabilising effects of Pershing 2, deplored the extent to which the NATO decision drove home the utter dependency of Europe on US protection, regretted that the decision would be likely to increase political repression within the Eastern bloc and concluded by demanding the modernisation of the French strategic 'deterrent' as the only hope of avoiding nuclear war in Europe.[30] But the PS as a body avoided making any official pronounce-ment on the NATO decision. They did, however, refuse to participate in a PCF-organised demonstration against Pershing 2 and Cruise, arguing that the SS 20 needed to be included in the protest.[31]

The uncertainty over France's strategic priorities was exacerbated in April 1980 with the publication of defence proposals from both the Giscardian and Gaullist parties. While Giscard attempted valiantly to cover all his political and military options (his preference went towards NATO, but he was dependent on Gaullist votes in the forthcoming presidential elections), the Gaullists opted massively for strategic nuclear missiles based on submarines, whose numbers they wished to increase from 6 to 15.[32] In face of these uncertainties, it became more than ever urgent for the PS to put forward its own defence proposals in time for the 1981 presidentials. This was to be the task of the Socialist Project, published in January 1980.[33]

The Socialist Project contained a number of significant shifts in comparison with the text voted only two years previously at the national convention on defence. First, the commitment to eventual abandonment of all forms of nuclear weaponry, which had still been the starting point in 1978, had completely disappeared. Secondly, whereas in 1978 the preservation of the 'deterrent' had been presented as a quasi-temporary measure pending the outcome of general disarmament talks, by 1980, it had come to be seen as an instrument of diplomatic pressure to get those talks under way.[34] Thirdly, the French arsenal was now clearly presented as an instrument of control in Europe to restrain the belligerent tendencies of the superpowers: 'Because it is capable of scuttling the hypothesis of a battle in Europe, the French deterrent is henceforth a factor of stability for the entire continent'.[35] Finally, whereas we saw that the 1978 document was intended by the PS majority as an expression of independence within the Alliance, the 1980 text leans much more heavily in the direction of 'neutralism' and insists repeatedly on the need to break down both blocs and both military alliances.

How far did the Socialist Project reflect the minority opinion of its drafters, Jean-Pierre Chevènement and the CERES, with whom Mitterrand had struck a political deal the year before in order to stave off a challenge to his presidential aspirations from Michel Rocard? The PS was still maintaining official silence on the NATO 'two-track decision' and throughout the summer of 1980, in a series of major interviews, François Mitterrand continued to insist that there existed rough parity between the superpowers in Europe. However, he noted that the idea of bargaining Pershing 2 against the SS 20 was beginning to make headway in diplomatic circles and he was clearly not averse to such an equation, even if he made it clear that he saw the matter largely as a question of nuclear diplomacy.[36] But Mitterrand is far too astute a politician to allow any of his options to slip out of his grasp and one can submit all of his pre-electoral statements on defence to the most powerful analytical microscope without finding any really unambiguous statement of policy.

A good example of this socialist propensity for fence-sitting is to be found in the debate over the neutron bomb which monopolised the attention of the defence establishment throughout much of 1980. In France the N-bomb rapidly acquired symbolic rather than military or strategic importance. To be in favour of it was seen as tantamount to Atlanticism and to negation of the Gaullist notion of 'deterrence'. When, in May 1980, the UDF published a statement in favour of the new device, specifically in the context of battle-fighting techniques, the suspicions which many had harboured since 1976 were instantly confirmed, even if the President himself postponed any decision on production.[37]

Within the PS, the same old divisions surfaced anew. On 25 June 1980, an official statement was issued to the effect that the party was not opposed to pursuit of the 'technical mastery' of the N-bomb,[38] but that it rejected production for the time being. The CERES refused to go along with this decision. The right-wing of the party, in the person of Michel Rocard, went to the other extreme, arguing that there was no reason not to go ahead with production immediately.[39] It was left to Charles Hernu to produce the military rationale behind the party's decision not to follow the Gaullists and the communists in denouncing the new weapon. He considered that, in the context of France's doctrine of the tactical 'ultimatum' shot, the N-bomb might be an appropriate warhead with which to equip Pluton.[40] In this way, the PS was able to have its N-bomb without being accused of reintegrating NATO or preparing for the 'forward battle' in Europe. But as 1980 turned into presidential year 1981, while the rest of Europe flocked to the demonstrations organised by the various peace movements, France once again shut out external problems and concentrated on her own domestic political battles.

Mitterrand's campaign manifesto, drawn up at a special socialist congress on 24 January 1981, was a far cry from either the 1978 or the 1980 documents on defence. Gone was all mention of abandoning nuclear weapons. Gone was all reference to the strategic 'deterrent' as being the instrument to prevent superpower confrontation in Europe. Gone was all mention of a referendum on the issue. Instead, there was vague reference made to simultaneous dissolution of the military blocs, a promise to prevent proliferation, a call for a European security conference and a call for withdrawal of the SS 20 alongside non-deployment of the new NATO missiles. Otherwise, the document stressed Mitterrand's penchant for the independent strategic 'deterrent', reduction of military service to six months and a redefinition of the scope and content of the Atlantic Alliance.

Defence issues, however, played virtually no part in the campaign, with the exception of a tripartite clash over numbers of nuclear submarines.[41] Mitterrand remained curiously silent about the specific clauses of the Alliance that he wished to see discussed, curiously silent about the balance of forces in Europe, enigmatic about the way in which he saw France's role in the defence of Europe and significantly silent about French strategic doctrine, all of which subjects were at the heart of the defence debate. The CERES group tried to break through this barrier of silence with a series of articles in *Le Monde*.[42] Their arguments were by now well known. The real debate, they insisted, was about bloc politics. Giscard's historical role, they charged, had been to realign France with NATO and thereby demolish all her credibility as an arbiter or intermediary between the superpowers.

Only a strong, nuclear France, totally independent of both blocs, could take the sorely-needed initiative on European disarmament. Was the CERES trying to force Mitterrand's hand before it was too late? Or did they feel that their ideas were shared by the socialist candidate? The events of the Mitterrand presidency have provided partial answers to some of these questions.

Defence Policy under President Mitterrand

When François Mitterrand assumed power in May 1981, several major questions relating to defence and military policy required urgent answers. During the final year of the Giscard *septennat*, defence had remained in a state of advanced ambiguity. There were four important issues on which defence experts looked to the socialists for a clear lead. First, what line would the new government take on the 'euromissiles' and on arms control and reduction talks in general? Second, which way would the socialists swing the balance of priorities as between nuclear and conventional defence systems? How would they react to rapid advances in military technology and the need for 'modernisation' which was being pressed on successive governments by the military planners? Third, what strategic theory would underpin the choice of weapons systems? If the priority were given to nuclear weapons, would this imply a preference for Gaullist precepts of strategic 'deterrence', or would new emphasis be placed (as it had been under Giscard) on battle-fighting, tactical nuclear weapons? On the other hand, if there was to be a major effort in the field of conventional weapons, would this signal closer links with NATO? Fourth, how would the socialists handle the long overdue question of the restructuring of the land army? Would they honour their electoral promise to reduce military service to six months? Would the new, professional force which seemed bound to emerge have a new role to play in the defence of Europe?

A flurry of defence activity followed Charles Hernu's appointment as Defence Minister on 22 May 1981. But those hoping for some early sign of socialist intentions were to be disappointed. Hernu discovered, on taking over at 14, rue St. Dominique, that the delays in implementing the procurements provisions of the 1977-82 defence white paper were much more serious than had been publicly admitted by the outgoing administration. He therefore decided to delay the drafting of a socialist programme until the existing (Giscardian) one had been fully implemented. Although this decision was justified in terms of the need for a minimum of continuity, it suggested that the differences in strategic doctrine between Mitterrand and Giscard were less absolute than certain socialists had often claimed. Above all, the delay gave the socialist government a breathing space in which to finalise its own ideas on defence.[43]

The other immediate decisions taken by Hernu, however, implied change rather than continuity. The controversial proposals to extend the Larzac military camp were scrapped. There was much political and environmentalist mileage to be derived from this, but the decision also made sense militarily since the extension had been intended mainly as a tank base and socialist defence doctrine had been moving rapidly away from the more classical notions of tank warfare. Similarly, Hernu's early statements on the nuclear arsenal underscored the government's decision to give priority to strategic nuclear weapons as opposed to tactical ones.[44]

As for the other immediate decisions, they gave no hint of what was to come. If military service was maintained at twelve months, this was explained in terms of the need to avoid abrupt changes in the strength of the army.[45] If nuclear testing was temporarily suspended in the South Pacific, this was purely coincidental since recent accidents at the test site would have required suspension in any case.[46] Perhaps the most visible innovation in the early months was the new socialist message of 'global defence'. In a major interview, Hernu argued that defence would only be effective if French society were united and considered by all its members to be worth defending. In this sense, suggested Hernu, the Minister of Labour, by putting men back to work, and the Minister of Education, by instilling a notion of justice and history in young people's minds, were also 'Ministers of Defence'. As for himself, he added, he was merely the 'Minister of Military Defence'.[47]

The Euromissiles and the Problems of Nuclear Diplomacy

One revealing indicator of socialist intentions came during the summer of 1981 when Mitterrand and Hernu first began to make pronouncements on the 'euromissile' question. While, as we have seen, Mitterrand had gradually been coming round to the idea of linking the SS 20 to the Pershing 2 and Cruise missiles, Charles Hernu had, until comparatively recently, held very different views. In a book entitled *Nous Les Grands*, published in December 1980 (one year after the NATO 'two-track' decision), he had summarily rejected all talk of Soviet superiority in Europe or elsewhere as NATO propaganda, referring scornfully to the 'circulation of the most fantastic figures and statistics'. On strategic systems, he argued that the USA had a commanding lead, in warheads, guidance systems, fuel systems and undetectability: 'On the whole range of weapons systems, the USA have about a generation's advance over the USSR [...] To speak of an imbalance in favour of the USSR is simply not serious.'[48] He accepted that the SS 20 was a qualitatively different weapon from the SS 4 or the SS 5, but even so did not feel that it had altered the balance of forces in Europe as a whole. He waved aside the oft-repeated assertion of a 5:1 Soviet advantage in tanks as 'meaningless' in view of the West's anti-tank weapons. After reviewing naval and air forces, he concluded unequivocally: 'The truth is that American superiority is total'. Hernu's book was unavailable in bookshops by the summer of 1981, and even the PS's own bookshop could not seem to locate a copy...[49]

For by that time, Mitterrand's own views on these matters were diametrically opposed to those expressed by his Defence Minister only six months previously. The matter was already very complex, but two interrelated secondary issues rendered it even more so. First, Mitterrand's stated intention of 'renegotiating' certain aspects of the Atlantic Alliance. Second, his decision to appoint four communists to his government. Vice-President Bush, visiting Paris immediately after this latter decision, ominously warned that relations between France and her Alliance partners could be seriously affected by the appointment of communist ministers. Mitterrand's margin of manoeuvre was tightly circumscribed. Retreat into a defence strategy based solely on France was as unthinkable as was complete reintegration into NATO. He could not afford to alienate the Americans for two reasons: France still depended on US satellite and other technology for her own defence systems; and US potential for economic sabotage of the French socialist experiments was considerable. All these considerations no doubt help to explain the President's decision, in July 1981, to offer enthusiastic support for the deployment of Pershing 2 and Cruise: 'I believe that peace is linked to the balance of forces in the world. The installation of the SS 20s and the Backfires has disturbed this balance in Europe. I cannot accept this and I believe that Europe must rearm in order to re-establish equilibrium. [...] I believe [...] there is a Soviet supremacy in Europe and I see a real danger there. But the USA has the means to re-establish the balance.'[50]

It is clear from the outset that Mitterrand's enthusiastic support for the NATO 'two-track' decision was based more on a diplomatic gamble than on strategic principle. Irrespective of the eventual outcome of the euromissile crisis, the risks for France in supporting

NATO were high. By arguing in favour of increasing both the American and the French nuclear arsenals, he risked blurring the distinction between superpower systems and the 'independent' French system. Moreover, he was overtly prejudicing France's hopes of acting as an 'honest broker' between the US and the USSR with a view to bringing them to the negotiating table (the stated principal aim of French diplomacy).[51] On the other hand, Mitterrand felt there was much to be gained from demonstrations of Franco-Atlantic solidarity. The sympathy of Ronald Reagan and of Helmut Schmidt was essential for the defence of the franc which was under heavy pressure already on the money markets. Moreover, Mitterrand clearly believed that 'nuclear diplomacy' works and that the Soviet Union would eventually concede to a united western front what it would not have yielded to a less resolute negotiating partner. France (and the 'West') might just get something for nothing.

The military or strategic aspect of the question is of far less immediate importance to Mitterrand. Having, in his July 1981 interview in *Stern*, spoken of clear Soviet superiority in Europe, he later stated, in the same interview, that he 'would like to know precisely what the state of the forces [was] between the two camps' and promised to 'study this matter very carefully'. What was it he did not yet know? Evidently quite a lot since only ten weeks later, in his major press conference of 24 September 1981, he reversed his previous judgement on Soviet superiority and accepted, as did Charles Hernu,[52] the notion of approximate parity between the superpowers. On these occasions, the decision to support NATO policy was justified on the grounds of a *potential* Soviet lead later in the decade.

In the long term, of course, Mitterrand is clearly very concerned about the military/strategic aspect of the euromissile question. He was disarmingly frank, in December 1981, in acknowledging that if the SS 20 had caused an imbalance in one direction, Pershing 2 would create another, equally intolerable imbalance in the other direction.[53]

Yet the basic tactic of the Mitterrand administration has been to play to the full the game of nuclear diplomacy. In an important speech to the IHEDN, Charles Hernu recognised that any meaningful redressing of the 'Eurobalance' by American weapons might take up to a decade, but what was important was 'the fact of announcing' the new deployments.[54] Similarly, Foreign Minister Claude Cheysson, in welcoming Reagan's 'zero option' proposals, analysed them in purely diplomatic terms. First, he said, they were intended to reassure Europeans who had been alarmed by previous statements from the White House about 'limited nuclear war-fighting in Europe'.[55]

Second, Cheysson interpreted the Pershing 2 missile as essentially a political weapon with which to counter the 'decoupling' propensities of the SS 20.[56] And finally, according to Cheysson, once the superpowers had been led to the negotiating table, they would be sure to find a satisfactory formula.[57]

Nuclear diplomacy is not seen by Mitterrand simply as a way of entering into the debate between the superpowers. It also has a bilateral dimension to it. The aim is to show both superpowers that France remains mistress of her own destiny. Thus, while Claude Cheysson, in the interview referred to above, insisted on France's desire to improve relations with the Soviet Union at every level, the President continued to refuse to meet the Soviet leaders while they maintained troops in Afghanistan. Yet, at the same time, France vigorously resisted US attempts to impose commercial sanctions on the socialist bloc and, after the imposition of martial law in Poland, successfully killed off US attempts to prevent European states from signing gas-pipeline contracts with the USSR. Similarly, although Mitterrand has been vociferous in his support for Reagan's nuclear diplomacy, he has been outspokenly opposed to US foreign policy on almost every other issue: Central America, North/South, Africa, international economic policy.

The main bilateral thrust of Mitterrand's nuclear diplomacy has come in the field of Franco-American relations. It was in the context of his much-publicised desire to 'renegotiate' aspects of the Atlantic Alliance that he made his dramatic flying visit to Washington on 12 March 1982. The object of the exercise, it was argued by many, was for Mitterrand to consecrate his position as 'spokesperson for Europe' which he felt France's nuclear arsenal gave him the right to claim. What he actually said to Reagan is still subject to conjecture, but a certain consensus has emerged around the likelihood of his having raised four basic points. The first was that the Alliance had to be seen as a comprehensive unit in which mutual duties and responsibilities, diplomatic, political and economic as well as military, needed to be carefully weighed.[58] Second, that at the European end the most vital task was to ensure that Germany be recemented to the Western bloc and prevented from sliding towards 'neutralism'. In order to achieve this, Mitterrand discussed with Reagan the prospect of much closer military collaboration between the two continental European powers. His third aim was to persuade the American President that, while nuclear diplomacy was a necessary game to be played, it had to be played sincerely and intelligently. It was he argued, vital not to provoke the Russians, not to bury détente altogether, and not to scuttle the Europeans' chance of establishing a viable *modus vivendi* with their Eastern neighbours. Finally, he wished to reassert France's absolute refusal to consider participating in the INF talks in Geneva. In this way, while offering France's enthusiastic support for one aspect of US nuclear diplomacy, Mitterrand was able to show the Americans that he was by no means a slave to the Pentagon. The same trip had the collateral effect of reminding the Russians, in case they should imagine that the gas-pipeline contracts signaled a 'weakening' of Western resolve, that Washington was only three hours away on Concorde, even if it did mean eating two breakfasts.[59]

While Mitterrand was pursuing nuclear diplomacy, the PS leaders were tussling with the need to prepare a statement on disarmament for the United Nations Special Session on the issue due to be held in New York in June 1982. In view of the party's support for both French and American contributions to the arms race, this was a difficult document to draft, and the finished product reflects these difficulties. The document is a curious mix of paradox and contradiction.[60] While proudly reasserting the traditional socialist concern for 'peace', it scornfully denounces 'pacifism' as an impasse (many people would have been forgiven for believing that 'pacifism' *was* the traditional socialist approach to peace). While asserting that the PS has a 'realistic' understanding of the requirements for maintaining peace, there is a complete absence of any theoretical assessment of those requirements. While reiterating socialist calls for disarmament, it repeats just as regularly the socialist call for France to build up her nuclear arsenal. While demanding the dissolution of the military blocs, it offers unequivocal support for the NATO position at Geneva. While recognising that all over Europe the political credibility of nuclear deterrence is being challenged and questioned, it asserts that the French 'deterrent' works and that the French people feel quite secure in the midst of their nuclear stockpile. Two concrete proposals somewhat enhance the value of what otherwise stands as a confused compromise text, which tries hard to please all the conflicting tendencies within the party. The first proposal is a renewed call for a European Disarmament Conference comprising all the nations involved in the 'Helsinki process'. The second is for a conference of all five nuclear powers with a view to producing a global approach to nuclear disarmament. In July 1983, the former of these proposals was finally accepted and the Conference on European security and co-operation, meeting in Madrid, finally agreed to organise an all-European disarmament conference which will meet in Stockholm on 17 January 1984.[61]

Not surprisingly, 1983, the year of Pershing 2 and Cruise, produced an intensification of France's participation in the game of nuclear diplomacy. This was the result of a variety of new developments. The new Soviet leader, Yuri Andropov, reacting to the unquestioning support for NATO which was forthcoming from France under Mitterrand, proposed that a solution to the stalled INF talks in Geneva would be for the USSR to reduce its intermediate-range nuclear missiles to the level of the combined French and British totals, in exchange, of course, for non-deployment of Cruise and Pershing 2. Mitterrand's 'independence bluff' had been called. In January, former President Giscard broke his self-imposed silence and openly criticised the socialist government for its public support for NATO military decisions. He was quick to spot the Achilles heel of the socialist stance and warned that France was in the process of destroying her own case for not having her nuclear arsenal discussed at Geneva. Two days later, one of Giscard's former senior diplomatic advisers, Gabriel Robin, pressed the attack on the government by arguing that the SS 20 had hardly affected the balance of forces in Europe since the Soviets, with their SS 4 and SS 5, had for years possessed the capacity to destroy the continent several times over. What, asked Robin somewhat disingenuously,[62] did the SS 20 add to that capability? Quite apart from the internal political capital that the Giscardians stood to gain from entering the controversy in this way (the Mitterrand line was becoming increasingly controversial, both with the general public and with the PCF) the ex-President's low-profile approach to arms control contrasted sharply with that of Mitterrand.[63] Moreover, sensing that Reagan's 'zero option' was increasingly perceived in the West as an unrealistic starting point for arms control negotiations, Giscard pressed home his attack in February 1983 by suggesting that it should be reformulated as 'objective zero' and by arguing in favour of a compromise which would generate a process leading to gradual disarmament.[64]

But François Mitterrand was not deterred. On 20 January 1983, he addressed a specially convened session of the German parliament and urged the German people to welcome Pershing 2 onto their soil as the only way of establishing a nuclear balance in Europe. To enthusiastic applause from Christian Democratic benches, and mortified silence from his fellow socialists of the SPD (including his personal friends Willy Brandt and Helmut Schmidt) Mitterrand put the entire weight of his authority behind the NATO 'two-track' decision which was, to some extent, at the heart of the forthcoming German election campaign.[65] The right-wing Bavarian leader, Franz-Josef Strauss, later estimated that Mitterrand's speech had been worth an extra three per cent of the votes for the right-wing candidates.[66] Yet so great was Mitterrand's fear lest an SPD victory at the German polls break what he considered to be the ongoing dynamic of nuclear *diplomacy*, that the *politics* of his speech was obviously of no concern to him. There is an element of self-fulfilling prophecy in nuclear diplomacy which involves the players in getting more and more deeply involved the longer they play. The Williamsburg summit brought this lesson home to the French president in no uncertain terms.

In May 1983, Mitterrand allowed himself to be manoeuvred by Mrs Thatcher and President Reagan into signing a joint communiqué on the security of the Western world.[67] The anomaly of the Williamsburg communiqué derived not only from the fact that this was the first time an economic summit had given rise to a defence statement, but also from the fact that the presence at the conference of Mr Nakasone implied an extension of the Atlantic Alliance to include Japan. The French protested energetically against any such interpretation.[68] Moreover, it is clear that Reagan and Thatcher had hoped to use the statement as a reassertion of the non-negotiability of the 'zero-option', and it was due to resistance from both Mitterrand and Kohl that a sentence was included in the statement to the effect that 'the negotiations will determine the level of deployment' of any new missiles. This turned out to be a highly significant development in more ways than one.

In the first place, it represented the first occasion on which Mitterrand had openly departed from the official 'zero-option' position on Geneva. By the summer of 1983, it had become clear that the rigidity of that position was merely an obstacle to progress. In this sense, the Williamsburg statement can be seen as a united western move in the direction of flexibility. In the following weeks, Mitterrand was to stress on numerous occasions that he found both the American starting position ('zero-option') and the Soviet starting position (slight reductions in the SS 20 levels in exchange for non-deployment of the NATO missiles) unacceptable. After a series of discussions with German leaders, he began to promote with some degree of energy the 'walk-in-the-woods' compromise solution which had been elaborated by the US and Soviet negotiators in the summer of 1982 (no deployment of Pershing, and reduction of Cruise levels to around 300, with corresponding reductions in the SS 20 to about 100 missiles).[69] This was in fact a tacit admission that time was running short and that if nuclear diplomacy were to produce any result at all, the West would have to change its negotiating stance.

But that shift in position after Williamsburg also produced a new line from the PCF. They interpreted the joint communiqué as a *hardening* of western resolve, since not only was this the first time France had signed a statement to the effect that 'the security of our countries is indivisible', but also the reference to the negotiations deciding the level of missile deployments was seen as acceptance of the fact that *some* western missiles *would* be deployed. Therefore, on 31 May 1983, the political bureau of the PCF, in an important statement critical of the French position at Williamsburg, argued that since the various governments had taken this line on Geneva, the INF talks should be opened up to all European countries.[70] From all sides the criticism of Mitterrand began to pour in. The Gaullists[71] and the Soviet Union[72] joined forces in denouncing his return to 'Atlanticism'.

In the summer of 1983, the diplomatic battle over the euromissiles saw France at the centre of the controversy in various ways. First, the Soviet proposal that France's arsenal should be put on the table at Geneva became a major sticking point in the INF negotiations. Second, the decision of the French government to break a seventeen-year isolation and act as host to the NATO Council meeting, which was held in Paris in June, gave rise to predictable criticism from Gaullists and Communists, not to mention the Kremlin.[73] Third, in his speech to the NATO meeting, Mitterrand came out openly in favour of the 'walk-in-the-woods compromise', which had recently found favour with the SPD,[74] and formulated the hope that Geneva would fix the INF 'balance' at 'the lowest level possible'. This may well have been in part in an attempt to stave off a mounting challenge to the French position from a combination of the PCF, the peace movement and the Soviet Union. For the fourth development was precisely such a challenge.

On 19 June 1983, the PCF-dominated MDP held a highly successful 'peace picnic' in the forest of Vincennes, which many commentators interpreted as the moment of take-off for the French peace movement.[75] Although the slogans for this demonstration remained as vague as ever, the position of the PCF itself had shifted quite markedly since the Williamsburg declaration. With increasing regularity, the PCF was beginning to agitate for France to accept the Andropov proposals that the French nuclear arsenal should, together with the British, be 'balanced' against the SS 20s.[76] These proposals were made quite explicit after a surprise visit by Georges Marchais to Moscow on 12 July. Despite a public-relations exercise which consisted of conjuring up a false 'quarrel' between Marchais and Andropov, it rapidly transpired that what was afoot was an agreement between the PCF and the CPSU on taking the French weapons 'into consideration' at Geneva.[77] The repercussions of this major breach in the 'presidential majority' are still not clear, but it is possible that, despite PCF reassurances to the contrary, this could prove to be a turning point for the communists in government in France.[78] The ambiguities in the defence policies of the various components of the 'presidential majority' finally burst out into the open in the summer of 1983 when the CERES joined in the chorus of criticism.[79]

At this stage, one can only speculate as to why Mitterrand has chosen to give such unswerving public support to Pershing and Cruise. Quite apart from his conviction that nuclear diplomacy is an appropriate occupation for a country like France, he is clearly convinced that there exists a danger of Soviet supremacy in Europe from the mid-1980s. He greatly fears the potential impact of such an imbalance on the attitude of Germany towards the Soviet Union, and is determined to do everything in his power to continue to weld Germany to the West. However, his initial faith in the bargaining process has worn rather thin, and there are signs that his irritation with Washington has become as severe as his posturing towards Moscow. The political price of unswerving support for Reagan has begun to prove rather high, and it has exposed the conflicts and contradictions not only as between the PS and the PCF, but also within the governing PS. It seems clear that, before Williamsburg, he felt that, whatever the impact of his position on the Russians, he was building up a stock of credit in the White House which he presumably felt he would later be able to cash in on other issues. But his total failure to persuade the US administration to alter its monetary and fiscal policies has destroyed that illusion as well.[80] It is clear that American economic pressures on the socialist government have been highly successful in 'keeping Mitterrand in line'. In order to fully understand the direction of French defence policy in the years to come, we must now look at the item which, in late 1983, remains very much at the heart of the euromissile debates: the French independent 'deterrent'.

The French 'Deterrent'

If all the signs had suggested that Giscard d'Estaing had subtly been restructuring France's entire defence panoply, including her nuclear arsenal, with a view to *rapprochement* with the NATO doctrine of 'flexible response', there have been many indications that Mitterrand wishes to be seen as trying to reverse that trend. The first defence budget, published in October 1981, was the occasion for confirmation that France would construct a seventh nuclear missile-launching submarine (of a completely new type), would develop a new, mobile, surface-to-surface strategic missile (the SX), with which to replace the vulnerable fixed-silo S 3, and would replace the ageing Pluton tactical missile with the longer range Hades. While the first two decisions confirmed the government's stated intentions of affording absolute priority to strategic systems, the decision on Hades came as something of a shock to many socialist deputies who had been under the impression that tactical weapons might be phased out.

The fact that they are not being phased out is significant. Senior politicians and military leaders have repeatedly stressed, in recent months, that the 'all-or-nothing' strategic approach to 'deterrence' is not at all credible. France, they insist, needs an intermediate stage in the strategy of *du faible au fort* which will allow her to make clear her intentions. Under the socialist administration, there has been an unequivocal public return to the doctrine first theorised under the Gaullists, by General Lucien Poirier, of the 'test' or 'ultimatum' shot. According to this theory, the tactical missile is to be used, on the political authority of the President, only in the event of an enemy advance which seems to be threatening France's 'vital interests'. The very act of firing it is intended as an unambiguous statement that the enemy must now stop its advance or else the strategic weapon will be fired almost immediately. In speech after speech, beginning with Pierre Mauroy's first lecture to the IHEDN on 14 September 1981, this interpretation of the tactical weapon has been driven home time and again.[81] Moreover, the same spokesmen have insisted that the Giscardian notion of tactical missiles as part of a war-fighting or battlefield panoply within the strategic context of 'flexible response' is anathema. In this respect, therefore, there appears to have been a very clear break with the direction in which Giscard seemed to be taking France under his presidency.[82]

But strategic nuclear weapons cost money, and at the height of the economic crisis that particular commodity was beginning to be in short supply. As early as January 1982, Pierre Mauroy had ordered the Defence Minister to freeze approximately 25% of his expenditure, and in the summer came a general wages and prices freeze, together with deep cuts in government spending. More than ever, it was incumbent on the socialists to make clear their defence priorities. When the 1983 defence budget was made public before the parliamentary defence commission on 30 September 1982, those priorities were unequivocal. Top priority was given to the strategic arsenal, with substantial resources being channelled into R & D for the mobile SX missile, the seventh nuclear submarine and plans for the new mirved M 5 submarine missile with which it was to be equipped.[83] But if such absolute priority was being afforded the strategic nuclear arsenal, what role was left, within a constantly decreasing level of resources, for France's conventional weaponry?

The Land Army

The question of the conventional armed forces was important, not only internally, where it had implications for military service as well as for the career structure of the professional soldier, but also, perhaps even more significantly, externally, where it had direct bearing on France's role in the defence of Europe. As early as 1974, the socialist party had made public its proposals for a drastic restructuring of the land army.[84] With the onset of the economic crisis and the specific difficulties in which the socialist government found itself in 1982, it became clear that draconian cuts could be expected in the army budget. The army began to hum with rumours. Some officers had already read the report commissioned by François Mitterrand and published in December 1981 by François Bloch-Lainé which had presaged sweeping cuts in army personnel, an important shift in military strategy and technical modernisation of the land army. Their fears were increased when Pierre Mauroy addressed the IHEDN in September 1982 and spoke of the imminent organisation of a 'new model army' with fewer men and more sophisticated equipment.[85] The fact that the government had still not completed its plans for a long-term military programme, and was therefore unable to disclose in any detail its intentions with regard to the armed forces, lent an element of uncertainty to the doubts which persisted throughout the winter of 1982-1983. The debate over the defence budget in November 1982 gave the right-wing opposition the opportunity to launch a vigorous attack on the government's austerity measures with regard to the armed forces, certain deputies accusing Mitterrand and Hernu of having no defence policy worth speaking of.[86] A minor scandal broke out in December when *Le Matin* published a confidential letter written three months earlier by the Supreme Commander of the land army, General Delaunay, to the Supreme Commander of the armed forces, General Lacaze, in which he argued that the proposed army reforms would lead to an army 'diminished' in men, 'weakened' in structure, with 'old-fashioned' equipment and generally 'demoralised'. This affair proved to be little more than a storm in a teacup since it soon transpired not only that the General's fears had been totally unfounded, but that he himself, in the meantime, had come to agree that the new measures would make the army technically more mobile and efficient.[87]

But before the precise reforms in the army were made public in the socialist *Loi de programmation militaire 1984-1988* in May 1983, a completely new strategic context began to emerge. On the very day when Hernu made clear his intentions to afford absolute priority to strategic nuclear weapons (30 September 1982) it so happened that General Bernard Rogers, Supreme Allied Commander in Europe, made a speech in Brussels to launch what was rapidly interpreted in France as a new war-fighting scenario for NATO, in line with the new American strategy of the 'Air-Land Battle'[88] which had been formulated a month previously in the USA, without any consultation with NATO. If France and her NATO allies appear united on deployment of Pershing 2 and Cruise as an element of nuclear diplomacy, the new American proposals for the defence of Europe seem liable to create very serious disruptions in Franco-NATO relations. There are two somewhat separate wings to what has increasingly come to be known as the 'Rogers doctrine'. The first is the desire to increase conventional defence capability in Europe so as to be able to 'raise the nuclear threshold' and possibly make a 'no early use' (of nuclear weapons) declaration. The second, which is much more closely associated with the notion of 'Air-Land Battle', is the prospect of abandoning thirty years of defensive posture on the part of NATO and preparing consciously to adopt an offensive strategy which would, in the early stages of conflict, carry the war into socialist-bloc territory using, if necessary, a combination of conventional, chemical and nuclear weapons. The two separate wings of this strategic theory are, of course, contradictory rather than complementary, and it is the case that while General Rogers himself gave regular publicity, throughout 1983, to the question of raising the nuclear threshold and increasing conventional defences, the more aggressive, war-fighting aspects of the Air-Land Battle scenario have remained confined to the specialist military journals.

Charles Hernu publicly rejects both aspects of the new American theory. One month after the initial Rogers speech in Brussels, Hernu addressed the delegates to the Western European Union and denounced the first part of the Rogers plan in ringing terms, criticising the attempts to raise the nuclear threshold as a covert effort to withdraw the American nuclear umbrella from Europe and as a misguided gamble which would in fact make war more likely. Moreover, Hernu sensed that there was much more behind the Rogers speech which had not been made public in Europe: 'I have the impression that General Rogers has only told us half the story. If he doesn't tell us the other half, there is every reason to be very concerned'.[89] Hernu continued, on many subsequent occasions, to offer public (and increasingly negative) criticism of the 'Rogers doctrine', stressing above all its incoherence and the considerable degree of uncertainty which surrounded it,[90] although he has so far refused to make any public statement on the Air-Land Battle scenario.

The strategic doctrine implicit in either aspect of the new American approach to the defence of Europe conflicts on a number of major points with the professed military thinking of the socialist administration in France. This conflict may appear to be masked on the surface by the resemblances between French and NATO military modernisation plans at the conventional level. These changes were introduced in France with the important *loi de programmation militaire* which was finally passed by the National Assembly in May 1983. During a much-publicised visit to the military camp at Canjuers on 15 October 1982, Mitterrand tried to allay the fears of many army officers by insisting that the land army would continue to play a major role in French defence policy.[91] But he made it clear that that role was to be one of 'global deterrence' in which conventional defence, like the tactical nuclear missiles, is considered to be one element in an overall defence policy whose key is the strategic nuclear arsenal.[92] The basic argument is that all three elements are considered to be part of the 'global deterrent'. The 'deterrent' operates against any threat to France's 'vital interests' (which, in order to increase the level of uncertainty, are never defined). Since it is vital to know whether an enemy, by engaging in a certain form of military action, is seriously intending to threaten those 'vital interests' (as opposed to merely manoeuvring in the hope of gaining some minor advantage), it is necessary, according to French military strategy, to force that enemy to make his intentions crystal clear. If the conventional defence forces are sufficiently well organised, trained and equipped, then only a major attack from an enemy could hope to defeat them. A major attack would immediately be interpreted as a threat to the nation's 'vital interests', and would therefore introduce at once the prospect of recourse to the strategic nuclear arsenal. The tactical nuclear missile might come in at an intermediate stage in this process, but the main point is that every aspect of French defence policy is geared to preventing war from breaking out rather than to actually fighting it. If it were to break out despite these precautions, then the doctrine is clear: escalation to the level of strategic nuclear fire would be almost immediate. Such is the theory behind the French notion of 'global deterrence'. It is a very different theory from that of 'flexible response'.

Of course, the distinction lies essentially at the level of the *political* usage of the available systems. And since the systems are essentially the same whatever the government in power, it is quite conceivable that their political usage can vary very considerably from administration to administration. This aspect of the question no doubt helps to explain why the Mitterrand administration has seemed so genuinely shocked by Soviet suggestions that the French nuclear arsenal should be included in the Geneva talks. Mitterrand, Hernu and Cheysson argue that France's nuclear strategy (global deterrence) is quite distinct from that of NATO (flexible response). Therefore, the argument goes, because the doctrine governing the systems is so different, the systems themselves cannot be lumped together for arms control purposes. By the same token, Giscard's belief that France's strategic posture is (and should be) no different from that of NATO means that his only hope of keeping the French arsenal off the negotiating table is by keeping a very low profile on NATO. All this is very confusing and it is hardly surprising that the opinion polls indicate almost universal ignorance about the strategic theories underlying France's weapons systems.

That ignorance and that confusion were not dispelled by the publication of the socialists' military white paper or *loi de programmation militaire* for 1984-88.[93] For it was less the strategic theory underlying the use of the new armed forces which was given prominence in the press coverage of the bill, than the actual weapons systems themselves.

The LPM involves military expenditure rising to 830,000 million francs (£83,000 million) over a five-year period. It contains very few surprises and, for the most part, merely gives programmatic form to a variety of decisions which had already been taken. The priority to strategic nuclear deterrence is re-asserted, 30% of the overall equipment budget going to nuclear hardware. The land army is scheduled for massive restructuring, the main feature being the planned creation of a rapid deployment force for use either in Europe or overseas. The reduction in officer personnel, which so many professionals had feared, is to be kept down to 35,000 men, with natural wastage accounting for the totality of this figure.

The most significant feature of the bill is the projected rapid deployment force (FAR). Details of the composition of this force were fleshed out in mid-June 1983 when the new Supreme Commander of the land army, General Imbot,[94] addressed a gathering of the military top brass in Paris. The FAR is composed of 47,000 men and involves five separate divisions: the 11th parachute division; the 9th marine infantry division; the 27th Alpine division; the 6th light armoured division; and the 4th air-borne division — all under one unified command. There are three main thrusts to this reorganisation: polyvalence, mobility and firepower. Polyvalence because the FAR embraces a variety of elite and highly trained units; mobility because it will be armed with the lightest equipment and based on new helicopter gunships or light tanks; firepower owing to its massive armoury of anti-tank PGMs and other 'fire and forget' self-targeting munitions. The air-borne division alone will have at its disposal almost 600 anti-tank weapons, ranging from the most sophisticated missile-firing helicopter to modern artillery pieces.[95]

At one level, there are remarkable similarities between this type of modernisation and the rapid deployment preparations being made by NATO in the context of the Air-Land Battle. The emphasis is on speed and the ability to carry the war rapidly into enemy territory. In presenting the new force, Charles Hernu specifically indicated that discussions would take place with the NATO allies as to how and under what circumstances it might be deployed in conjunction with other allied forces. And under questioning from the parliamentary defence commission on 21 June 1983, he admitted that deployment could only take place with the agreement of the NATO Supreme Commander, since the FAR would be dependent on NATO for air and logistical support.[96] These developments began to look extremely suspicious in various quarters. The PCF issued a strong criticism of any plans to use the FAR in Europe,[97] and similar worries were expressed by the dean of post-Gaullist defence strategy, General Poirier, in an article in *Défense Nationale*.[98] But both Hernu and the Supreme Commander of the French armed forces, General Lacaze, have publicly insisted that the FAR will not be used automatically in the event of hostilities in Europe, still less will it be used to cover a section of the West's defences along the 'Iron Curtain'. Moreover, they have repeatedly stressed that FAR is a war-prevention force rather than a war-fighting force. It will be under the political authority of the President of the Republic and his decision to deploy would symbolise the determination of the state to go to the ultimate extreme if hostilities did not cease immediately.[99] Thus the three legs of the French strategic 'deterrent' are structurally linked in a cohesive unit.

That, at any rate, is the professed theory behind the FAR. There is likely to be vigorous debate in the coming years over several aspects of the doctrine. First, whether the stated usage is in fact the real one. Second, whether the FAR could be put to different strategic usages (it is clear that it could easily be adapted to fit in perfectly with current NATO strategy). Third, whether the theory itself is viable, whether there is any meaningful correlation between the theory and the practice: could such a political and indeed cerebral approach to 'deterrence' have any real meaning, let alone any chance of success in the heat of battle between the superpowers.[100] The pages of the specialist journals will no doubt address these issues over the coming years. At the heart of them, of course, is the fundamental question of the relationship between France and the defence of Europe.

France and the Defence of Europe.

The euromissiles, the Atlantic Alliance, the status of the French 'independent deterrent', and the reforms in the land army are all problems which have no meaning outside the key strategic issue of France's role in the defence of Europe. There are, in France, two extreme positions which constitute the outer poles of the debate. On the one hand, certain hard-line Gaullists and the occasional CERES maverick consider that the independent nuclear arsenal allows France the luxury of being largely unconcerned with the rest of Europe. 'Pure sanctuarisation' implies that, until an enemy puts a toe in the Rhine (or on an Atlantic beach?) there is no cause for alarm. While such purists are concerned only with France's geographical frontiers, others see only her *political* frontiers and would be content to abandon 'independence' in favour of total reintegration into the Atlantic Alliance. They are to be found mainly in the centrist political family which ranges from the right-wing of the PS to the Giscardian party. However, neither of these polarised positions enjoys much credibility or respect in France these days.

This marginalisation of the poles makes for an extremely rich discussion in the space lying between them. That space is the geographical and political solidarity of *Europe* (as opposed to 'the West' or the 'North Atlantic'). The Europeans, increasingly, wish to participate more fully in their own defence. But here again we find in France two polarised positions, both of which can be located within the PS. For some members of the CERES, the solution is for Europe to dispense to the greatest extent possible (and, ideally, altogether) with the American 'umbrella'. Jean-Pierre Chevènement has recently revived the notion expressed in the Socialist Project, whereby the

French 'deterrent' should serve as the spearhead of a European defence force independent of the USA.[101] This strategy is conceived within the context of bloc dissolution and the emergence of an 'autonomous' European continent. For others, like Pierre Mauroy, the defence of Europe should be assured by greater cooperation among the European states, but within the overall framework of the Atlantic Alliance.[102]

The degree of 'Atlanticism' implicit in this second approach can vary considerably. While the preference of the CDS, and probably of most of the Giscardians, would go towards nuclear cooperation between France and Great Britain,[103] this option tends to be less popular among the socialists, most of whom see Britain (especially under Mrs Thatcher) as something of an American poodle (if not a Trojan horse). Most socialists seem to prefer some sort of special cooperation with West Germany.

That, at any rate, has been the direction taken by François Mitterrand. The cooperation is, of course, fraught with problems, as is the entire European defence issue.[104] But Franco-German relations have certainly been pursued with energy. In the nine months after Helmut Kohl became Chancellor, he and Mitterrand met specifically for Franco-German 'summit' talks on no fewer than six occasions. Much of the initiative seems to have come from the French, who are keen to forge a new relationship with West Germany, but the Germans are obviously keen to listen. At the same time the socialists must not appear to be compromising French 'independence', while the Germans clearly have no desire to play second (conventional) fiddle to the French nuclear panoply, still less to exchange the US 'umbrella' for a hypothetical and highly problematic French one.

Nevertheless, since there is now universal doubt about the best strategic approach to Europe's defences, the Germans and the French are very keen to go on talking. Indeed, that talking has, since October 1982, been institutionalised by the establishment of a permanent Franco-German defence commission which has met and is scheduled to go on meeting regularly, every three months.[105] Clearly, the experience of working with Reagan has made Mitterrand and Kohl more conscious than ever of the specificity of Europe's problems. But for the moment, we have no indications whatsoever, other than negative ones,[106] as to what sort of decisions are being shaped in this historical military cooperation between the two traditional continental rivals.

Currently, there is a plethora of proposals as to with whom, with which weapons systems and according to which strategic doctrine

France might cooperate in the defences of Europe.[107] There are, indeed, as many different approaches as there are authors and strategists. In the space of a generation, Europe has been 'protected' by doctrines as diverse as those of 'massive retaliation', 'mutual assured destruction', 'flexible response', the 'seamless web' and now 'air-land-battle'. All of them, except the last which has only just been elaborated, were discarded because they eventually lacked credibility. Currently, Europe is at a military, diplomatic and strategic turning point. The future role of France in her defences remains pretty much of an open question. The way it is resolved could well be one of the most crucial issues in what remains of this century.

Notes

1. The old Socialist Party (SFIO) had become so discredited for a variety of reasons that it had been replaced in 1969 by a new grouping of several socialist organisations. Mitterrand took over this party as general secretary in 1971.

2. Jean Jaurès (1859-1914) was the founding father of 'modern' French socialism and its greatest theoretician. See Harvey Goldberg, *The Life of Jaurès* (Madison, 1962) and, on the tradition of the 'citizen soldier', Richard D. Challener, *The French Theory of the Nation in Arms, 1866-1939* (New York, Russell, 1965).

3. In the minds of the socialist and labour movements, by the turn of the century the army was especially associated with political repression. Although it had lost most of its foreign campaigns throughout the nineteenth century, it had not failed to quell political revolt (1848, 1871) or to shoot down striking workers (1891, 1900, 1907, 1908, 1909 etc.).

4. See *La Nef*, October-December 1965 and Franz-Olivier Giesbert, *François Mitterrand ou la tentation de l'histoire* (Paris, Seuil, 1977), p. 224.

5. Charles Hernu, *Soldat-Citoyen: essai sur la défense et la sécurité de la France* (Paris, Flammarion, 1975), p. 49.

6. For the text of these various motions see ibid., pp.51-66; see also Pascal Krop, *Les Socialistes et l'Armée* (Paris, PUF, 1983), pp. 63-64.

7. *Changer la Vie. Programme de gouvernement du Parti Socialiste* (Paris, Flammarion, 1972) (Defence section, pp. 197-207).

8. Ibid., p.28. Mitterrand was to pursue this line of reasoning in his speech to the party congress at Grenoble in 1973, when he argued that a great power like France could not have a defence policy based solely on negations. See, on this evolution, François Bourg, 'Dégager l'alternative: le Parti socialiste et l'étude des problèmes de défense', *Nouvelle Revue socialiste*, 6 (1974), p. 6.

9. The CPG called for 'abandonment of every aspect of the French strategic nuclear

126 Defence and the Mitterrand Government

strike force; an immediate halt to the production of the strike force; reconversion of the military nuclear industry into peaceful, civil, nuclear power', *Programme commun de gouvernement* (Paris, Editions sociales, 1972), p. 171. It should be noted, however, that the CPG did not call for destruction of France's existing nuclear stocks, as the PCF's own programme had done (see *Changer de Cap: programme pour un gouvernement démocratique d'union populaire* (Paris, Editions sociales, 1971), p. 221. On the difference between the PCF and the PS at this juncture, see Jean Klein, 'La Gauche française et les problèmes de Défense', *Politique Etrangère*, 5 (1978), pp. 508-20.

10. Hernu, *Soldat-Citoyen*, p. 68.

11. Literally, 'the priest in battlekit': the old slogan of the republican left, for whom the egalitarian principles of the Republic and the unity of the nation required that everybody without exception should be subject to military service.

12. Morris Janowitz, Professor of military sociology at Chicago University, author of numerous works on the sociology of armies, including his classic *The Professional Soldier* (1960) became quite widely known in France during a year as visiting Professor at Paris University (1977-78).

13. The main extracts from this document are reproduced in Hernu, *Soldat-Citoyen*, pp. 131-40 & 236-42. It should be noted also that the pro-nuclear 'Atlanticists' in the PS, under Robert Pontillon, had contributed in no small measure to the elaboration of these theses. See P. Krop, *Les Socialistes et l'Armée*, pp. 93-94.

14. The CAN published a first series of journals (*Armée Nouvelle*) between May 1974 (No.1) and January 1978 (Special No.8) A second series began in November 1979 (No.1). The most recent issue is June 1983 (No.8). The present address is: 25, rue du Louvre, 75001 Paris.

15. It was on this occasion that Mitterrand expanded his base, and his options by bringing into the party the right-wing of the PSU (Michel Rocard). See *Pour le Socialisme. Le livre des Assises du Socialisme* (Paris, Stock, 1974).

16. Ibid., pp. 84-87.

17. General Méry's controversial article, 'Une armée pour quoi faire et comment?' in *Défense nationale*, June 1976. Giscard's speech to the IHEDN on 1 June 1976 was published in *Le Monde*, 4 June 1976 and analysed extensively in subsequent issues.

18. Méry and Giscard had actually stated that the old Gaullist notion of an 'all-or-nothing' deterrent was no longer credible and that flexible response was now called for, together with its panoply of tactical, battlefield weapons.

19. There were many substantial attacks on Giscard's policy. Perhaps the most influential came from the father of French nuclear theory, General Pierre M. Gallois, *Le Renoncement: de la France défendue à l'Europe protégée. L'Appel* (Paris, Plon, 1977). The controversy has been reactivated recently by the general secretary of the Giscardian UDF, Michel Pinton. Writing in *Le Monde* on 16 June 1983, 'Une nouvelle Ligne Maginot?', Pinton insisted that the French arsenal no longer enjoyed any credibility and ought to be scrapped. His views were repudiated by the UDF and by the RPR, but the controversy continues...

20. See, on this important issue, François de Rose, *La France et la Défense de*

l'Europe (Paris, Seuil, 1976).

21. At the same time as he appeared to be giving priority to conventional weapons, Giscard also cancelled the planned sixth missile-firing nuclear submarine. He was later obliged to reverse this decision after fierce political bargaining from the Gaullists.

22. In May 1976, the CDN produced a document entitled 'Organisation générale de la défense'. See *Armée Nouvelle*, No.7, (1976), pp. 1-7. This implied definitive acceptance of nuclear weapons and François Mitterrand, in a television appearance in June 1976, had implied the same thing.

23. The Kanapa report was published in *L'Humanité* 12 May 1976, pp.5-6 and as a special PCF pamphlet under the title: *Défense Nationale: indépendance, paix et désarmement* (Paris, 1976), 31 pages. See also Yves Roucaute, *Le PCF et l'Armée* (Paris, PUF, 1983), pp. 171-83.

24. The meeting had originally been scheduled for December 1977, but was postponed only three days before it was due to convene, ostensibly on account of a threatened rail strike. In fact, as many rank and file militants were prepared to testify, more time was needed in order to pacify the dissent rising from the base. See B. Pingaud & J-P. Worms, 'Nous n'avons pas changé', *Le Monde* 7 January 1978, p.10. A good detailed analysis of the various motions put to the Convention is in P. Krop, *Les Socialistes et l'Armée*, pp. 104-112.

25. The spirit of the amendment was explained by Pingaud and Worms in the article cited above: 'the "maintenance" of nuclear weapons must not, under any circumstances, serve as a cover for qualitative improvements in our nuclear force for technological reasons. Still less does it imply acceptance of the principle of deterrence and its terrifying corollary, demographic targeting.' See, on Hernu's reaction to the tabling of the amendment, J.Isnard, 'L'Imbroglio', *Le Monde*, 8-9 January 1978, p. 2; and, on the 'resistance' of the anti-nuclear lobby, Patrick Viveret, 'Comment nous avons résisté in *Alternatives non-violentes*, No.46, Décembre 1982, pp. 24-32.

26. The CERES position was published in *Le Monde*, 26 October 1977. During the convention debates, Mitterrand referred to Chevènement as the 'high-priest (*thuriféraire*) of nuclearisation'. The complete text of the final compromise resolution is in *Le Poing et la Rose*, Supplement to No.73, August 1978, 'Textes de Référence', pp. 32-5. In an interview with the author on 4 August 1983, Didier Motchane stated that the CERES did not openly propose total withdrawal from the Atlantic Alliance (as they had done at Suresnes in 1972) but that such withdrawal was the logical consequence of their proposals.

27. P. Delahousse, 'Pour une initiative française', *Le Monde*, 14 July 1979. At the 1979 July 14 parade, for the first time in 15 years, the nuclear 'deterrent' was conspicuous by its absence.

28. This proposal was first floated in a special interview with Buis and Sanguinetti published in *Le Nouvel Observateur*, 20 August 1979, pp. 26-28. Needless to say, press comment concentrated on little else for weeks afterwards.

29. J.-P. Cot, 'La France doit participer à SALT 3', *Le Monde*, 9-10 September 1979; D. Motchane, 'Pour une politique d'indépendance', *Le Monde*, 20 September 1979.

30. J.-P. Chevènement, 'La défense américaine de l'Europe: une impasse', *Le Monde*, 15 December 1979. These views were more or less echoed, in slightly different language, by Charles Hernu, 'Guerre ou Paix', ibid., 21 February 1980 and Jacques Huntzinger, 'Désarmement et Sécurité', ibid., 27 February 1980.

31. Mitterrand explained the socialist refusal in his book, *Ici et Maintenant* (Paris, Fayard, 1980), p. 234.

32. UDF, *Une Doctrine de défense pour la France*, Paris, 1980, 68 pages; RPR, *Une Politique de défense pour la France*, Paris, 1980, 150 pages.

33. *Projet Socialiste pour la France des Années 1980* (Paris, Club socialiste du Livre, 1980) (section on defence: pp. 346-50).

34. 'It is in the power of France, because of her nuclear weapons, to take the initiative in this direction', ibid., p. 346.

35. Ibid., p.349. This idea occurs regularly in CERES publications, but its strategic implications are never spelled out in any great detail. The basic notion appears to be that, if there were a real threat that the superpowers might go to war in Europe, the French deterrent would be used to threaten both Moscow and Washington and bring the two of them to their senses.

36. In his 'presidential manifesto', *Ici et Maintenant* (see note 31), Mitterrand said (p.245.): 'Pershing 2s, deployed in Germany, can reach Kiev in 6 minutes. I understand why the Russians are alarmed. For them Pershing 2 is an intolerable imbalance.' And in response to the question, 'Do you want the Americans to abandon them?', he replied: 'Yes. And that the Russians accept, at the same time, to *talk about the SS 20*' (my stress -JH).

37. The highly restrained defence correspondent of *Le Monde*, Jacques Isnard, openly spoke of this decision of the UDF as representing a clean break with Gaullist defence principles, 'Un changement de cap', *Le Monde*, 28 May 1980, p. 38.

38. *Maîtrise technologique* was a term Mitterrand himself invented as sounding more politically acceptable than 'research and development'.

39. Rocard's statement was made on *France-Inter* on 2 July 1980. The furore it aroused was reported in *Le Monde*, 5 July 1980, including disavowals by both Hernu and Chévènement.

40. Hernu's ideas were first published in an editorial in *Armée Nouvelle*, No.2, 3ème trimestre, 1980, pp. 1-2. Interestingly enough, his close collaborator at the *Conventions*, Jean Paucot argued a case against the N-bomb which was much closer to the CERES line: 'A propos de neutrons', *Armée Nouvelle*, No.2 ibid., pp. 1-3 and 'Des neutrons pour quoi faire?', *Le Monde*, 20 June 1980.

41. Mitterrand promised to build two more (bringing the total to eight). Chirac accused Giscard of having tried to keep the total down to five and proposed, on behalf of himself and the RPR, to increase the fleet to 15 by the year 2000.

42. Georges Sarre, 'Une initiative européenne pour le désarmement', *Le Monde*, 17 April 1981; Jean-Pierre Chevènement, 'Le Pourissement de la doctrine militaire', ibid., 5 May 1981.

43. When Pierre Mauroy addressed the IHEDN on 14 September 1981, he frankly admitted that the government had not had time to deliberate on defence matters, *Défense Nationale*, October 1981, p. 15. Two weeks later, the Commander in Chief of the Armed Forces, General Lacaze, spoke on socialist defence policy 'in so far as it can be inferred from' assorted statements emanating from government circles, ibid., November 1981, p.7.

44. For these early decisions, see *Le Monde*, 11 July 1981. On the issue of tactical nuclear weapons, it was remarkable that one of Hernu's principal collaborators, Jean Paucot, pleaded, in an op.ed. article, in favour of absolute downgrading of Pluton and total concentration on strategic ones, 'Les Socialistes et le refus de la guerre', *Le Monde*, 14 July 1981.

45. Hernu also confessed that he had no desire to increase the ranks of the unemployed: see interview with J. Isnard in *Le Monde*, 11 July 1981.

46. See, on this question, Françoise Berger, 'La pollution nucléaire a doublé dans les trois derniers mois à Mururoa', *Libération*, 6 November 1981 and Debora Mackenzie, 'Mururoa sinks under a *force de frappe*', *New Scientist*, 15 April 1982, pp. 170-71.

47. Hernu interview in *Le Monde*, 11 July 1981 and similar ideas by Mauroy in *Défense nationale*, October 1981.

48. C. Hernu, *Nous...les Grands* (Lyon, Boursier, 1980), pp. 47-51.

49. I was informed of the existence of this work in the summer of 1981 by the bookseller at PS headquarters. After trying in vain for over a year to order one through various booksellers, I finally managed to obtain a copy from a member of Hernu's staff.

50. Interview published in the German magazine *Stern*, 8 July 1981.

51. The USSR has traditionally demanded that the French and the British arsenals be included in disarmament discussions, but during the SALT talks, the Americans had persuaded them to accept the notion that these arsenals were 'intermediate' rather than strategic. However, once Mitterrand came out openly in favour of increasing the American intermediate arsenal, the Soviets launched a veritable avalanche of demands that the French and British weapons be included in the Western 'arithmetic'. See *Temps Nouveaux*, 20 July 1981; *Pravda*, 9 July 1981, and *Izvestia*, 13 July 1981. In December 1982, Yuri Andropov made inclusion of the French and British weapons into the main Soviet demand at the INF talks.

52. Mitterrand: 'My personal conclusion is that in fact a genuine strategic balance will be maintained until 1984-85, but that after 1985 it may swing in favour of greater power to the Soviet Union.' *Le Monde*, 26 September 1981, p.6. Hernu: 'it is quite useful, as regards the degree of balance betweeen the superpowers, to speak, as the Soviets do, of a "global correlation of forces", but we foresee a potential serious risk that this balance may be broken in favour of the Soviets in the middle of the decade.' *Défense Nationale*, December 1981, p.7. However, Hernu argued that the potential new destabilising factor was not so much the SS 20 as the new Soviet tactical weapons, the SS 21, SS 22 and SSX 23.

53. TV interview with Mitterrand; transcript published in *Le Monde*, 1 December

1981. This, of course, was a point he had made a year previously (see above, footnote 36).

54. *Défense nationale*, December 1981, p. 8.

55. Ronald Reagan had caused a considerable stir in Europe in October 1981 by stating that he could imagine circumstances under which the USA would engage in a limited nuclear war in Europe without having recourse to the American strategic weapons.

56. Most French leaders have argued that the main aim of the SS 20 is to 'decouple' the USA from Europe, since the Soviet missile does not threaten American territory. However, for every commentator who has seen Pershing 2 as a way of 're-coupling' the two halves of the Alliance, there is another who interprets it as further evidence of 'decoupling' since the Pershing 2 will actually be fired from Europe. On 're-coupling', see *The Modernisation of NATO's Long-range Theatre Nuclear Forces*, Washington D.C., 1981. For the response to this, see Mary Kaldor, 'Nuclear Weapons and the Atlantic Alliance', *Democracy*, January 1982, pp. 9-23.

57. Complete text of Cheysson interview in *Le Monde*, 2 December 1981. For a general study, see Wilfrid L Kohl, *French Nuclear Diplomacy* (Princeton U.P., 1971).

58. In his first interview as President, Mitterrand had stated pointedly that 'one cannot both hope for greater political and military homogeneity within the Alliance and, at the same time, put up with 'every-man-for-himself' in economic matters'. *Le Monde* 2 July 1981.

59. See, for analyses of the Mitterrand visit, *Le Nouvel Observateur*, 13 March 1982; *Le Point*, 15 March 1982; *L'Express*, 19 March 1982.

60. PS, *Déclaration sur la Paix, la Sécurité et le Désarmement* (Paris, 1982), 20 pages.

61. Thierry Maliniak, 'Enfin un accord entre l'Est et l'Ouest', *Le Monde* 17-18 July 1983.

62. G. Robin, 'Hors des Pershing, point de salut', *Le Monde*, 18 January 1983.

63. Mitterrand had been one of the most scathing in his attack on Giscard after the latter, by visiting Brezhnev in Warsaw in May 1980, had broken the diplomatic blockade of the Soviet Union which the West had imposed after the invasion of Afghanistan. For an overview of Giscard's diplomacy, see Paul-Marie de La Gorce, 'Bilan d'un septennat: la politique extérieure française', *Politique étrangère*, 1, (1981), pp. 89-104.

64. V.Giscard d'Estaing, 'Une occasion historique pour l'Europe', *Le Monde*, 19 February 1983.

65. See *The Guardian* 21 January 1983 and *Le Monde*, 22, 23 and 24 January 1983.

66. See André Fontaine, quoting *Die Welt*, 'Entre la "Suite" et le "Requiem"', *Le Monde*, 26 January 1983.

67. The text of this communiqué and a long analysis of the circumstances under which it came into being, in *Le Monde*, 31 May 1983.

68. Claude Cheysson, in addressing the press at the same meeting at which the

communiqué was read out, was categorical in stating that under no circumstances was France prepared to even entertain an extension of the Atlantic Alliance 'geographically or functionally', ibid., 31 May 1983, p. 6. However, it would seem that Cheysson's protests were mainly for the public back home.

69. Helmut Schmidt spent two days (2-3 June 1983) at Mitterrand's country house at Latche, and on 19 July, Chancellor Kohl had an informal meeting with Mitterrand at Dabo (Moselle). In an article published in *The Washington Post*, 22 May 1983, Schmidt had already expressed his opinion that the 'walk-in-the-woods' compromise was 'totally acceptable'.

70. *L'Humanité*, 1 June 1983 and *Le Monde*, 2 June 1983.

71. Philippe Seguin, RPR deputy for the Vosges, stated on France-Inter that Mitterrand had made 'a major concession' to Reagan by signing the communiqué (*Le Monde*, 1 June 1983, p. 2); and the former Foreign Minister Michel Jobert, speaking on RTL on 5 June, referred to France's 'good faith' having been 'caught napping' and regretted that France had now placed herself 'under the wing of the American broody hen', *Le Monde*, 7 June 1983.

72. *Pravda*, on 1 June 1983, spoke of 'substantial shifts in French deterrence theory' after the Williamsburg communiqué.

73. Details in *Le Monde*, 10 June 1983.

74. Text of his speech and details of the 'walk-in-the-woods' formula in ibid., p.8.

75. *L'Humanite*, 20 June 1983. See André Fontaine, 'Quelles armes contre la guerre?', *Le Monde*, 18 June 1983 and J.-M. Colombani, 'Le pacifisme peut-il prendre en France?', ibid., 19-20 June 1983.

76. Maxime Gremetz had been the first to make this proposal in a little-noticed speech on May 20, and this had been followed up by a speech by Georges Marchais on May 26 which had caused rather more of a stir. Michel Tatu analyses the issues in 'La France et les euromissiles', *Le Monde*, 23 June 1983.

77. See, on the manoeuvring which surrounded Marchais' visit, M. Tatu, 'Où sont les "désaccords" entre M. Marchais et M. Andropov?', ibid., 19 July 1983.

78. Appearing on the TV programme 'L'Heure de Vérité' on 9 June 1983, Charles Fiterman, the senior communist minister, categorically denied that the euromissile issue would ever be responsible for the communists leaving government (*Le Monde*, 11 June 1983). But the fact remains that, once the PCF feels it has the masses behind it on this issue, it is unlikely to relinquish its pressure on Mitterrand, even though it will not voluntarily leave the government on a foreign policy issue.

79. Didier Motchane had already been highly critical of Williamsburg (*Le Monde*, 3 June 1983). Then, in an article in the pro-CERES monthly, *Enjeu* (July-August 1983), Motchane extended the range of his disagreement with the government to cover France's position on the euromissiles, the strategic implications behind the new defence white paper and the entire attitude of France's leaders towards the Alliance in general and the USA in particular. In an interview with the author on 4 August 1983, he said that he was now more or less convinced that the PS leaders had embraced Atlanticism, and that the rest was mere window-dressing.

80. Philippe Bauchard, in an article in *Témoignage Chrétien*, 11-17 July 1983, revealed that, in a series of private conversations with journalists, Mitterrand had confessed that he no longer expected anything from Reagan.

81. The most recent and most categorical statement of this case was in General Lacaze's speech to the IHEDN, published in *Défense nationale*, June 1983. 'Politique de défense et stratégie militaire de la France', pp. 16-18.

82. For an analysis of the theory of the tactical 'ultimatum' shot, and of Giscard's attempts to alter that theory, see General Lucien Poirier, *Essais de Stratégie théorique*, Paris, 1982.

83. See Hernu's presentation of his budget in *Le Monde*, 1 October 1982, p. 15. Unfortunately for him, between the time he presented his budget to parliament and the debate in the Assembly several weeks later, Mauroy imposed severe cutbacks on all spending departments and the M 5 missile was one of the victims of the cuts.

84. In the *Fiche de Synthèse* (see above, note 13).

85. P. Mauroy, 'Vers un nouveau modèle d'armée', *Défense nationale*, November 1982, pp. 9-28.

86. See articles by Arthur Paecht (UDF) and Yves Lancien (RPR) in *Le Monde*, 8 October 1982.

87. See the 'revelations' in *Le Matin*, 6 December 1982, and Delaunay's message to the army, in *Terre Informations*, January 1983.

88. On Air Land Battle, see 'Une nouvelle stratégie atlantique?', *Le Monde* , 5 October 1982; Konrad Ege & Martha Wenger, 'La nouvelle doctrine "Air Land Battle"', *Le Monde Diplomatique*, February 1983; A.M. Thomas, 'L'Air Land Battle et l'engagement américain en Europe', *Défense nationale*, April 1983.

89. Hernu's speech was published in *Défense nationale*, January 1983, pp. 167-168 and reported in *Le Monde*, 2 December 1982.

90. Hernu hjad already cast doubt on the Rogers Plan in his speech to the IHEDN on 16 November 1982, *Défense nationale*, December 1982, p. 13. During a trip to the USA in January 1983, he made a point of publicly demanding further information about the new strategy, *Le Monde*, 20 January 1983. In his closing speech to the colloquium on Science and Defence on 27 April 1983, he overtly dismissed the Rogers plan as misguided and in any case incapable of making France change her strategic plans, ibid., 30 April 1983. Claude Cheysson, during the meeting of the NATO Council in Paris in June, also made a point of rejecting the logic behind the Rogers plan, ibid., 9 June 1983. See also, on this subject, Claude Le Borgne, 'Le Général Rogers, l'Amérique et l'Europe', *Défense nationale*, February 1983, pp. 25-32.

91. *Le Monde* 17-18 October 1982.

92. On 'global deterrence' see Hernu's and Lacaze's speeches to the IHEDN, in *Défense nationale*, December 1982 and June 1983.

93. *Journal Officiel*, Assemblée Nationale, No.1452, 'Projet de loi portant

approbation de la programmation militaire pour les années 1984-1988', 22 pages.

94. General René Imbot replaced General Delaunay after the latter announced his early retirement in March 1983.

95. See Jacques Isnard's interview with Hernu when the details of the FAR were released, *Le Monde*, 18 June 1983.

96. *Le Monde*, 24 June 1983.

97. See Louis Baillot's comments, on behalf of the central committee's defence commission, in *L'Humanité*, 8 June 1983.

98. Lucien Poirier, 'La Greffe', *Défense nationale*, April 1983. Poirier admitted that he hoped the explanations given by Hernu were the correct ones, but added that the FAR remained very much an unknown quantity. In an interview with the author on 6 August 1983, Admiral Sanguinetti expressed the view that the FAR *was* intended to be used as part of NATO's panoply.

99. Jean-Yves Le Drian, *Le Monde*, 20 May 1983; Hernu, ibid., 18 June 1983; Lacaze, *Défense nationale*, June 1983, p. 21.

100. Michel Pinton, the General Secretary of the UDF, ridiculed this overly theoretical aspect of the deterrent in his highly provocative article in *Le Monde* on 16 June 1983. Pinton's personal attack on the theory of deterrence has been formally disavowed not only by the RPR, but also by his own party (ibid., 24 June 1983).

101. Chevènement's comments, in an interview on France-Inter (17 January 1983) reported in *Le Monde* 19 January 1983.

102. In his speech to the IHEDN, *Défense nationale*, October 1981, p. 18.

103. Paul Delahousse, 'L'Europe, objet ou acteur?', *Le Monde*, 9 December 1981.

104. For the complexities of the differing attitudes towards this problem among the political parties represented in the European Parliament, see J-L. Burban, 'La Communauté européenne et la défense', *Défense nationale*, July 1980, pp. 97-108 and special issue of *Politique Etrangère*, No.6 (1978), 'Défense de l'Europe ou défense européenne?'.

105. Reports on the meeting between Kohl and Mitterrand on 21-22 October 1982 in *Le Monde*, 22, 23, 24-5 October 1982 ('MM Kohl et Mitterrand annoncent un renforcement des consultations militaires et stratégiques entre les deux pays').

106. While stating that this new cooperation would be less concerned with military matters than with strategy, Mitterrand went to great lengths to give reassurances that 'There is no question of associating the Federal Republic with French nuclear strategy, nor of a transfer of nuclear technology to Germany, nor even of any financial contribution by Germany to the French force levels.' Report on 21-22 October meeting in *Défense Nationale*, December 1982, p. 155 (the review incorrectly puts the date of the meeting as November).

107. François de Rose, *Contre la Stratégie des Curiaces* (Paris, Julliard, 1983); Léo Hamon, *Le Sanctuaire désenclavé* (Paris, Cahiers de la Fondation pour les Etudes de

Défense Nationale, 1982); Michel Manel, *L'Europe sans Défense* (Paris, Berger Levrault, 1982); Jean-Paul Pigasse, *Le Bouclier d'Europe; vers une autonomie militaire de la Communauté européenne* (Paris, Seghers, 1982); Robert Close, *Encore un effort... et nous aurons définitivement perdu la troisième guerre mondiale* (Paris, Belfond, 1982).

5 FRENCH NUCLEAR WEAPONS
Patricia Chilton

The French nuclear weapon stockpile is small by superpower standards: less than a fortieth of the size of the United States arsenal and matched twenty-five to one by Soviet nuclear devices. However, it is at present larger than the British stock, not far behind that of China, and significantly more diversified than those of either Britain or China.[1] Among the second-division nuclear powers, France alone has developed a mini-triad of strategic nuclear forces comprising land-based missiles, submarine-launched missiles and strategic bombers, to which has been added a tactical triad of tank-launched missiles, medium-range bombers and carrier-based combat aircraft, all equipped with nuclear weapons.

The weapons themselves, and the delivery vehicles and support systems associated with them, are built almost exclusively in France. This arises partly from the conscious decision of post-war France to pursue autonomy in arms production as a prerequisite to political independence and national security, and partly from necessity following the American restriction of the flow of nuclear information to France. This dealt a severe blow to French interests in cooperating on nuclear weapons development, not just with the Americans, but equally with the British, who were anxious to avoid sharing secrets with France which might prejudice their privileged exchanges with the USA on nuclear matters. Though the denial of access to American facilities imposed lasting strains on France's economy and scientific resources, the national pride resulting from the achievements of the country's own military-industrial complex has brought its compensations.[2] Certainly the national and international stature of French firms which lead in this field today is impressive: Dassault-Breguet with its legendary fighter planes and 60 to 70 per cent foreign sales; Aérospatiale (SNIAS), France's largest aerospace group, selling helicopters and tactical missiles abroad and developing strategic missiles for France's land- and sea-based deterrents which are not for sale; SNECMA and Matra, leading exporters, respectively, of aircraft motors and missiles; Thomson-CSF, France's principal defence electronics firm, exporting over a third of its military production; the

Délégation générale pour l'armement (DGA) producing all types of armaments, many of them for export, under the direction of the Ministry of Defence; and the *Commissariat à l'énergie atomique* (CEA), which is responsible for nuclear warhead design and the manufacture of nuclear charges.[3] The French arms industry is thus heavily export-dependent and at the same time subject to tight government control, since all of the leading producers are either government agencies (CEA and DGA), public corporations (SNIAS and SNECMA), or nationalised industries (Dassault, Matra and Thomson). Both the excellent export record of these companies and their close links with government have helped in the development of a comprehensive nuclear weapons programme. Firstly by offsetting the loss of potential export revenue involved in the production of nuclear weapons (restrictions on the sale of nuclear weapons components and technology do exist in France, despite the French refusal to sign the Non-Proliferation Treaty[4]); and secondly by giving government more room to manoeuvre in directing funds towards its high priority research and development projects within the relevant industries. A third feature which has helped to make economic sense of France's independent nuclear weapons programme is of course the success of its civil component, the nuclear energy industry, with its own complex economic and political rationale, and its own special contribution to the cause of national independence and security, over and above the mutual justifications it shares with the nuclear weapons industry.[5]

However, even though France has made itself the foremost conventional arms exporter in the world (relative to size of population), has consistently allocated 15 to 20 per cent of its defence budget to its nuclear forces,[6] and has become self-sufficient in plutonium production, the country has nevertheless experienced continuous financial difficulties in the pursuit of an independent nuclear programme since its inception in the 1950s. Currently there is a crisis of confidence in the government's ability to pay for a modernisation of its nuclear arsenal between now and the end of the century — a modernisation which is already much more modest than had been hoped for in many military and opposition quarters. Between the budget debate in late 1982 and the passage through parliament of the *Loi de programmation militaire 1984-1988*[7] during the early months of 1983, the government has revealed its five-year plan for military spending, arms procurement and development, as well as for the restructuring of the armed forces. This plan will shape the defence postures of France through to the beginning of the next century, and will usher in important changes in the scale, form, and strategic implications of the French nuclear deterrent. Apart from fears that 830 billion francs[8] will simply not be enough to meet the costs envisaged in the plan, there is concern that failure to invest much larger sums of money in the arms race could soon leave France out of the running. One of the most outspoken critics[9] of the *Loi de programmation militaire* points out with some justification that the technology gap between France and the superpowers is widening exponentially: whereas French nuclear technology was only four years behind that of the United States in 1958, it will be twenty years behind by the year 2000, and fifteen years behind the Soviet Union. And this is presuming that there are no further delays or cancellations in following through the provisions of the present plan — which seems unlikely given past experience, and the fact that a mere five per cent annual inflation has been allowed in calculating the amounts necessary for defence spending over the next five years.

But the story of over-ambitious research programmes, cancelled orders, and schedules over-running is familiar enough (the previous five-year plan, scheduled for 1977 to 1982, has taken until 1983 to complete, and many procurement projects have been cut or extended into the future[10]), and in the end the economies will be grudgingly accepted.[11] It is other aspects of the defence plan's response to the 'twofold technological challenge of counterforce strategy and the military use of space'[12] which may prove a sticking-point, as the defeat of the *Loi de programmation militaire* on its first reading in the Senate revealed.[13] For in responding, even within its own financial restraints, to the technological challenge posed by the two superpowers, France has been forced to talk about something other than the perennial shortage of cash. Reluctantly, the military and political elites have come to discuss the logic of the deterrent. France's double triad is being dismantled and a considerably less comfortable image of nuclear deterrence is being projected for the 1990s. Changes envisaged in both the strategic and tactical arsenals, together with some significant reorganisation of the armed forces, have left the role of France's tactical weapons open to fresh doubt and speculation. Two distinct notions are current. The first, that the use of tactical nuclear weapons will always be linked with an imminent strategic strike, the one following virtually automatically on the other 'warning' shot, is the official doctrine of *dissuasion* reiterated by the present government.[14] The second, that tactical nuclear weapons will be integrated into the conventional weaponry of the armed forces so that they may have recourse to them if they are needed,[15] seems to coincide more exactly with the practical changes outlined in the rest of the defence plan.

These include a massive investment in tactical nuclear weapons, a tacit acknowledgement that France is not likely to achieve autonomy in the all-important area of satellite intelligence and communication, and the creation of a rapid deployment force (FAR) which, being specifically aimed at cooperation with NATO troops in Europe, could well draw France's nuclear arsenal closer to the battlefield.[16]

Strategic Nuclear Weapons (FNS)

The distinction between strategic and tactical weapons, while it raises problems that are discussed elsewhere in this volume,[17] will be maintained according to the classification commonly adopted in French military discourse, where 'strategic' means that the device can be targeted on the Soviet Union, or, theoretically, on any other country of equivalent distance and accessibility. Such weapons are often termed 'eurostrategic' or 'intermediate-range' missiles in Anglo-American literature. The *Forces nucléaires stratégiques* (FNS) were created as the major innovation of the first five-year defence plan in 1960. As a command structure, they represented the first step in the restructuring of the armed forces that was to diminish the role of the land army, and of which the latest defence plan is a continuation. For although the strategic triad has a land-based component, that component is under the command of the air force, along with the command of strategic bombers. The strategic command structure is therefore bipartite, consisting of an air force command, the *Forces aériennes stratégiques* (FAS), and a naval command, the *Force océanique stratégique* (FOST).

Strategic Bombers (FAS)

The Mirage IVA is a relatively small medium-range supersonic bomber developed by Dassault in the late 1950s and first deployed in 1964. Historically the first, and for seven years the only delivery system of the French nuclear deterrent, it constituted the original *force de frappe* and still retains some of the glamour of its early mission, though it was conceived as a stop-gap while French engineers produced their own ground- and submarine-launched missiles without the hoped for American help. The plane was designed to deliver atomic bombs into the heartland of Soviet Russia, and this is certainly feasible, but it is by no means a long-range bomber.[18] Missions of up to 4,000 km are accredited to it, dependent on in-flight refuelling, or around 2,500 km without refuelling, flying at subsonic speeds. At high speeds (twice the speed of sound) and high altitudes its range is greatly reduced, and its average combat radius is reckoned to be about 1,600 km,[19] which could make the return trip from Moscow somewhat uncertain. It can carry either conventional bombs, or a single 60 to 70 kiloton thermonuclear bomb, the AN22 (this is apparently its usual payload, though it is occasionally cited as a one- or three-weapon system,[20] and Soviet sources make it four[21]). High claims are made for the aircraft's performance and versatility, but it lacks the sophistication of the most recent Soviet and American planes and has long been vulnerable to attack from a wide variety of Soviet defensive weapons. Indeed current estimates of arriving warheads in the event of this system being used put the number at six.[22] It is therefore due to be phased out, but the ageing plane seems destined to play its stop-gap role well on to the end of the century. Out of a total of 62 Mirage IVAs built, there are at present 34 operational, with a further 14 available for training, reconnaissance and in reserve. These are organised in six squadrons, and supported by eleven C135F refuelling tankers. Though the FAS headquarters are situated at Taverny, near Paris, the Mirage squadrons themselves are dispersed on bases throughout France,[23] from Bordeaux on the west coast to Orange in the south and Luxeuil near the German border.

Only 18 of the Mirages[24] (to be reclassified as Mirage IVP) will remain in service after 1985, and as from 1987 their free-fall bombs will be replaced by the new ASMP missile being developed for the tactical combat aircraft. The Mirage IVA will, in effect, 'convert to theatre role',[25] and ultimately be replaced by the new Mirage 2000N tactical bombers, though the *Loi de programmation militaire* has it maintaining its strategic presence until at least 1996,[26] when it may be notionally replaced by the land-based SX missile discussed below. It is now clear that there is no new strategic bomber in the plans, and no intention of funding a research project in this area.[27] The decision to phase out the strategic bomber may be linked to observations that a successor to the Mirage IVA would only make sense as a cruise missile carrier (like the American B52 and the Soviet Backfire bomber), and to the subsequent shelving of cruise missile development in France. However that may be, the original form of the *force de frappe* will certainly disappear between 1985 and 1987, leaving a ten-year gap in the strategic triad, and an experimental SX missile, which may well have other roles to fulfil, on the drawing board.

Strategic Missiles (FAS)

The land-based component of the strategic triad is the *Groupement de Missiles Stratégiques* (GMS), a fixed-silo intermediate-range ballistic missile system also commanded by the *Forces aériennes stratégiques*. Though it was originally conceived as an interim deterrent while a launching system from nuclear submarines was being perfected in the 1960s, the first two squadrons of SSBS S2 (*Sol-sol balistique stratégique*) missiles did not become operational until 1971 (the same year as the first nuclear submarine) and 1972. Plans for a third squadron were suspended in 1974, but improvements have proceeded on the existing two groups. Between 1980 and early 1983 the underground silos in which they are housed were hardened, and converted to receive the new SSBS S3 missile. This, like its predecessor, is a two-stage solid-fuel missile, but its range has been increased from 2,750 km to over 3,000 km and instead of the 150 kiloton warhead carried by the S2, the S3 has a one megaton thermonuclear charge and improved penetration capabilities to counter enemy defences. The missiles can reach most of European Russia, and, given the small size of the force (just 18 missiles in all), the estimated number of arriving warheads for this system is high, being set at eight. The system is maintained on permanent alert, and all 18 missiles could be fired within one minute. The two groups of nine launch areas are dispersed over a site of a thousand square kilometres on the Plateau d'Albion in Haute Provence, not far from Avignon. Each group is commanded by a heavily protected, subterranean, central fire control room, buried deep under the French Alps, and linked to the FAS headquarters by attack-proof communication networks. The nearby Saint-Christol air base provides the necessary logistic support facilities, including vector and warhead storage and assembly.

The SSBS installation plays a singular role in French deterrence theory on account of its acknowledged vulnerability. On the one hand, official communiqués adopt an optimistic tone in their talk of hardening, dispersal and survivability, and the press can even *boast* that it would take 20 megatons of explosives (more than was used throughout the duration of the last war) to destroy the Plateau d'Albion.[28] On the other hand, even those who know that modern nuclear weaponry includes in its range single warheads with a greater yield than 20 megatons can still argue the case in favour of the SSBS. Its vulnerability is transformed into an asset: any would-be aggressor would have to declare himself by a pre-emptive nuclear strike against this target, since it cannot be destroyed by conventional means, and as such an unambiguous attack would elicit the automatic riposte of the submarine missiles, it would never be attempted... This is the theme[29] which recurs throughout the strategic discourse on the use of the SSBS S3, and may even result in its being preferred to its probable successor, the SX.

There is much uncertainty about both the form and the role of the experimental SX missile, and the *Loi de programmation militaire 1984-1988* has done little to clarify matters beyond confirming that the SX is to be a mobile strategic missile, and that it is scheduled to come into service in 1996. This is considerably later than expected. Announced as a French response to the threat of the Soviet SS20,[30] it was originally suggested that it might be deployed in the mid-1980s, or by the early 1990s at the latest. The delay has led to suspicions that the programme is not making progress. The defence plan also states that the SX will replace the 18 Mirage IV bombers converted to ASMP which will be kept in service until that date. However, it has been widely assumed in recent years that the SX would be replacing the vulnerable SSBS S3 system. Certainly there is no sign of any other alternative system or further modernisation in respect of the S3, which is only billed to last until 1996.[31] It had also been assumed, and assurances given,[32] that the SX would be able to utilise hardened installations on the Plateau d'Albion as a base after the S3 system had been withdrawn, but the Minister of Defence refused to commit himself when pressed on that point in the Defence Commission. Regarding the manner of deployment of the SX missile, he would only say that it was to be 'transportable from one site to another'.[33] It seems possible, therefore, that the S3 missiles may remain in their silos, while some three dozen SX missiles, each armed with three of the miniaturised thermonuclear warheads at present being tested in the Pacific and with a range of some 4,000 km, are moved around on heavy lorries or in army transport planes. On the other hand, there are indications that the SX may yet have to replace both systems,[34] in which case it would be the only remaining component of the FAS.

In this connection it is worth mentioning the French interest in cruise missiles — not the American Tomahawk, but a rival made-in-France version — which would seem in many ways more appropriate than the SX to replace both the few remaining strategic bombers and the vulnerable S3 ballistic missiles. This appeared to be a serious option for the French in the late 1970s.[35] It was even suggested that a French *missile de croisière* programme would have advantages over the present concentration on submarines, both on the grounds of cost (air-launched cruise missiles are much cheaper to finance and maintain than submarines) and invulnerability (should there be a breakthrough in submarine detection). However, the cruise missile idea has been quietly dropped, and there is no hint of it in the present defence plan. There is one paramount reason for this, which has far-reaching implications for France's participation in the nuclear arms race, over and above the choice of a strategic missile system for the next decade. While the design of a small pilotless plane with appropriate propulsion and terminal guidance system is well within the scope of French aerospace and electronics engineers, the information needed to programme such a machine to make it usable would have to be gathered by satellite,[36] and it is precisely this facility that the French do not have at their disposal.[37]

Submarines (FOST)

France's fleet of five nuclear-powered missile-launching submarines or SNLEs (*sous-marins nucléaires lanceurs d'engins*) is still regarded as the mainstay of her strategic defences. Its destructive power, albeit compulsively over-rated in both popular and expert opinion,[38] is much greater than that of either of the other two strategic systems. The estimated number of arriving warheads is 26, and this could be doubled by the addition of the sixth submarine in 1985, and increased six fold or more if modernisation proceeds as planned by the end of the century. More significant than fire-power or accuracy in strategic defensive doctrine is the ability to escape detection and destruction in order to ensure a second-strike capability, and here the submarine has reigned supreme since the Americans launched the first Polaris missile in 1960. Submarines are more expensive to build, man and maintain than any of the alternative air- and land-based systems, but their relative invulnerability has persuaded France, like Britain, to invest heavily in a system which also makes the most of their maritime opportunities.

After a relatively slow start — the first French nuclear submarine, *le Redoutable*, did not become fully operational until 1971, though it had been launched in 1967 — the fleet was built up steadily with *le Terrible* in 1973, *le Foudroyant* in 1974, *l'Indomptable* in 1976 and *le Tonnant* in 1980. Each of these submarines carries 16 two-stage solid-fuel ballistic missiles in vertical launch tubes, with a range of over 3,000 km and equipped with a single one megaton warhead apiece. This version, the M20, was first deployed in 1977, replacing earlier versions, the M1 (1971) and M2 (1974), which had had ranges of 2,500 km and 2,900 km respectively. The sixth submarine, *l'Inflexible*, due in 1985, will be equipped with the new M4 three-stage solid-fuel ballistic missile which was successfully tested in the Pacific at the end of 1980.

The history of the M4 is a fine example of a certain tendency to over-rate the state of nuclear technology in France. By 1980 there had been ample and accurate public description[39] of the projected new submarine-launched ballistic missile, the M4, which was to have an MRV system with inertial guidance, permitting the six separate but not independently targetable 150 kiloton warheads to be scattered over an area of approximately 350 km by 150 km.[40]

But confusion between the M4 and its possible successor the M5, and between MRV and MIRV systems, together with indiscriminate application of the word *mirvé* and some deliberate fudging in official statements on an embarrassingly delayed programme, combined at the beginning of the 1980s to produce the myth of a MIRVed M4 which has persisted in high places. The M4 is neither MIRVed nor MARVed; it is not comparable with Trident, nor even Chevaline. It is certainly more sophisticated than the M20: it has a range of 4,000 km and a hardened re-entry vehicle, as well as its six 150 kiloton warheads, but these cannot be accurately aimed at six different targets.

The M4 will be progressively fitted to all the existing submarines except for the first in the series *le Redoutable*, which is scheduled to be withdrawn from service in 1997, and the retrofit is due to be completed by 1989. As opposed to the 80 M20s presently deployed, there will therefore be 96 M4 missiles with a total of 576 warheads and 16 remaining M20s deployed by the 1990s. It is worth noting, however, that before January 1983 no more than two SNLEs were on patrol at any one time, and that it is only since that date that the number has been increased to three, not without some strain on the present system.

Work on a seventh submarine, of a fundamentally new design, has been given the go-ahead in the *Loi de programmation militaire 1984-1988*, but this is unlikely to be operational before 1994 at the earliest, and it should be noted that not only the *Redoutable* but also the *Terrible* will have been withdrawn by 1999. Complete silence has descended on the M5 project for a new type of missile, possibly with manoeuvrable multiple warheads[41] like Chevaline, to replace the M4 missile. There are fears that the programme is proving prohibitively expensive.[42] It had been assumed that the M5 would at the very least be ready for the seventh SNLE, but the *Loi de programmation militaire* announces that this vessel will be equipped with M4 missiles, so it appears that no new submarine-launched missile technology is anticipated in the next ten years. This is a startling admission, especially after the M4 build-up which turned out to have so little substance. However, it is perhaps less surprising when one recalls that the real technological threat facing the FOST is the likelihood of a breakthrough in submarine detection by one or both of the superpowers. As this is almost certain to depend on satellite surveillance systems which are beyond the scope of the French, there is perhaps little they can do. It is no doubt the optimum use of their resources in the circumstances to commit them to a research programme for a faster, quieter, deeper-diving, more resistant submarine, which may be able to keep one step ahead of developments in submarine detection, even at the expense of a prestige weapon system. Meanwhile, the FOST can pride itself on the fact that, in the first ten years of its existence, more than a hundred successful operational patrols were effected without discovery or interception.

The operational base of the FOST is at Brest, and logistical support for the missile system is provided by the Ile Longue Naval Base in Brest Bay, where there are the assembly and storage facilities necessary to keep the missiles in operational readiness. The command headquarters are located in old mine-workings at Houilles in the Paris suburbs, but there are alternative headquarters in Brest and Toulon should anything go wrong. In addition to the SNLE, the FOST command structure also covers the fleet of SNAs (sous-marins nucléaires d'attaque) which is particularly favoured by the *Loi de programmation militaire*.[43] The first SNA, the *Rubis*, has just come into service, and the second, the *Saphir*, will follow shortly. By 1988 there will be four SNAs operational and four more on order. These are relatively small (2,500 tons) nuclear-powered hunter-killer submarines. Their performance is limited compared with their American or British counterparts, which are bigger and faster, but they are nevertheless considered the key element of any future naval operation. They have the dual role of protecting the navy's surface vessels as well as the SNLE fleet, and are heavily armed, mainly with Exocet SM39 missiles, but do not carry nuclear weapons themselves. Nevertheless, their integration into the strategic command structure is an interesting development. It becomes even more significant when one considers the pressures towards integration of conventional and nuclear weaponry which exist at the so-called tactical level.

Tactical Nuclear Weapons (ANT)

The *Armement nucléaire tactique* (ANT) derives from no fixed programme or strategic doctrine, and the decisions governing its creation during the 1970s were neither momentous nor contentious.

Nevertheless, in the seven years from 1972 to 1979 all three of the armed forces acquired their own nuclear unit, leaving virtually no gap between the setting up of the strategic triad and the evolution of the *Armement nucléaire tactique*.

As with the strategic deterrent, authorisation for the use of tactical nuclear weapons is the responsibility of the President of the Republic, but this has never seemed such a clear-cut issue in the case of the ANT, to the extent that it has had to be vigorously restated in the *Loi de programmation militaire 1984-1988*. The rationale of the ANT has always been an embarrassment, making a mockery of the pure *dissuasion* doctrine, which has never quite been abandoned at the political level. The discussions surrounding the present defence plan have shown how great are the pressures to separate these weapons from the deterrence posture by integrating them fully into the range of conventional weapons available to troops in the event of war fighting. The *Loi de programmation militaire* takes a firm stand against this tendency in its declaratory policy. Yet the defence spending programme it outlines is heavily oriented towards an investment in tactical nuclear armaments,[44] belying its prominently reported claim to give 'priority to the strategic nuclear arsenal'. The structural reforms of the defence plan are ambiguous. They propose a review of the command structure which will take operational control of tactical nuclear weapons out of the hands of the army, simultaneously safeguarding and upgrading them.

In its present composition, the ANT mimics the triadic structure of the strategic arsenal, having a land-based component, an air-borne component, and a sea-based component.

Tactical Missiles

Pluton is a land-mobile surface-to-surface tactical nuclear missile mounted, together with its launching ramp, on a modified AMX 30 tank chassis. It is very much an 'army' weapon. The missile has a range capability of from 20 to 120 km, and alternative warheads: the 25 kiloton AN51 (which contains the same MR50 nuclear charge as the AN52 free-fall bomb carried by French air force Mirage III and Jaguar aircraft and the carrier-based Super Etendard), intended for important targets in an enemy's rear; or a 15 kiloton device which is meant to be employed nearer to the main battle area. Classified as a battlefield support weapon, it is similar to the American Lance missile, and is theoretically supposed to support the three divisions of French troops still deployed in West Germany. Positioned in France, however, its use has always been problematic.[45]

Its conception dates back to a French land army requirement, at the time of the withdrawal from NATO in 1966, for a replacement for the American Honest John missile which had equipped NATO-integrated French forces in West Germany up till then. Though the research programme was initiated in November 1966, and the first missiles test-fired in 1969, initial production contracts were not awarded until 1972, and deliveries only began early in 1974, when the system became operational. Up to 120 Plutons were originally planned, but there are currently 30 launchers (42 including reserves), together with appropriate support and re-supply units, equipping five *régiments d'artillerie nucléaire* (RAN) stationed in the north-east of France (at Laon, Suippes, Mailly, Oberhoffen and Belfort). Each regiment is made up of 1,000 men, and although the crew specified for each of its six launch vehicles is only four, much has been made of the direct participation of ordinary conscripts (who make up over 80 per cent of personnel) in the operation of this nuclear weapons system, making it unique in the French nuclear armoury, even a 'manifestation of citizen support for the Nation's nuclear defences'.[46]

This justificatory feature is due to be sacrificed, however, in favour of the 'unified command structure' of tactical nuclear weapons outlined in the *Loi de programmation militaire*. The creation of an autonomous section to manage the next generation of land-based missiles, directly under the control of the Supreme Commander of the Armed Forces, will remove from the land army their only operational contact with these prestige weapons. That the move is presented as a reaffirmation of political control over this 'purely deterrent' weaponry is indicative of how clearly the trend in the opposite direction has been perceived.[47] Whether the new investment in tactical weaponry and personnel will ensure a reversal of this trend is open to doubt.

It is all the more doubtful, considering the nature of the new generation of tactical missiles themselves. The setting up of the new command structure is timed to coincide with the introduction of the Hades missile as a replacement for Pluton in 1992. The *Loi de programmation militaire* forsees the deployment of Hades in one regiment from 1992,[48] with up to five other regiments being similarly equipped by the year 2000. Research on a 'Super Pluton' was already in hand by 1977, and the Hades project was disclosed in 1980. It is at present envisaged as a semi-ballistic missile, whose warheads, varying between 20 and 60 kilotons, might be manoeuvrable in the final stages of their trajectory. Mounted in pairs on a wheel-based launch vehicle, it would be more mobile than the tank-based Pluton, and its range has been increased to over 350 km. Superficially, this has the advantage of enabling it to reach Warsaw Pact territory, but it also poses problems of targeting[49] which the present state of French electronic intelligence systems is unlikely to solve alone. And this has the most serious implications for the coordination of French manoeuvres within NATO command structures, from whose resources the necessary information would be forthcoming.

This is not to say that French efforts in this field have been slack. On the contrary, research and development programmes for both Pluton and Hades have given equal weight to the design of highly specialised equipment intended to provide the necessary information for selecting appropriate targets in a battlefield situation.[50] The Pluton system, in addition to an AMX 30 launching vehicle, comprises a command vehicle containing data-processing equipment organised round the IRIS 35M computer of the *Plan Calcul Militaire*. This is capable of operation under severe environmental conditions, and target data can be obtained in real-time from an R20 drone equipped with a Cyclope passive IR reconnaissance system. Along with the Hades missile is being developed simultaneously the CL 289 pilotless reconnaissance aircraft. Like Hades, this will come into service in 1992, and it will be used for the prior identification of targets —assisted by Mirage IIIR reconnaissance planes, the 13th parachute regiment and French monitoring of enemy radio transmissions. But an essential element will still be the 'information gathered in Europe by American forces'[51] with their access to satellite observation and communication.

There is another dimension to the Hades missile which should be borne in mind: it is the natural vehicle for the neutron bomb,[52] being technically capable of carrying enhanced radiation weapons as alternatives to the warheads specified above. France had successfully developed and tested an enhanced radiation weapon by the summer of 1980, and was due to reach the stage when regular production would be possible during 1983. Though the *Loi de programmation militaire 1984-1988* makes no commitment to the manufacture of the neutron bomb, it leaves open the option of placing it on the order book during this period. There is certainly widespread speculation that it will be available as part of the Hades system in 1992. This is bound to place new emphasis on counterforce strategy in military thinking, whatever political protestations are made to the contrary, because this is the only context in which justification of enhanced radiation weapons has been attempted.

And counterforce strategy, with its need for improved accuracy and information feedback,[53] is bound to lead to greater reliance on those command, control, communications and intelligence systems which may force France to compromise her independence in military decisions if she wishes to avail herself of them.

Tactical Bombers

By far the largest contingent of the ANT is furnished by the *force aérienne tactique* (FATac) which has had nuclear capability since 1972, two years before the more publicised Pluton missiles became operational. There are currently 30 Mirage IIIE and 45 Jaguar A aircraft permanently assigned to nuclear-dedicated squadrons, and over a hundred of each type of plane available in total, though only about half of these could be considered mission-ready. The two Mirage squadrons and three Jaguar squadrons, based at Saint-Dizier and Luxeuil in the north-east and Istres in the south of France, benefit from dispersed and specially hardened shelters, and specific communication links with operational headquarters. Planes are maintained fully armed, and intensive 'realistic' training is a regular feature for both pilots and ground personnel, who are all highly qualified and professionalised, in contrast to the largely conscripted Pluton regiments.

The Mirage IIIE, which had already been in service for eleven years when the nuclear unit was created, is a single-seater jet plane designed for high-speed precision attack at very low altitudes. The Jaguar A, deployed since 1973, is a single-seater twin-engine jet with similar all-weather navigation and attack features and an in-flight refuelling facility in addition. Both planes have a fairly limited average combat radius of 600 to 700 km, though they can achieve much higher ranges in optimum conditions. Their free-fall AN52 bombs carry basically the same 25 kiloton nuclear warhead as that used for the Pluton missiles, and are exactly the same as the weapons deployed on the sea-based bombers.

Up until now these weapons have been the basic equipment of the entire tactical strike force. Indeed, it has been a matter of some pride, stressed in military propaganda,[54] that the same nuclear bomb, which is 'entirely of French design and manufacture', has been common to the nuclear units of all three of the armed forces. This arrangement reflects the sense of a 'minimum' deterrent which is still quite strong in France, and may have had managerial advantages in preventing inter-service rivalry. But this cosy state of affairs is coming to an end. By the time the Hades system introduces its new and as yet undefined range of warheads, and upsets the balance between the services with its new command structure, a major escalation in the build-up of France's tactical arsenal will already have taken place, and the AN52 will have given way to a much more versatile and aggressive weapon system. As from the mid-1980s a new plane, the Mirage 2000N, will progressively replace the Mirage IIIE and Jaguar A squadrons, and new weaponry, the ASMP (*air-sol moyenne portée*) missile, will equip not only the Mirage 2000N for which it was designed, but also the sea-based Super Etendard bombers and what is left of the Mirage IV strategic bomber force.

The Mirage 2000N made a successful test flight in February of 1983. A product of French, German and British collaboration,[55] and already billed as 'the plane of the century', it is an extremely versatile two-seater low-altitude attack aircraft with advanced radar equipment, in-flight refuelling and an estimated combat radius of up to 1,400 km even without refuelling. When the additional range of the ASMP missile to be fired from this plane is taken into account (as much as 300 km), the Mirage 2000N may be seen as comparable in many respects with the Mirage IVA strategic bomber which some sources report it as 'replacing'.[56] Development has not gone smoothly: delays have been reported regularly over the last few years, attributed by Dassault to the difficulty they have experienced in perfecting the sophisticated radar equipment and jet engine. There have also been fears recently that money would not be available to purchase the 200 or so planes originally called for once they came into production. The *Loi de programmation militaire*, however, confirms credits for the first 15 Mirage 2000N bombers (by contrast, credits for the 25 non-nuclear Mirage 2000 interceptors due to be ordered in 1982 have been temporarily frozen and will not be unblocked before 1984-85[57]), and anticipates delivery of 36 planes by 1988, when the Mirage 2000N is due to come into service. A full series of 112 planes is envisaged eventually, equipping five squadrons.

Without doubt the most significant aspect of the modernisation programme in this area is the qualitative change which will occur in the weaponry of the tactical bombers with the deployment of the new *air-sol moyenne portée* (ASMP) missile as from 1987. This is a development along the lines of the Exocet and Otomat missiles which the French are acknowledged to be very good at. The ASMP is a ramjet-powered air-to-surface missile which can travel 100-300 km (depending on launch height) to reach its target after being fired from an aircraft remaining outside enemy defences. This, together with the fact that its trajectories can be varied from very high to very low altitudes, makes its degree of penetration much greater than that of the traditional bomber (estimates of arriving warheads for the present tactical bomber squadrons would not expect more than one aircraft per squadron to successfully deliver a bomb[58]). It also carries a much bigger 150 kiloton nuclear warhead. It will be fitted first to the 18 converted Mirage IVP aircraft in 1987, and then from 1988 to the new Mirage 2000N, of which at least 15 are due to become operational in that year. At the same time it will replace the AN52 weapons of the 36 carrier-based nuclear bombers. As this involves some 69 planes in the first instance, it is not surprising that CEA engineers have recently voiced disquiet that, for financial reasons, the number of ASMPs on order has now been reduced from 100 to only 60.[59] On the other hand, there is nothing very unusual in cuts, delays and financial stringency hitting the ambitious nuclear weapons programmes of successive French governments. Neither does it mean that the programme, even when pared down, will be without impact on French — and international — defence planning.

Aircraft Carriers

The sea-based tactical bomber force (*aviation embarquée*) is the most recently formed contingent of the ANT. It did not become operational until January 1979, with the deployment of the Super Etendard and the conversion of the first aircraft carrier to nuclear capability. Now both of France's aircraft carriers, *Clemenceau* and *Foch*, based with the Mediterranean fleet, are equipped to store and fit the AN52 nuclear bombs which the Super Etendard, like the aircraft of the FATac, carries. Unlike the Mirage IIIE and Jaguar A, however, the Super Etendard has the capacity to carry the new ASMP missile, with which it will be fitted after 1987. It also carries the Exocet AM39 conventional weaponry.

The Super Etendard is a small single-seater fighter plane with a powerful jet engine which enables it to sustain speeds of up to 1,200 km per hour at very low altitudes. Its normal combat range is similar to that of the FATac planes, about 700 km, which may be extended by in-flight refuelling. It was the first French fighter plane to be equipped with radar-linked inertial navigation and attack systems, and its radar is specially adapted to the identification of naval targets. There are at present three squadrons, comprising 36 Super Etendards in all, aboard the two existing aircraft carriers. An increase in the total number of nuclear-dedicated planes would seem to be indicated in plans for the transformation of Super Etendards from AN52 to ASMP.[60] Initially 10 planes were scheduled to be transformed between 1984 and 1986, and 40 more by 1988, which means an enlargement of the total force as well as its modernisation. On the other hand such increases are difficult to square with the aforementioned reductions in ASMP orders. Whatever the final numbers, however, and in the event they are nearly always lower than forecast, it is clear that the qualitative transformation in this area will be just as significant as in the FATac and the new Hades regiments.

And yet this thoroughgoing changeover to bigger, more accurate, longer-range, less destructible weapons in the tactical field often goes unnoticed in France, and is relatively uncommented abroad, especially in the case of the *aviation embarquée*. Much more contentious has been the issue of the aircraft carriers themselves, which are 20 years old already, and scheduled to be withdrawn in 1995 (*Clemenceau*) and 1998 (*Foch*). Whereas the Defence Council had approved in 1980 the construction of two nuclear-powered aircraft carriers to replace both *Foch* and *Clemenceau* in the 1990s,[61] the present defence plan proposes only one new carrier to replace *Clemenceau*, with *Foch* simply being converted in 1985-86 to ASMP operation. The new carrier will be nuclear-powered, but similar in size and design to the existing models, a 32,000 ton vessel with a runway and launching catapults, capable of carrying about 40 aircraft. There had been speculation in the late 1970s that the new generation of aircraft carriers would be smaller, faster and more manoeuvrable, provided that the French could develop a Harrier-type jump-jet which would require less runway space.[62] It appears that this idea had already been dropped by the time of the 1980 decision, but much retrospective justification has been found during the last twelve months, in the light of the South Atlantic experience, for the retention of conventional carriers and their fleets of Super Etendards.[63]

Much attention has also been given to the provision of support and protection vessels, with both anti-aircraft and anti-submarine defences, so that, theoretically, this mobile strike force can participate wherever the need arises, in either sea- or land-battles, using either conventional or nuclear weaponry. Interchangeability has perhaps been taken farther in the carrier fleet than in any of the other nuclear units, but it is an unobtrusive characteristic, which passes almost without comment. The economy measure announced in respect of the *Foch* caused an outcry in military and political circles in France. The vulnerability of any aircraft carrier, nuclear-powered or not, in any exchange involving the sort of tactical nuclear weapons which will shortly be in place (see Table), has given rise to comparatively little discussion.

EVOLUTION OF FRENCH NUCLEAR FORCES 1964-2000

Year	Strategic	Tactical
1964	1st Mirage IVA	
1971	36 Mirage IVA 9 SSBS (S2) 1 SNLE (16 M1)	
1974	36 Mirage IVA 18 SSBS (S2) 3 SNLE (48 M2)	30 Mirage IIIE 45 Jaguar A 30 Pluton 1st Super Etendard
1983	34 Mirage IVA 18 SSBS (S3) 5 SNLE (80 M20)	30 Mirage IIIE 45 Jaguar A 42 Pluton 36 Super Etendard
1988 (projected)	 18 SSBS (S3) 6 SNLE (80 M20, 16 M4)	18 Mirage IVP (ASMP), 15-36 Mirage 2000N (ASMP), remaining Mirage IIIE and Jaguar A 42 Pluton 36-50 Super Etendard (ASMP)
1996 (projected)	1st SX 7 SNLE (16 M20, 96 M4)	75-112 Mirage 2000N (ASMP) 30-42 Hades 50 Super Etendard (ASMP)
2000 (projected)	36 SX 5 SNLE (80 M4)	112 Mirage 2000N (ASMP) 42 Hades 50 Super Etendard (ASMP)

The Conventional Context

While the FNS have been an autonomous section of the armed forces since their creation at the beginning of the 1960s, and the ANT is to be accorded a similar status if the recommendations of the present defence plan are followed through, neither France's nuclear weapons systems nor French strategic doctrine can be understood in isolation from the conventional forces which still account for 80 per cent of the French defence budget. Restructuring of the armed services over the past 20 years has always been closely connected with the role of the nuclear arsenal, and many of the functions of the conventional forces are either concerned with support systems which are essential to the operation of the nuclear forces, or have implications for the deterrence theories associated with them. There are three elements of the present defence plan which are of the utmost importance in this respect. They are (1) the creation of the rapid deployment force (*Forces d'Action Rapide*, FAR), (2) the reorganisation of local and civil defence (*Défense Opérationelle du Territoire*, DOT), and (3) the development of systems to cope with the problems of command-control-communications-and-intelligence (C3I).

Military Restructuring

The total armed forces in France, which has a population presently approaching 54 million, number just under half a million,[64] of whom rather more than half are conscripts, and some 12,000 are women. The army is preponderant in numerical terms, with over three fifths of the entire armed forces personnel. The air force has approximately one fifth, and the navy slightly less. Over and above these forces, the paramilitary Gendarmerie provides a further 83,000 trained troops, placing it between the navy and the air force in numerical importance. Conscripts are unevenly divided between the services. They account for roughly two thirds of the land army's personnel, but only about one third of the air and naval forces, and currently ten per cent of the Gendarmerie.[65] Of the combined forces, almost 20,000 are directly concerned in the operation of the FNS: 10,600 air force personnel; 5,500 from the navy; 2,800 from the army; and at least 800 *gendarmes*. In addition, there are the operators of tactical nuclear weapons systems in each of the three services: five Pluton regiments; five strike squadrons of the FATac; and three strike squadrons of the naval air force.

By far the most massive cuts in military personnel ever to be implemented in modern France were brought about during the 1960s through the medium of de Gaulle's first two defence plans. These halved the numbers for the combined armed forces, which had stood at well over a million throughout the Algerian War of 1957-62, bringing them down to 575,000 by 1968. A decade later, Giscard's 1977-82 defence plan further reduced the land army (from 330,000 in 1977 to 314,000 in 1982). This was partly compensated by an increase in the Gendarmerie (from 76,000 to 83,000 in four years, 5,000 posts being created by a single cabinet decision in March 1978), resulting in the present overall level of 566,000.[66] Mitterrand's defence plan for the 1980s proposes an even more substantial reduction in the total number of military personnel, a reduction by 35,000 men altogether, of whom 22,000 are to go from the land army. This represents a reduction in manpower of nearly seven per cent.[67] In the terms of the *Loi de programmation* itself, these cuts are to be compensated by fundamental changes in the organisation and equipment of the army, with the emphasis on mobility and sophisticated conventional weaponry. By the mid-1990s it is envisaged that this army will consist of some 290,000 soldiers, equipped with 1,100 tanks, 250 combat helicopters, 450 pieces of modern heavy artillery, and about 8,000 armoured cars.[68] Anti-tank weapons like the HOT and Milan PGMs figure high on the list, as do the air-launched Exocet and Otomat missiles. In addition to the 450 fighter planes maintained by the air force, almost a hundred transport planes[69] will stand by for transportation of troops at short notice. There is to be investment in low-altitude air defence systems, and night-operation equipment is to be a priority.

The present defence plan marks the third major restructuring of the armed forces in the lifetime of the Fifth Republic. De Gaulle's reforms, from 1960 onwards, implemented a new organisation of the armed forces into (1) the Territorial Defence Forces (*Forces de Défense Opérationelle du Territoire*, DOT), (2) the Mobile Forces (*Forces de Manoeuvre*), and (3) the Strategic Nuclear Forces (*Forces Nucléaires Stratégiques*, FNS). The DOT combined the forces of both the Gendarmerie and the bulk of the land army (hence most conscripts), and was conceived as a home-based defence force whose reponsibilities began at the French frontiers. The *Forces de Manoeuvre* comprised both the French divisions stationed in West Germany, and the *Forces d'Intervention* which were intended for rapid deployment outside France, principally in Africa, being 'trained to fight on terrain very different from the European theatre'.[70] The FNS provided a new command structure for the pre-tactical generations of nuclear weapons, giving key roles to the air force and navy and further downgrading the land army by effectively excluding it from the control of this prestige area.

In 1977, Giscard rationalised the command structure, bringing the military personnel of the DOT and the *Forces de Manoeuvre* into one integrated body of military forces, and concentrating on the standardisation of the basic divisions stationed the length and breadth of French territory, in a structure commonly referred to as '*quadrillage du territoire*'.[71] At the same time, increasing emphasis was placed on the specialisation of certain units, especially those participating in the revamped *Forces d'Intervention*, or *Forces d'Assistance Rapide*, as they were now called. Also, a major investment was made in the Gendarmerie force, considerably strengthening its paramilitary and surveillance aspects. Retention of the FNS was taken for granted, but most of the later generations of nuclear weapons, the so-called tactical weapons, remained outside this command structure.

As from 1984, Mitterrand's military restructuring will in some respects reverse the trend of the last decade, for example, in replacing *quadrillage du territoire* by the strengthening of traditional army 'frontier' positions, particularly in the east and north-east of France. In other respects, it builds upon what may well be seen in retrospect as a period of consolidation, during which the Giscard government's reforms prepared the ground for what have been presented by and large as the 'new departures' of the latest defence plan, namely the creation of a rapid deployment force and the upgrading of the Gendarmerie in relation to the DOT. Henceforth the land army will comprise (1) the rapid deployment force (*Forces d'Action Rapide*, FAR) which will constitute one sixth of the entire land army by the 1990s, (2) the vestiges of a territorial defence (DOT) based essentially on the Gendarmerie, and (3) the remainder or *Première Armée* situated in West Germany and on France's eastern borders. The responsibilities of this latter section will remain largely unchanged, except with regard to its tactical nuclear weapons, which will eventually be reconstituted under a new, non-land-army command, similar in status to the FNS. This will leave the armed forces with three highly sensitive command centres, the new *unité nucléaire tactique*, the FNS, and the FAR, all of which are concerned with highly professionalised forces, and all of which are expressly intended to be used as *political* weapons,[72] under the direct control of the President of the Republic.

The FAR

The idea, and indeed existence, of a rapid deployment force in the French military is not new. The creation of the *Forces d'Intervention* by de Gaulle in the 1960s went along with the traumatic withdrawal of the French army from its North-African base, and the continuing process of decolonisation on that continent. A solid core of professional soldiers, though permanently based in France, continued to train for operation in Africa, and the agreements made with former French colonies required France to equip itself for possible external intervention on their behalf. By the beginning of the 1980s, the *Forces d'Assistance Rapide*, as they were then called, had been increased to 20,000 men, and already included two of France's crack divisions, the 11th parachute division, an air-borne contingent with its headquarters in Toulouse, and the 9th marine infantry division, specialised in amphibious operations, and based in Saint-Malo. To these was added on 1 July 1981 the newly created and wholly professionalised 31st brigade, equipped with heavy artillery, but also specialised in amphibious and helicopter operations. This is now to become the 6th light armoured division, made even more mobile by a concentration on armoured cars, and these three existing divisions are to be joined by two further divisions, the 4th air-borne division, consisting of some 250 combat helicopters armed with over 500 Milan and HOT anti-tank weapons, and the 27th Alpine division. Together these five divisions will form the *Forces d'Action Rapide*, with their unified command headquarters at Saint-Germain-en-Laye, near Paris.

Apart from the increase in size (to 47,000 men or one sixth of the restructured land army) and the generous equipment budget, the novelty of the FAR as it is presented in the 1984-1988 defence plan lies chiefly in its new and separate command structure, and in the fact that its use is envisaged first and foremost in Europe, 'possibly alongside the NATO Allies'. The reorientation is sharp and unambiguous, despite references to the multi-purpose nature of the FAR and its continuing role in Africa and the Middle East. Speaking in May 1983,[73] General Lacaze, Supreme Commander of the French Armed Forces, listed in the following order the missions of the new FAR: (1) fighting alongside the [NATO] Allies, (2) supporting armoured divisions of the land army, (3) participating in territorial defence (DOT), and (4) providing rapid assistance overseas. Lucien Poirier[74] is even more unequivocal in his appraisal of the 'increasingly significant' step of 'grafting a new force' onto the French defence system which may have 'far-reaching consequences' in terms of France's reintegration into NATO. And fears have been widely expressed[75] of France's falling in with the US preparation of 'Air Land Battle 2000', according to which 'the land army would improve its capacity to wage all forms of combat, conventional, nuclear, electronic or chemical,[76] either separately or in combination'.[77]

The political and popular anxiety expressed on this topic has been couched overwhelmingly in terms of the relationship between France and the NATO allies, especially the USA. But the implications for the potential engagement of France's tactical nuclear weapons in the European battlefield are clear. And since it is in this area of French nuclear weaponry that the most rapidly increased investment is concurrently taking place, it is more than likely that expectations will progress along this path. The assurances built into the current planning documents by the creation of an autonomous command structure for France's tactical nuclear weapons, and their removal from the traditional divisions of the French land army, must be balanced against the likelihood of a closer collaboration in the future between the new tactical nuclear unit and the NATO command structure. In view of the operational dependency of French systems on US support services, particularly satellite information, it would indeed be strange if such collaboration did not take place. And it is certainly not impossible to envisage looking back at the present provisions as a period of consolidation, building up to a fuller integration, rather than as an assertion of uncompromising independence.

The DOT

The role of the Gendarmerie in French military planning is often forgotten, but has been highlighted by the major role ascribed to this ambivalent force in the 1984-1988 defence plan. From being explicitly associated with territorial defence in de Gaulle's restructuring phase, the role of the Gendarmerie became less prominent under Giscard's planning, which insisted upon the responsibilities of *army* divisions for all levels of territorial defence in its concept of *quadrillage du territoire*. At the same time, however, the manpower of the *gendarme* force was increased by twelve per cent during the Giscard presidency, and investment was channelled into a comprehensive computer-and-communications network on the one hand, and modern military equipment such as helicopters and armoured cars on the other. The generally improved status and bigger budget accorded to the Gendarmerie under Giscard undoubtedly laid the foundations for the Mitterrand government's decision to return the full responsibility for the DOT to this revitalised force, a decision which is accompanied by an extensive programme for upgrading its buildings and equipment. The present plan provides for between 7,000 and 9,000 new accommodation units for the expanded force, 25,000 FAMAS assault guns (as supplied to the army since 1979) for issue to *gendarmes*, substantial investment in helicopters and armoured vehicles, and further modernisation of the specific telecommunications network and information-processing facilities.[78]

The Gendarmerie's 4,000 territorial brigades ensure dense implantation in all areas of France, both urban and rural, and, together with its nationwide communications network, make it well suited to its permanent surveillance task. In times of tension, its prime task would be the guarding of 'sensitive installations', among which the most important would be all nuclear weapons installations, other nuclear plants, and communications networks, and it is clear that any 'reserves' brought in at this stage would be those from within the specific security arrangements for individual installations. The Gendarmerie is involved with security of nuclear weapons systems at all levels, and at all times. Special units of *gendarmes*, the first of their kind, have even been created on board France's two aircraft carriers to guard the stocks of nuclear weapons now stored there.[79]

Contingency plans do however include the mobilisation of reservists through the DOT, in operations of general territorial resistance. On the one hand, it is noted that the accent seems now to be on 'prolonged resistance' rather than immediate fighting.[80] On the other hand, the very notion of a territorial defence in which reservists would play any role whatsoever is very much in doubt, given the 'nature of the threat'.[81]

As for civil defence, this also comes under the aegis of the DOT, though, as critics from many different viewpoints have pointed out,[82] provision for the protection of the civilian population in the event of war breaking out is sadly lacking in France. In the event of a nuclear attack, it is non-existent. However, the present government has undertaken to study the subject. In September 1981 Prime Minister Mauroy announced that civil defence (*la protection civile*) formed an integral part of the policy of *dissuasion*, and should be used to reinforce its credibility. Since 1982, a liaison officer has been working with the Ministry of Defence and the Ministry of the Interior to create a 'substantial organisation' to protect France's urban centres. More specially trained reservists are to be involved, for example in the army's functions in connection with natural disasters and major accidents, so that they will be prepared for 'all emergencies' in any future conflict.[83] It is interesting to note that, if the French government stands by its undertaking to 'inform' as well as to 'protect' the civilian population, it is bound to encounter the problem of the credibility of the civil defence exercise itself.

C3I Systems

Of all the support systems provided by the French military in general for the forces' nuclear contingents, those facilities which have come to be known by the nickname C3I — command, control, communications and intelligence-gathering systems — are the most crucial for the operation, and therefore credibility, of the nuclear deterrent. The defence plan debate obliquely acknowledges that this is one of the weakest areas in the present state of French defences.[84] It notes the challenge, without necessarily furnishing satisfactory assurances that this challenge will be met. For there are serious doubts as to how 'independent' France has been able to remain in practice in this respect, and certainly fears that she will be unable to remain so in the future, as the superpowers move into their 'star wars' phase.

This is not to say that France has little to show in this field. On the contrary, it is one which has seen extensive development over the last decade, and in which considerable efforts are being made at present. Hardened communication systems have evolved for the FAS, the FOST, and the FATac, incorporating features of redundancy and of resistance to atmospheric disturbance and electromagnetic impulsion. The most sophisticated radar equipment is being used in the new Mirage 2000 plane. The use of reconnaissance drones linked to advanced computers is commonplace, as in the operation of Pluton and eventually Hades. Then there is the elaborate telecommunications network specific to the Gendarmerie, which is likewise coupled with sophisticated data-processing equipment, and even so earmarked for 'modernisation' in the *Loi de programmation militaire*. Also detailed for completion is the integrated network for automatic transmissions (*réseau intégré des transmissions automatiques*, RITA) which came into operation in 1980 to facilitate command in the land army. The defence plan points suggestively to 'a coherent programme for the acquisition of *complementary* means of surveillance, detection and location of targets'.[85] So it comes as something of a surprise to read in its small print that the relatively modest RITA system, which was supposed to be a creation of the last government, is still not complete, and that its related information-processing systems will not begin to be operational before 1988.

It is also widely admitted that France is very vulnerable to aerial attack. The air-defence system at present in use is the automatic STRIDA II, with its ten radar stations, but France relies heavily on NATO warning systems on her eastern borders, and is singularly vulnerable on her Mediterranean flank. Hence the urgent improvement planned for radar cover in general (high and low altitude), and the emergency purchase announced in the defence plan of low altitude defence systems (*détection aéroportée*) from abroad — probably America. This is an unusual choice for France, which is technically capable of producing this kind of plane itself. The move has been justified on the grounds of urgency, yet the final choice of system will not be made before 1984, and two 'batches' will be bought in by 1988.

Also due to become operational by 1988 are the air-borne transmissions system Astarté and its ground network Ramsès. General Lacaze cites these two programmes as the main thrust of the French C3I programme, and the system is clearly regarded as part of the 'modernisation of France's nuclear weapons'. Claims for its qualities of resistance to 'all atmospheric interference', and for its capacity to 'ensure the security of liaison in mainland France' whatever the conditions, underline the deterrent credibility factor associated with these systems. That being so, it is perhaps surprising that only four planes with Astarté command posts are ordered for 1988, and that the total investment in this system is similar to the cost involved in the construction of one SNLE.[86]

The sum of French developments in this sphere pales into insignificance, however, beside the superpowers' current C3I ventures, which are an extension of the space race. One of the most-asked and least-answered questions of the present defence plan debates has concerned the future of the French satellite programme. 'France will be lucky to get any satellites off the ground before her enemies are ready to shoot them down' was the disgruntled conclusion.[87] The so-called SAMRO programme for the launching of a French military observation satellite is still officially endorsed by the French government,[88] but statements on its feasibility have been increasingly ambiguous, and it is widely considered to be postponed indefinitely.[89] Jean Lecanuet, in the Senate debate, drew hard-hitting conclusions from this failure: 'you have developed the tactical nuclear weapons — Hades missiles, Mirage 2000N, ASMP — but you make no provision for the modern indispensable means of defining targets which are essential for these weapons to be fully effective —like the SAMRO satellite...' While Jacques Genton, the Senate *rapporteur*, even referred to SAMRO as 'of capital importance for the operation of the FOST'.

Nor has the military failed to stress the need for credible and independent C3I back-up to sustain a credible and independent nuclear deterrent. Indeed, there are signs that the 'electronic arsenal' is well on its way to *replacing* the nuclear arsenal in its deterrent value to would-be aggressors. General Gallois,[90] in particular, impressed the parliamentary defence commission (*Commission de la Défense Nationale et des Forces Armées*) with his exposition of the way the familiar arguments in French strategic theory — the contradictions between the all-or-nothing posture and the flexible response approach — have in his opinion been superseded by the new strategic possibilities opened up by counterforce technology, which invalidates the credibility of the anti-city 'deterrent',[91] and by the new challenge of the military use of space by the superpowers. His warning of the loss of *independence* imminent for France in the wake of the latest superpower initiatives in the space/arms race would not go unheeded. But the solution is not simple. Gallois, along with many others, is convinced of the need for European collaboration, suggesting that France, Great Britain, Germany, and maybe Italy and others, should mount a collective project to meet the superpower challenge. The European Space Agency project and recent successful launches of the rocket Ariane are obviously of interest in this regard.[92]

France has been exerting diplomatic pressure for several years for the setting up of an international satellite monitoring agency (ISMA) to assist with arms control verifications.[93] While this has met with negative response from the USA and USSR, anxious to preserve their arms-development advantages in this field, it is felt to be increasingly unlikely that the US-Soviet monopoly on military reconnaissance satellites can continue unchallenged, and that other countries will acquire such a capability.[94]

It would seem that France has a series of defence choices that have *not* been faced in the *Loi de programmation militaire*. Either the independent nuclear deterrent is abandoned altogether; or France becomes dependent on American C3I support, which implies integrating the French nuclear forces into NATO; or the technology gap is made up by the sharing of resources in a joint European programme.

Implications

The key question for an outsider considering the significance of the French nuclear arsenal in a global context must be the weight it carries in the East-West balance of terror. How does it measure up against the superpower arsenals? How does it relate to NATO? How does it differ from the British 'independent' deterrent? And what are the implications of current technological developments for France's future as a nuclear 'great power'?

On the one hand, one must be careful not to underestimate the strength of the French arsenal.[95] In sheer destructive power, regardless of the relative crudeness of their targeting procedures and the vulnerability of many of their delivery systems, the credibility of the French claim to a 'strategy of sixty million dead' is beyond doubt. For the present decade at least, and probably the next, the French are assured of the technical capacity to devastate most Soviet cities, independently of NATO or the United States, and even after suffering a pre-emptive or 'surgical' strike. Whether the political will to do so would exist in any imaginable circumstances is another matter.

Compared with British nuclear capability, the French showing is impressive. France has more weapons, a greater variety of delivery systems, and a much more independent military and political control. Yet even the French bid for an independent nuclear strategy, though initially resisted by the USA, is increasingly recognised as indirectly serving US interests.[96] Apart from the greater national effort willingly sustained by France in comparison with other NATO countries, which has been an important consideration during the recession years, there is the theory of the 'wild card' in the nuclear poker game. The element of uncertainty thrown into the game by France's independent posture automatically strengthens the US hand — but there is no way France can withdraw this support without undermining the basis of its own deterrent theory.

Furthermore, there are a number of developments taking place in the field of French nuclear weapons which tend to support the Soviet claim that French warheads should be counted in with NATO ones for the purposes of negotiations on strategic arms reduction. The multiple warheads feature of the new generation of strategic weapons, M4 and SX, has made an impact (which would be even greater if full MIRVing were to be achieved); so has the SX programme in itself, which has, with a good deal of US encouragement, been conceived as a part of the western world's response to the Soviet SS20 deployment; and Hades, though classified as a battlefield support weapon, will effectively be targeted on Warsaw Pact territory and therefore possessed of some 'strategic' value. The tactical build-up too, with its accent on medium-range weapons systems easily capable of threatening Warsaw Pact territory, is just as significant in Soviet calculations. Then there is the fact that France has virtually ceased trying to be ambiguous about the direction in which its nuclear missiles are pointing.[97] Like NATO's, they are targeted against the Soviet Union, and there is no denying the importance of the threat they represent.

On the other hand, it is hard to see France maintaining its independence, even in the limited sense of the independent military command of its own weapons systems, without falling hopelessly behind in terms of technological credibility. Collaboration, either with NATO, or on a European basis, seems imperative if the French nuclear deterrent is to be maintained at all. The Quixotic nature of France's small-power stand against the nuclear 'giants' may not hold out indefinitely.

Notes

1. 'Military record of CBR/atomic happenings', *Aviation Studies Atlantic* (London), September 1982. The figures given are USA: 30,420; USSR: 17,470; China: 942; France: 720; UK: 640. For a fuller discussion of units of account and a comparison of estimates currently available see *SIPRI Yearbook 1983*, pp.LII-LIII; also Ruth Leger Sivard, *World Military and Social Expenditures 1982* (Leesburg Virginia, World Priorities, 1982), pp.12-13.

2. Christian Mellon, in a BBC interview, 23 April 1983, analysed the 'nuclear consensus' in France primarily in terms of French pride in their own French-built nuclear weapons, and noted that there would be an outcry if ever American missiles were placed in France.

3. Edward A. Kolodziej, 'French arms trade: the economic determinants', *SIPRI Yearbook 1983*, pp.371-90.

4. The Non-Proliferation Treaty, negotiated from 1967 and in force since 1970, bans the transfer of nuclear weapons technology from nuclear to non-nuclear states. France is not a signatory, but claims to abide by its provisions voluntarily. Transfer of *civil* nuclear technology, in which France is extremely active, is permitted under the treaty.

5. See Chapter 9 on the nuclear power issue.

6. Compared with 3 per cent of the defence budget spent on the nuclear deterrent in Britain. Defence spending in general in France represents approximately 17 per cent of

the national budget, or 3-4 per cent of GNP.

7. It is standard parliamentary practice in France to take as government bills the somewhat irregular 5-year plans, begun in 1960, which usually contain some measures of reform in the armed forces, as well as a review of defence expenditure, and almost inevitably statements of defence doctrine. This is the fifth in line, the previous plans covering the periods 1960-64, 1965-70, 1971-75 and 1977-82. For a discussion of the party-political issues surrounding the present debate, see Chapter 4.

8. 830,000,000,000 F.F. is the sum set aside for all military expenditure during the 5-year period. The equipment budget accounts for 50 per cent, and of this 30 per cent is allocated to the nuclear weapons programme, that is 131,500,000,000 F.F.

9. Yves Lancien, RPR, speaking in the Assembly debate on the defence plan: *Journal Officiel*, Assemblée Nationale, 20 May 1983, p.1240. His remarks are based on the delaying of the M5 programme until 'around the year 2000'.

10. Jean Gatel, PS, makes this point, ibid., p.1267, with particular reference to delays in the Mirage 2000 programme between 1977 and 1979. Giscard also faced repeated criticism with regard to delays in the nuclear submarine programme: *Le Monde*, 25 May 1980 and 9 May 1981, for example.

11. The Assembly voted in favour of the *Loi de programmation militaire* by 330 to 152 votes: see *Journal Officiel*, Assemblée Nationale, 20 May 1983, p.1292.

12. Assemblée Nationale, *Rapport d'information déposé par la commission de la défense nationale et des forces armées sur la programmation militaire*, No. 1440, p.14. This defence commission report clearly considers this to be 'one of the major questions to which an answer must be provided in one form or another in the course of the present defence review'. It will be clear from the present chapter that this question has not yet been resolved.

13. The Senate voted against each article of the *Loi de programmation militaire* by substantial majorities, in some cases as high as 2 to 1 : see *Journal Officiel*, Sénat, 15 June 1983, pp.1624-5.

14. Charles Hernu, in his presentation of the defence plan to the Assembly: *Journal Officiel*, Assemblée Nationale, 20 May 1983, p.1219; and in a rare interruption of the fiercely critical Senate *rapporteur*: *Journal Officiel*, Sénat, 15 June 1983, pp.1591-2.

15. This is a *political demand* of the parliamentary opposition, well represented by Jacques Genton, UCDP and *rapporteur* in the Senate defence debate, who argued that it was unacceptable to create a FAR which might now find itself obliged to participate in a NATO 'forward battle' without benefit of battlefield nuclear weapons: ibid., p.1624. It is also increasingly a *military assumption*: see Hubert Haenel, *La Défense Nationale* (Paris, P.U.F.,1982), p.78, describing the current ANT as 'totally integrated into the conventional forces'; and Lucien Poirier, 'La Greffe', *Défense Nationale*, April 1983, pp.5-32.

16. Ibid.; also A.-M. Thomas, 'L'Air Land Battle et l'engagement américain en Europe', *Défense Nationale*, April 1983, pp.51-67.

17. See Admiral Sanguinetti's remarks in Chapter 6.

18. Cf. the American B52 and Soviet TU95 long-range bombers, with ranges of over 12,000 km: see Paul Rogers, *A Guide to Nuclear Weapons* (London, Housmans, 1981).

19. IISS, *The Military Balance 1982-83*, p.137. Average combat radius assumes high-level transit, low-level penetration of air defences and average payload, unrefuelled.

20. Gwyn Prins ed., *Defended to Death* (Harmondsworth, Penguin Books, 1983), p.317.

21. M. D. Oustinov, *Pravda*, 25 October 1979, cited in Alain Joxe ed., *Demain la Guerre?* (Paris, Editions Ouvrières, 1981), p.228.

22. IISS, *The Military Balance 1982-83*, p.137. Estimates of arriving warheads are calculated on the basis of: Warheads available x Survivability x Reliability x Penetration.

23. Mirage IVA bases: Luxeuil, Saint-Dizier, Bourges-Avord, Bordeaux, Mont-de-Marsan, Cazaux, Orange; C135F bases: Bourges-Avord, Mont-de-Marsan, Istres. *Le Monde*, 13 July 1977.

24. This number was increased from 15 by the present defence plan. See also 'Fewer Mirage IVs to retire', *Flight International*, Vol. 119, No. 3749, 14 March 1981, p.717.

25. IISS, *The Military Balance 1982-83*, p.34.

26. Assemblée Nationale, *Rapport fait au nom de la commission de la défense nationale et des forces armées sur le projet de loi portant approbation de la programmation militaire pour les années 1984-1988*, No. 1485, p.49 and p. 111. The plane's *reconnaissance* role is also stressed in this report.

27. Jean Lecanuet, president of the foreign affairs and defence commission, deplores the fact that no new-generation strategic bomber is envisaged, despite the fact that this is an area where France leads the world technologically: *Journal Officiel*, Sénat, 15 June 1983, p.1598.

28. Jacques Isnard, *Le Monde*, 23 May 1980, p.28, quotes this assessment from *Stratégique*, premier trimestre 1979, Hôtel National des Invalides, Paris.

29. P. M. Gallois, 'The Future of France's *Force de Dissuasion*', *Strategic Review*, Vol. 7, No. 3, Summer 1979, pp.34 ff; also Assemblée Nationale, No. 1485, p.49.

30. *Le Monde*, 28 June 1980.

31. Assemblée Nationale, No. 1485, p.49.

32. By Charles Hernu, as reported in *Le Monde*, 30-31 January 1983.

33. Assemblée Nationale, No. 1485, p.92.

34. Jean Gatel, fervent supporter of the government's defence policy, states categorically that the SX has the advantage of being able to replace *both* the Plateau d'Albion missiles *and* the Mirage IV bombers: *Journal Officiel*, Assemblée Nationale, 20

May 1983, p.1266.

35. *Le Monde*, 13 July 1977, reported that a French cruise missile was 'being developed'.

36. Lawrence Freedman, *Britain and Nuclear Weapons* (London, Macmillan, 1980), p.72.

37. *Le Monde*, 16-17 March 1980.

38. Cf. Maurice Leman, 'La Dissuasion nucléaire française', *Défense Nationale*, January 1981, p.108, claiming that the M4 would render the FOST, after calculation of 'arriving warheads', capable of separately targeting and destroying 120 Soviet cities. This is not possible without full MIRVing, which the M4 does not have.

39. For example, *Le Monde*, 13 July 1977; and *Le Monde*, 11 June 1980.

40. For a good up-to-date account see *Le Monde*, 24 March 1983; also Per Berg, 'British and French eurostrategic forces', *SIPRI Yearbook 1983*, p.36.

41. *Le Monde*, 6-7 December 1981.

42. Jacques Isnard reports in some detail the suspicions of CEA engineers in *Le Monde*, 24 March 1983.

43. Assemblée Nationale, No. 1485, p.61.

44. See the analysis of the French defence budget by Thomas Ohlson and Rita Tullberg in 'World military expenditure and production', *SIPRI Yearbook 1983*, p.146, which shows a particularly rapid increase in spending on tactical nuclear weapons.

45. Pierre Lellouche, of the prestigious *Institut français des relations internationales*, and not a noted critic of France's nuclear policies, told Stuart Simon in a BBC interview: 'I have no idea. Nobody in France knows what [the Plutons] are for. No number of seminars and meetings with political and military analysts has enabled me to find out.' *The Listener*, 28 April 1983, pp.5-6.

46. *Armées d'aujourd'hui*, No. 72 (July-August 1982), p.15.

47. Hernu insists on the need for a new command structure 'to dissipate the dangerous illusion that the Hades regiments can be used as a sort of battle artillery': Assemblée Nationale, No. 1485, p.85.

48. Ibid., p.83. It was due in 1991, and the number has been cut back from 180 to 120: *Le Monde*, 24 March 1983.

49. Jacques Isnard, defence correspondent of *Le Monde*, and Jean Paucot, director of the *Institut de Polémologie*, discuss this problem in *Le Monde*, 30 October 1982 and 20 April 1983 respectively.

50. *Jane's Weapons Systems 1982-83* (London, Jane's Yearbooks).

51. *Le Monde*, 16 December 1982.

52. *Le Monde*, 15-16 November 1981.

53. General Lacaze outlines the importance of C3I for the efficacy of the 'test' doctrine in the use of the ANT: 'It is essential to be able to acquire precise and ongoing information and feedback on potential objectives, not just at the point of contact with enemy troops, but in the full depth of their theatre of operations, including the logistical infrastructure necessary to support them, details of command posts, transmission centres, depots and launch-sites ... and the appropriate information must be capable of being relayed in a hostile electronic environment.' *Défense Nationale*, June 1983, p.18.

54. *Armées d'aujourd'hui*, No. 72 (July-August 1982), pp.9, 16, 17.

55. Mary Kaldor, *The Baroque Arsenal* (London, André Deutsch, 1982), pp.200-201, also notes that 'practically no European country can now afford to go it alone in the development and production of a major combat aircraft'.

56. See, for example, William Arkin, 'Nuclear Weapons in Europe', in Mary Kaldor and Dan Smith eds., *Disarming Europe* (London, Merlin Press, 1982), pp.46-7. The confusion arises partly from the fact that a *strategic* Mirage 4000 was at one time planned, but quickly abandoned in favour of concentrating resources into large numbers of high-performance *tactical* Mirage 2000 planes.

57. *Le Monde*, 3-4 October 1982; Assemblée Nationale, No. 1485, p.67 and p.130.

58. IISS, *The Military Balance 1982-83*, pp.136-7. The estimate gives 8 arriving warheads in all, including sea-based squadrons.

59. *Le Monde*, 24 March 1983. Cf. 'Cent missiles "ASMP" sur avions', *Air et Cosmos*, No. 864, 13 June 1981, p.105.

60. Assemblée Nationale, No. 1485, p.51.

61. *Le Monde*, 25 September 1980.

62. *Le Monde*, 28 November 1978.

63. See, for example, General Méry, *Défense Nationale*, April 1983, p.171; also Assemblée Nationale, No. 1440, p.17, Note (1).

64. IISS, *The Military Balance 1982-83*, pp.34-6. When the Gendarmerie is taken into account, the figure is well over half a million.

65. This accounts for discrepancies in figures quoted for the proportion of conscripts in the armed forces. When the Gendarmerie figures are integrated with those for the other services, the proportion of professional 'soldiers' is shown as 57 per cent, and the proportion of conscripts falls to 43 per cent. Conscription in the Gendarmerie is however being increased — from around 5,000 in previous years to 8,698 in 1983: *Journal Officiel*, Assemblée Nationale, 20 May 1983, p.1221.

66. INSEE, *Tableaux de l'économie française*, 1980, p.155. This figure does not include some 10,000 personnel on inter-service central staff, which would bring the overall total to 576,000.

67. Presented by the French Minister of Defence as '5 per cent' in Assemblée

168 *French Nuclear Weapons*

Nationale, *Projet de loi portant approbation de la programmation militaire pour les années 1984-1988*, No. 1452, p.12.

68. Assemblée Nationale, No. 1452, pp.10-11.

69. General Gallois notes however that the Super-Transall transport plane was 'added halfway through the programme', as something of an afterthought: Assemblée Nationale, No. 1440, p.98.

70. Pierre Messmer, speaking as Minister of the Armies in 1962, in Lothar Ruehl, *La politique militaire de la Ve République* (Paris, Presses de la Fondation Nationale des Sciences Politiques, 1976), p.338.

71. See Chapter 6 for elucidation of this concept.

72. A point always made about the old Mirage IV *force de frappe*, and now related to the new FAR and Tactical Nuclear Command is that their *visible* mobilisation is a threat in itself, and makes them useful as *political* weapons.

73. General Lacaze, 'Politique de défense et stratégie militaire de la France', *Défense Nationale*, June 1983, pp.20-21.

74. Lucien Poirier, *Défense Nationale*, April 1983, pp.5-6.

75. See, for example, Pierre Lellouche in *Le Point*, 4 October 1982.

76. France has a declared policy of non-use and negotiated banning of all chemical weapons, but is known to produce and stockpile them at present. See Assemblée Nationale, No. 1452, p.6; and *SIPRI Yearbook 1982*, pp.330-31.

77. A.-M. Thomas, *Défense Nationale*, April 1983, p.58.

78. Assemblée Nationale, No. 1452, p.20.

79. *Armées d'aujourd'hui*, No. 72 (July-August 1982), p.16. See also 'Interview with Charles Hernu', *Le Monde*, 18 June 1983, pp.18-19.

80. Lucien Poirier, *Défense Nationale*, April 1983, p.31.

81. General Gallois in Assemblée Nationale, No. 1440, p.97.

82. For example, Yves Lancien in *Journal Officiel*, Assemblée Nationale, 20 May 1983, p.1242; and Pierre Bernheim in *Armée Nouvelle*, No. 8, 2me Trimestre 1983, p.9.

83. Ibid., p.10.

84. Among the questions which received no direct answer from the Defence Minister despite being put at every opportunity, were those on the SAMRO project, and on observation and communication satellites in general, along with the stock questions on the M5, SX development and the neutron bomb: see, for example, Assemblée Nationale, No. 1485, pp.87-97.

85. Assemblée Nationale, No. 1452, p.16.

86. General Lacaze, *Défense Nationale*, June 1983, p.15.

87. Jacques Baumel, *Journal Officiel*, Assemblée Nationale, 20 May 1983, p.1261.

88. The clearest indication of government policy on SAMRO was given eventually in a curt reply to close questioning of the Defence Minister: 'Funds are allocated in the defence plan for research on the satellite, but you know that there exist other possibilities.' *Journal Officiel*, Assemblée Nationale, 20 May 1983, p.1260.

89. *Le Monde*, 23 October 1982; *SIPRI Yearbook 1983*, p.146; and Jean Lecanuet, *Journal Officiel*, Sénat, 15 June 1983, p.1598, who remarks that the SAMRO project has been 'put off till kingdom come'.

90. Assemblée Nationale, No. 1440, esp. pp.13-14 and pp.97-107.

91. In this scenario France, subjected to a successful 'surgical strike', would be unable to retaliate, as use of its anti-city second-strike capability would only bring total destruction upon the hitherto 'relatively spared' population.

92. Of the two satellites successfully put into orbit by Ariane in the first half of 1983, one is to be the first operational satellite of EUTELSAT, retransmitting radio, television and telephone communications in Europe. The other is an AMSAT amateur radio enthusiasts' satellite.

93. The ISMA proposal was made by France at the first UN Special Session on Disarmament in 1978.

94. Jozef Goldblat, *Agreements for Arms Control* (London, Taylor & Francis, 1982), p.105.

95. This is done in a curious way by the French themselves, as their sources consistently and cumulatively *over*-estimate the kilotonnage of the Hiroshima bomb (e.g. 'the Hiroshima bomb equals 15-20 kilotons', therefore 'a French 70 kiloton bomb equals 3 Hiroshimas' and 'the 25 kiloton bombs are the equivalent of one Hiroshima'). As the Hiroshima bomb is normally rated at 12-13 kilotons, this can lead to a significant *under*-estimating of the explosive power of French nuclear weapons. Conversely, *over*-estimating of accuracy is equally common (see Note 38).

96. For a detailed analysis of this, see F. Roy Willis, *The French Paradox* (Stanford, Hoover Press, 1982).

97. Didier Motchane, of the CERES group of the PS, in *Le Monde*, 21 July 1983, points out the absurdity of the French position of distancing their nuclear weapons from strategic arms reduction talks between the blocs, while at the same time formulating a defence plan in which, 'for the first time in the history of the Republic, *one specified state* is designated as the enemy'. Thomas L. Saaty, *Mathematical Models of Arms Control and Disarmament* (New York, John Wiley & Sons, 1968), p.34, makes a similar point and concludes: 'Such bias may be damaging to France and to the rest of the world.'

PART TWO

VOICES OF DISSENT

6 FRENCH DEFENCE: A MILITARY CRITIQUE
Admiral Antoine Sanguinetti

Basic Definitions and Distinctions

Before we can begin to discuss the concepts of *force de frappe* and *force de dissuasion*, we have first and foremost to make a distinction between them in both political and military terms. The distinction is very simple. A *force de dissuasion* or deterrent is a political weapon, the only possible aim of which is to prevent war by the knowledge of the horror which it could unleash, and here we must insist on the conditional *could*, not can, or will unleash. A *force de dissuasion* is a peacetime weapon designed to put the potential adversary on his guard because he can never be sure that it will not be used, thereby making less likely the continuation of politics by those other means that we call war. On the other hand, a *force de frappe* or strike weapon is a military weapon designed for making war, a war-*fighting* weapon, and that makes all the difference.

As for the vocabulary invented to distinguish between these two types of weapon, it is worth pausing to consider its implications. At the specialist level, weapons of deterrence have become known as strategic weapons, and the new war-fighting weapons have been christened tactical weapons. All that one can say is that this expert classification has nothing to do with either strategy or tactics. In order to deter effectively, and in order to deter those who count in that they are powerful enough in the world today to start a world war by their actions, it is obviously necessary to deter them by threatening them directly, by threatening their own people, on their own soil. After all, what American or Russian is ever going to be effectively deterred from conflict by the prospect of wiping out the Europeans? And since these are the only powers capable of plunging humanity into the apocalypse, the only effective deterrent is to ensure that the apocalypse would take place on their own territories, thereby threatening to wipe out the protagonists themselves.

This has led to a second definition of the terms strategic and tactical. When a weapon has characteristics pertaining either to its range, or

173

simply to its deployment potential, such that it can fall on and destroy the territory of the Soviet Union or the United States of America, that weapon is strategic. When it can only fall on those unfortunate enough to be in between the two, the weapon is tactical. The latter is clearly more acceptable than the former to the superpower protagonists. If I wished to push this second definition further I might conclude that anything which is likely to fall on *my* head is strategic.

The point is that the distinction between these weapons is neither a question of size nor a question of range. It is rather a question of range in relation to deployment, and of where a warhead may fall by virtue of its deployment. Up until now, or at least until very recently, most strategic weapons, for example the American Minuteman missiles and indeed most of the French nuclear weapons, have carried nuclear warheads of up to one megaton, that is to say roughly fifty times the size of the Hiroshima bomb. Today a certain number of strategic weapons, thanks to progress made in multiple warheads, in precision, and in other technical aspects, have had the size of their individual warheads considerably reduced. For example the American Poseidon, whose submarine weapons account for the majority of American strategic weapons at the present time, is a system in which each Poseidon missile is armed with between ten and fourteen warheads of only fifty kilotons, that is to say barely two Hiroshimas. On the other hand, among those tactical weapons designed to confront each other on the European battlefield, there are a great many one-megaton weapons, and this has been the case for many years. These are fifty-times-Hiroshima weapons. Indeed the majority of our tactical weapons are in this category. And when we are told of small-scale nuclear weapons, of the type being developed for French land-based missiles, then we should note that even these are three-times-Hiroshima weapons, which is hardly a definition of a harmless little bomb. Take the Soviet SS20 warheads. The SS20 is always presented as such a monstrous weapon on account of its three warheads, whereas in the NATO armoury fourteen warheads is quite a common number. We are told that the Soviets have considerably reduced the size of these warheads, which is intended to show that they are conceived as counterforce weapons. The fact remains that one single SS20 warhead is nevertheless 140 kilotons or seven Hiroshimas. It would therefore be a mistake to set too much store on the distinction between the terms tactical and strategic to separate those weapons which are powerful from those which are not.

The truth is that, without exception, we are dealing with weapons whose very nature, regardless of their particular size, implies a total break with everything that humanity has known in the past, in the most bloody wars that have ever been waged. There is simply no comparison. And it is this fundamental change which concerns us as military men. We may have relished urging civilians to war in the past, but we can have no stomach for a war in which we shall be wiped out along with the rest of the population. This, broadly speaking, is what *armes de dissuasion* and *armes de frappe* are all about. The former are intended to avoid the holocaust, the latter to participate in it.

Now a second distinction must be made, and in making it we shall come back to the military and technical details of French nuclear weapon systems. The second distinction is that between first-strike weapons and second-strike weapons. And here the distinction is basically between land-based weapons, these being in general first-strike weapons, and sea-based weapons located on submarines, which in general are second-strike weapons. Why? Because in the case of land-based weapons, for example the USA's 1,000 Minuteman or 54 Titan missiles, or the great majority of Soviet inter-continental missiles, the exact position of every single one is known. There is no military secret in the world. Observation satellites scan the globe every day, and we all know exactly where everyone else has hidden their missiles. Which means that these land-based weapons can naturally only be used *before* they are destroyed, and that they can therefore only be of use if they are launched first. Before the attack. This is the sense of 'first-strike'. Today, the very possession of these weapons signifies an aggressive intent. On the other hand, second-strike weapons, otherwise known as the response to initial aggression, have been based on submarines, because no-one can at present detect for certain the position of nuclear submarines in the sea. For this reason, the western world in particular has based the vast majority of its deterrent weapons on submarines, which remain immune from destruction in any first strike by the Soviets. Strangely enough, for the Soviet Union, it is the other way round. The majority of their weapons are based on land, with submarines, perhaps because they require greater technical skill, accounting for only a small proportion, roughly twenty-five per cent, of their strategic nuclear weapons.

French Nuclear Strategy

Having made these basic definitions and distinctions, we can now look more closely at the evolution of French nuclear strategy. Let me begin at the moment when Charles de Gaulle, returning to power in France, inherited what had been prepared by his predecessors, and in particular by Pierre Mendès-France: the atomic bomb, which was nearing the end of its experimental stage in France, and which was to be tested at Reganne in the Sahara desert in 1960. A nuclear explosion on its own is one thing. It commands a certain amount of respect in the world. But it remains imperative, if it is to have any military significance, to mount it on a delivery-system, in order that it may be transported to the enemy. This was brought home to the French at the time of Suez when, together with the British, we were forced to bow to an undisguised threat from Soviet President Bulganin who warned us that if we did not leave Egypt immediately, he would destroy London and Paris on the same day. We got the point. And when Bulganin added words to the effect that the British and the French should understand, in this day and age, that the only nations which can afford to take political initiatives are those which possess nuclear weapons, we got that point too. And both the British and the French accelerated their own nuclear weapons programmes.

So it should be stressed that, from the outset, what France wanted to avoid with the deterrent was a repeat of any such threat. Whether it came from the Soviets, or, since, at the time of Suez, they had aligned themselves with the Soviets on that particular issue, from the Americans. We had wanted to create a pure *arme de dissuasion*. As for the delivery of that little bomb we started out with, we had to make use of the systems we were capable of producing ourselves at the time. And that in itself largely explains the genesis of the French deterrent. At the outset, what were we capable of producing? Aeroplanes. Marcel Dassault set to work and produced a reasonably good plane called the Mirage IV. Of course a plane is still a plane, whatever its specifications, and as such it is not the ideal vehicle for transporting a nuclear bomb into heavily defended enemy territory. But we made do with what we had, and that became our first generation of nuclear weapons.

After that, we set our engineers to work, much to their delight, and they prepared a second generation of nuclear weapons which was referred to as an 'interim generation'. This was a system of land-based missiles, and I have already explained how limited their use is. They can now only be used as first-strike weapons and one can hardly imagine the French making a first strike against either the Russians or the Americans, and bringing down retribution on their own heads afterwards. The second version of the interim generation consisted of ground-to-ground ballistic missiles sited on the Plateau d'Albion. But, from the outset, the guiding principle was to create the only valid kind of nuclear deterrent, the second-strike capability, one which would respond if necessary, or which would be capable of responding to aggression, and this principle gave us the submarine-based systems. Using this technically much more difficult method, we simultaneously prepared missiles and submarines, which became operational by degrees during the late 1960s.

Since, in the beginning, we only made weapons with relatively limited ranges, it was obvious that our deterrent theory could only be applied in the direction of the Soviet Union. As far as the other side was concerned, there was nothing to prevent us firing the missiles westwards from the Plateau d'Albion. At best, they would have come down in the Atlantic just west of Biarritz. No-one could claim that these missiles could intimidate the United States of America. With the submarines, however, size is a relative matter. For submarines, which throughout the world carry only intermediate-range weapons, have the unique advantage of being able to move in order to get close to their target, and that is what makes them strategic. One SS20 has a range roughly equivalent to that of any submarine weapon system, but as it is land-based, it can only fall on Europe and is therefore classed as tactical. Whereas in the case of an American weapon of the same range based on an American submarine of the Sixth Fleet in the Mediterranean, it can fall on the Soviet Union and is therefore strategic. We shall come back to this later.

Under de Gaulle, the French began with planes, moved on to land-based missiles, and finally submarine-based missiles. There was never any mention, throughout the de Gaulle era, of a tactical nuclear weapon. France was to have strategic weapons which achieve their object of making the enemy stop and think by their very existence. And that was that. The uncertainty of the enemy as to whether we would use them or not would lead inevitably to his choosing other methods of argument. Towards the end of de Gaulle's presidency, from about the time when France withdrew, not from the Atlantic Alliance, but from its integrated military structure — that is to say when de Gaulle removed the French military from its subordination to American command and put it under his own control — there began to be discussion in France of the strategy of omnidirectional defence or *tous azimuts*. This meant that, in addition to the Soviets whom we could already hit, the necessary arrangements were to be made to render us capable of striking American territory, should the case arise, in order to make them stop and think as well. It meant having the capacity, even with regard to the Americans, of dissuading other people from exercising too much political pressure on us. The result was almost immediate. General de Gaulle's Chief of Staff at the time was General

Ailleret, and he was soon to die in a mysterious airplane accident in the Indian Ocean. And Charles de Gaulle himself, within two years, had disappeared from the French political scene in a conjunction of circumstances made up of left-wing opposition, which was perfectly normal, but also of opposition from a large section of the right which had been supporting him up until that point, which was much less explicable. But disappear he did, and he was replaced by Georges Pompidou.

Georges Pompidou, despite his many political talents, was by no means an expert on military matters, at least not at this point in time. Under Pompidou we were to see the beginnings of a significant change in French strategic planning. Pompidou came up against pressure from the French army. It should be explained that the French army is a total enigma, even to the navy. It has two main mottoes, whose virtues are inculcated in its Military Academies. The first is *s'instruire pour vaincre* ('educated to conquer'). But to conquer you have to have a war, so they seem not very well disposed towards the theory of deterrence from the start. Effective deterrence means no medals and no promotion. The second motto is *mourir pour la patrie* ('to die for one's country'). Now speaking as a military man, and I have seen my share of campaigns in my time, I had always thought the idea was that the *other* man should die for *his* country! But the French army seems unable to get beyond the idea of having a war, and there is obviously no surer way of dying for one's country than by having a nuclear war. They were clearly so committed to this idea, that they beseiged Georges Pompidou to produce a tactical nuclear weapon. Something which would enable them to fight with nuclear weapons in Germany or even on French territory, because they did not have a very clear idea of what nuclear weapons were all about.

This led to the invention of a very curious doctrine, one which does not exist outside France, and which is called the 'test theory'. It was devised in order to avoid the situation in which we might be faced with a choice between 'all or nothing', between unleashing the holocaust or immediate surrender. According to this theory, it is simply not credible to threaten the Soviets by saying that, if they start a war against you, you will destroy them, because then they will destroy you too and you would have generalised suicide. The idea of the nuclear deterrent as a peace-keeping weapon which may be effective *before* war breaks out, but is worse than useless *after* it has broken out, seems to have gone by the board. So, the argument continues, the best thing to do after the Soviets have started to attack would be to give them a number of warnings. If they start a war, we shall use all the methods at our disposal, tanks, men, our world-famous intelligence, but if all these are to no avail we shall proceed to a so-called 'test of their intentions', as they approach the French frontier. The argument is very subtle. The Soviets launch an attack with millions of men and tens of thousands of tanks, they vanquish the two million NATO soldiers based in central Europe, and at that point the French Army decides it would like to know what the Soviets' intentions are. Now in order to discover what their intentions are, France is going to use tactical nuclear weapons — on German territory. And this is where the argument becomes anything but amusing. Because what it means is that France is afraid of threatening the Soviet aggressors directly on their own territory, so instead we are prepared coldly and deliberately to slaughter the population of some other country to show how resolute we are. We will opt for killing Germans, or Poles, in order to frighten the Russians. No matter what the Allies, or the Poles and East Germans themselves, may think about it. Such is the basis of the French theory, the so-called 'test theory'.

Not surprisingly, this theory, which was inaugurated under Pompidou, was substantially strengthened under Valéry Giscard d'Estaing. And this was precisely the area where we clashed, Giscard and I, with unfortunate results for myself. Now when Valéry Giscard d'Estaing came to power, supported simultaneously by his own personal following and by the Gaullists, the first thing he did was to affirm that he would not depart from Gaullist theory in any way. Defence doctrine was still going to be based on the theory of deterrence. In reality, from the moment of taking office, he set about scrapping the sixth nuclear strategic deterrent submarine, which Pompidou had started to build, and which had already cost something like 20 billion old francs. This was deliberately scrapped with the clear indication that there would be no new nuclear submarine for France under the Giscard presidency. But work began in earnest, on the other hand, on the manufacture of tactical nuclear weapons. Originally, under Pompidou, we had begun with aircraft-based missiles. The deployment of Pluton missiles had been planned, but it was Giscard who set to work in earnest on the manufacture of Plutons and he had succeeded by the end of his seven-year term of office. For there are now forty-two Pluton missile-launchers in service in the French army.

Acceleration of tactical weaponry was therefore a keynote of Giscard's policy. At the same time, he made a number of speeches which spelled out total rejection of the deterrence theory, as he informed us that he was preparing French troops for *la bataille de l'avant* or the forward defence of Europe. He even added, for good measure, that if there were a battle in Europe, there would only be one possible 'theatre' of war, and France would be included in that 'theatre'. He could not have indicated more clearly that he was abandoning the theory of deterrence. But even in saying that he was only telling half the truth. Because the French army was in fact already well ensconced inside German territory and prepared for forward defence fighting. This had been envisaged by de Gaulle, using conventional means. Giscard, however, all the time he was talking of forward defence, was planning to bring back a substantial part of the French army onto French territory. Why? It is extremely interesting to examine side by side both what Giscard was doing in France, and at the same time the doctrine being developed by James Schlesinger, Nixon's Defence Secretary, before the United States Congress in early 1975. It is interesting to study the Schlesinger theory for two reasons. First of all, for what it tells us about what Valéry Giscard d'Estaing was doing at the time with the French army. And secondly, for the light it sheds on what Nixon's successors, Carter and then Reagan, were to do in due course in terms of the euromissiles.

In 1975, James Schlesinger reported to the United States Congress[1] that the Soviet arms build-up was beginning to represent a serious threat. Soviet weapons were now easily capable of destroying United States territory several times over (just as the United States was capable of destroying the Soviet Union several times over). Consequently, argued Schlesinger, since it seemed always possible for a war to break out somewhere, and since it might be a war which would develop according to the 'flexible response' theory of his predecessor, Robert McNamara, the USA now needed to see to it that a war waged according to the flexible response theory in Europe would have no chance of escalating into a strategic exchange between the two superpowers. He urged that it was imperative for the US to disengage themselves from this possibility, and to take such measures as might be necessary to enable them to wage such a war honourably enough, giving commitments which would be sufficiently reassuring to the European allies, but which would certainly not permit the war to escalate to the point at which it might involve US territory or the American people. But Schlesinger added another element to his doctrine, concerning the armies of the NATO countries. He argued that at the time (the mid-seventies) the conditions for the outbreak of a war in Europe did not obtain — the Soviets did not want one and neither did the USA. So the major new function of the NATO armies for the time being was to ensure the internal 'political integrity or stability' of those nations belonging to the Alliance.

This is the Schlesinger theory. It is one which was to be borne out by events in many different places. For example, it is indisputable that, having gone through a certain amount of political reshaping, the Turkish army is now ensuring the internal political integrity of the Turkish nation. Just as the Spanish army is frequently tempted to ensure the internal political stability of the Spanish nation. What is more worrying is that, within days of the Schlesinger report, as from 20 February 1975, a process of reorganisation of the French army was begun in France, which gives food for thought. When Valéry Giscard d'Estaing took over the French army there were six major divisions on the frontiers. The most isolated one, a parachute division, was based on the Spanish frontier, and the other five in Alsace or in Germany. Valéry Giscard d'Estaing took these six divisions, and announced that in view of his 'forward defence' policy he was going to transform the French army, and increase it from six divisions to fourteen or fifteen. The French were quick to applaud their defence-minded President. He omitted to mention that he was going to take divisions of 18,000 men and transform them into divisions of 6,000 to 8,000 men, rather like over-sized brigades of riot police. He duly brought them back onto French territory in accordance with a plan expounded in the Chamber of Deputies on 19 June 1975 by General Bigeard.

Marcel Bigeard was Under Secretary for Defence at that time, and Yvon Bourges the Defence Minister. As the team responsible for reconstructing the armed services during the Giscard presidency, it is perhaps surprising that the one was renowned for his lack of political *finesse*, and the other for his complete lack of military experience, either in the French Army or in the Resistance. Yet reconstruct the armed services they did.

Bigeard explained to the Chamber of Deputies that while we did have divisions close to the forward defence positions, there was one thing that we had not thought of, which was that the Russians might get in by the back door. This thought had so impressed him that the whole of the French army was to be reorganised so as to place soldiers in positions where there was the greatest risk of infiltration by Soviet soldiers. The divisions of French soldiers were duly stationed in Saint-Brieuc, Limoges, Bordeaux, Toulouse, Marseille, Grenoble, Lyon, Rouen, Saint-Germain, Amiens and Lille. So any Russian peasant who succeeds in infiltrating French territory has had it! In fact, there are now fewer forces than previously left to provide a forward defence, since substantial parts of the army have been brought back home, in accordance with a policy that has become known as *quadrillage du territoire*. And the way it has been done leads one to conclude that, in reality, for several years now, the French army has been specifically prepared, from the point of view of armaments and organisation, to be able to act if necessary *within* the country, if there were to be, for example, a change in the internal political stability of the nation.

Socialist Defence Policy

This was not so well organised, however, that it could prevent the events of May 1981 from occurring. Perhaps it was partly the sense of invulnerability on the part of the incumbents that provoked the French electorate into voting in the left-wing opposition. Whatever the case, we find ourselves now with François Mitterrand at the head of a government composed of socialist and even communist ministers. The French socialists have spent many years working out their defence policy, in particular through the *Commission de défense*, made up of about 150 or 160 members, of whom many are from the military. This body has been trying to work out what a socialist policy for France might look like in the military sphere. It has produced a number of documents, the most important from the point of view of defence being the motion carried by the National Convention on defence held by the Socialist Party in January 1978. At this Convention, the Socialist Party, which was preparing to assume power, was clearly feeling the burden of its heritage. For no government which comes to power can live in a dream-world; it has a heritage in the existing armed forces, which it will have to accommodate to for a certain time. Changing the structure of the armed forces is extremely expensive, and, given the nature of the French state, it is highly unlikely that military spending will be viewed as a priority area. So the socialists had to face up to the fact that they would inherit this army in its current state: a strategic nuclear deterrent force; an army equipped with tactical nuclear weapons; and a military network liable to intervene internally at any point in France. And all of this could only be changed progressively.

With regard to strategic nuclear weapons, it must be said that some of us in the French military are far from displeased with the present situation, as long as two great nations of the world possess strategic nuclear weapons capable of destroying France. For when we talk about creating nuclear-free zones in Europe, we are talking about two kinds of nuclear weapons, those based in Europe which can be launched from Europe, but also those weapons based elsewhere which could be targeted on Europe. And ridding Europe of the first kind without affecting the other kind is tantamount to putting oneself at the mercy of the superpowers. So we accept that as long as the Soviet Union and the United States of America continue to make such fruitless efforts at disarmament, we shall maintain our strategic nuclear arsenal in its present state (*en état*). *En état* means that it will be scrupulously maintained, and subjected to such technical improvements as are necessary for it to remain credible. And that is what the Socialist Party texts prescribe. *En état* does not mean anything over and above that.

But there are many at the same time who maintain that the theory of the 'test', that is to say the destruction of innocent people, whether German or Polish, on the pretext of frightening off the aggressor, is intolerable, and that the use of tactical nuclear weapons in battle is intolerable, because tactical nuclear weapons used in battle leave no chance of survival for the people in whose territory they are used. This feeling was so orthodox within the PS that, in January 1980, immediately after the NATO decision to modernise its nuclear weapons in Europe as a so-called response to the Soviets' SS20s, François Mitterrand made an outstanding speech in the National Assembly, as spokesman of the Socialist Party. The theme of this speech was: 'Neither Pershings nor SS20s but Disarmament'. And that was how it was when he came to power.

From that moment on, however, the game was to produce subtle interpretations of what had been said before the PS found itself in office. Partly because, as I have mentioned, changing anything to do with the army takes many years because the costs are so enormous, and partly because basically, beyond all the fine speeches, most socialists really have very little idea what they are working towards. Every French government has been obsessed with saying that in matters of defence it is continuing the policies of the previous government. Valéry Giscard d'Estaing said it, and it was not true. Pompidou said it, and it was not true. I only hope, now François Mitterrand and Charles Hernu are also saying it, that it is still not true. I should like to think that our ministers are lying, but I am not yet sure of it. What is certain is that they have taken a number of decisions, some of which might be interpreted as going in the right direction, while others may require us to remain vigilant.

First of all, they announced that they were going to build a seventh nuclear missile-launching submarine (SNLE). The original deterrence theory was that France needed six SNLEs, of which four would be technically operational at any one time. For these six submarines there are just four nuclear weapon systems. There are always two submarines temporarily out of action, one being in the process of refitting (every four years a submarine has to spend one year in dry-dock being refitted), and the other undergoing a process of transformation (technically *en refonte*), that is being made ready to receive new equipment, new weapons systems, as the case may be, but still within the framework of being maintained *en état*. So when the socialists announced a seventh submarine, this seemed at first to be no longer a case of maintaining *en état* our strategic nuclear weapons, but of increasing them. Or it might be argued that when the Prime Minister announced the news, he was not being completely frank about its implications, because he said that this seventh submarine was for the middle of the next decade, and that it would come into service around 1995, with new weapons systems and a wholly new technology. Now by that time, there will no longer be six French nuclear submarines, because at least the *Redoutable*, which was launched in the 1960s, will have come to the end of its useful life, and been scrapped. Moreover, the decision has already been taken not to convert this vessel to take the new M4 missiles which will come into operation in 1985. As a result, there will still be, even with the new vessel, only six nuclear submarines. The announcement is therefore ambiguous. Did Mauroy speak of a seventh submarine in order to win the damp gratitude of the French Navy? Or did he simply make a mistake? I do not know. In any case there is no danger involved at the moment. This first decision *can* be interpreted as moving in the right direction, so long as there is no truth in the suggestion of *increasing* France's nuclear capacity.

It would be more worrying if there were no truth in the second decision, which on the face of it seems good. This is the move which is just beginning to make itself felt, a move towards what the socialists call a 'popular deterrent force', to replace the imposition of a military grid on France by the French army. The legacy of Giscard is that France is policed by a network of military divisions (the *quadrillage du territoire* model), which, through the use of information technology, can be marshalled in accordance with political criteria — divisions moreover which are backed up by reserve units subject to even stricter political control, since present provisions for these reserve units allow for the mobilisation of 60,000 chosen men out of a total of more than 4 million reservists, which shows the degree of selection possible. The PS, on the other hand, envisages a short period of military service. This would be reduced to the minimum required for training, and coupled with a programme for a potential rapid mass mobilisation based on *local* organisation. Being local, it would no longer allow for selection based on computerised files, of the sort which enables those whose profiles fail to fit to be sent away to Germany, while members of right-wing or extreme right-wing political parties are guaranteed a posting in France. Perhaps this reform then is also indicative of a move in the right direction. We shall have to see how it works out in practice.[2]

What I find totally unacceptable, however, is the fact that, even in the most recent speeches, the PS is clinging to the 'test' doctrine. That is to say, we are preparing to add to the destruction of Germany or Poland with our own weapons in order to show our determination. In a speech made by Pierre Mauroy before the National Defence Institute in the autumn of 1982, the Prime Minister reiterates in its entirety the 'test' doctrine which I have just described, insisting that it is absolutely necessary:

> Our country must therefore dispose of a tactical nuclear force, in order to be able to *test* the true intentions of an adversary possessed not only of such weapons, but also of superior numerical strength in the conventional sphere. In the absence of such a force on our side, the adversary would, in effect, be able to control the level of violence of the conflict, reducing our potential in conventional strength as it suited him, and forcing us into either an early use, or non-use, of our strategic arsenal.[3]

Maybe he is trying in this way to boost the morale of the French army, by reviving hope in its motto of *mourir pour la patrie*. But the problem is that at the same time Mauroy and Hernu are speaking in quite different terms, authorising not the scrapping of the Pluton missiles, but the replacement of Pluton by another system, the Hades. Subject to discussions with the German government, the Hades missiles will be installed by the early 1990s. They enjoy the distinct advantage of no longer being limited in range to West German territory. They will be able to reach East Germany or Poland, thus failing to resolve in any way what I choose to call the problem of the morality of these weapons.

There is also the fact that we have not yet made up our minds on the vexed question of the neutron bomb. As we know, Valéry Giscard d'Estaing, a year before he was ousted from the presidency, had announced that, in spite of the misleading speeches of Yvon Bourges, they had already decided several years previously to authorise research and development of a neutron bomb in France, and that this had been successfully carried out. Militants within the Socialist Party had counted on the cancellation of this programme with the change of government. And yet everything that François Mitterrand and his Prime Minister have said indicates that, on the contrary, the neutron bomb is still a feature of French research and development.[4] Now if this were simply a question of academic research there would be no problem. I agree that we have to keep up with advanced technology developments and innovation. But if at some point in the future the decision (which has not yet been taken) were to be taken in favour of the production of the neutron bomb, this would be certain to provoke the most serious crisis within the French left.

On the other hand, there are some very positive signs. Firstly, whatever else may be happening, in all the speeches of the socialist members of the French government, they are nevertheless still talking in terms of disarmament. They are still talking about the necessity of negotiations between the two superpowers. I should prefer them to talk about the necessity of negotiations, not just between the two superpowers, a fruitless exchange so far, but in the presence of those European nations doomed to destruction if ever nuclear war breaks out, that is to say within the framework of the Conference on European Security and Cooperation presently being held in Madrid, and previously in Belgrade and Helsinki.[5] For me this represents the only genuine example of disarmament discussion, bringing together as it does not only the two nations capable of destroying the world, but also the first nations which would be destroyed if war broke out and whose interests are therefore very much concerned in ensuring that we never get to that extremity.

The second positive sign concerns the dismantling of the two blocs. The dismantling of the two military blocs *is* part of the socialist programme, and it has not yet been abandoned in their political discourse. The proviso is always made that the dismantling of the two blocs should only take place after their replacement by another system of collective security. In fact, and this is a third positive sign, Pierre Mauroy does himself appear to be looking at the possibility of a form of collective security provided by an autonomous European defence. This is something which countless Europeans, emasculated by years of Atlanticist propaganda, have ceased to believe in, forgetting that as Europeans they far outnumber the Soviets and the Americans taken together, that they have the highest gross national product in the world, that they are well established as the foremost commercial power in the world, that they invented everything including civilisation, and that they can take care of themselves. To quote from Mauroy's recent speech again:

> We want to promote the construction of Europe, for
> Europe will never be truly protected, until the Europeans
> undertake to protect it themselves. The voice of Europe, so
> often silent in the international forum, will not shape the
> course of events until it becomes the expression of a
> common will, beginning with the will of the Europeans to
> ensure their own defence.[6]

That I take to be a positive sign, and perhaps it is this interpretation
that one should put on the comments about a possible attempt being
made by the French socialists at this moment to win over the West
Germans to their point of view, and to begin to build up a doctrine
which, in its first phase, would be based on the French nuclear
deterrent and the German conventional armed forces backed up by
French conventional forces.

   However that may be, I am going to resist the temptation to pass
judgement on what the French socialist government is doing right
now, especially in the present international situation. Let us consider
precisely what that situation is. I recollect an occasion not many years
ago, when another ally of the United States, Italy, was contemplating
what was called the 'historic compromise'. This may have involved
bringing a number of communist ministers into the Italian government. Not a majority by any means, but such as might safely be
swallowed up by their great Christian democracy. This was in July
1975, and there were unequivocal reactions in the United States,
numerous speeches by Kissinger and Ford around that time, saying
that they could never accept the Italians bringing communist ministers into their government. And Italian politics lurched from crisis to
crisis: from the fall of the lira on the European market to the
unmasking of the Lockheed affair in the United States Congress; from
scandals involving Italian ministers or generals, to scandals involving
the President of the Italian Republic himself. Finally it became
inevitable that Aldo Moro himself had to be removed from the political
scene, because he was refusing to play the game. Of course it was the
Red Brigade which kidnapped him. And of course the KGB had
something to do with it, at least according to popular wisdom. But, by a
curious coincidence, on the very day that the Italian Communist Party
joined the majority in government in Italy by voting for Andreotti as
Prime Minister, on that very day Aldo Moro was kidnapped, to be
found dead fifty-four days later. His successor announced immediately that the historic compromise was over.

Now France has gone a step further. Without committing themselves to any compromises beforehand, the socialists have taken four communists into the government. And there they are, in posts which are anything but token posts. We can safely assume that anything that was said at the time with regard to Italy applies equally to France — including the declarations of Helmut Schmidt after the summit meeting in Puerto Rico, indicating that a NATO intervention in Italy had been mooted at Puerto Rico if Italy appointed any communist ministers. In France the historic compromise is a *fait accompli*. So we may well imagine that all the strength of the Western Alliance, its real strength, measured in terms of capital and international finance, supplemented by the activities of the CIA, is directed towards the disappearance of the French socialist government from the present-day political scene, and towards a reversal of current French policy. And this could go a long way towards explaining why the present government may not be able to pursue all of its socialist programme at a stroke, and may be obliged to take things one at a time. Let us not forget that the French have leapt into the North-South fray with their Mexico and Cancun speeches, openly taking a stand for a new international economic order which is undoubtedly not in the interests of the United States at this moment. Is France really in a position, given this situation, to challenge the East-West balance as well? I doubt it. And I think this is one of the reasons why the French government must proceed slowly, and with great caution, if it is to achieve the slightest degree of military or strategic change in France at the present time.

Notes

1. *Annual Report, Fiscal Year 1976*: Report to the Congress, 5 February 1975; *The Theatre Nuclear Force Posture in Europe*, Report to the Congress, April 1975.

2. Although the 'popular mobilisation' measures referred to by Admiral Sanguinetti remain part of the PS platform, the military service bill which passed through Parliament in May 1983 did not see the long-awaited reduction of military service to six months for all. Instead, France now has military service of variable duration, depending on geography of posting and content of training. Some volunteer conscripts can actually *extend* their period of service by up to a further twelve months beyond the normal one year period.

3. Pierre Mauroy, address to the opening meeting of the 35th session of the *Institut des Hautes Etudes de Défense Nationale* (IHEDN), 20 September 1982.

4. Pierre Mauroy, ibid., refers to the neutron bomb as 'the nuclear weapon *par excellence*, [which] would enable us to reduce the scale of destruction necessary for the carrying out of military operations, [and which] will therefore conceivably find a place in our deterrent force'. And in June 1983, Charles Hernu confirmed that France has successfully tested neutron devices on Mururoa atoll in the South Pacific.

5. Although the Madrid conference has now agreed to convene a European Disarmament Conference, the French government has insisted that conventional weapons only be discussed.

6. Pierre Mauroy, IHEDN, 20 September 1982.

7 THE REBIRTH OF A PEACE MOVEMENT
Claude Bourdet

Militarism, Independence and the *Force de frappe*

When considering the role of militarism in post-war France, one must always remember that France has a long military tradition, much longer than that of the United States, and at least as long as that of Britain, Prussia and the other European countries. The army and its exploits are the objects of much reverence in French political culture. This is often forgotten when thinking of France as the 'defender of liberty' in the world. There was a time, in the period after 1940, when there was widespread disgust with the French army, because this military force, at the time one of the most powerful in the world, had proved utterly useless when it actually came to the crunch.

Fortunately for France, we rebuilt an excellent army,[1] which was based of course, like most good armies, not on military 'specialists' but on the people. That was the army of the Resistance, of the underground and of the Free French, which developed from 1940 onwards and showed its effectiveness in the battles of the British 8th Army and in the struggle of 1944-45. But then, this army of the Resistance rapidly acquired the characteristics of the old army. Most of the officers who had been active in the underground were soon ousted, and the same often happened to those coming from the Free French. The spirit of critical initiative, which had been the hallmark of the Resistance army, was snuffed out. Colonial wars, from 1946 onwards, enhanced brutality, racism and cruelty, just as if Hitler had left us his worst legacy. All this was barely perceived by the majority of French people, and although a new antimilitarism began to flourish, it remained a minority phenomenon. On an entirely different note, and a more spectacular scale, sections of the army revolted in 1961-62 against de Gaulle's peace policy in Algeria. But even these events were short-lived: many officers were ousted, some were pensioned off, some were jailed. That was the last act of insubordination from inside the ranks of the military, and its total failure explains, to some extent, why there are so few high-ranking officers today who question official military policy as many do in the US, in the Federal Republic, in the Netherlands and elsewhere.

Nuclear weapons, however, were bestowed on the army by the politicians. After the fiasco of Suez in 1956 and the Russian nuclear threat, the French and the British decided to go nuclear. When de Gaulle took over in 1958, the substratum of French nuclear policy was already there, although the General was to give it a much stronger impetus, for reasons which are easy to grasp. De Gaulle was above all a military statesman and saw power and 'grandeur' as the consequences of military might. At the same time, he was genuinely in favour of an alternative, independent policy. He abhorred the word 'neutralism', but his policy had a definite flavour of non-alignment. He followed this line with his usual pragmatism, in many different ways. During the war, he resisted the British and the Americans. After he took over in 1958, he tried to build a Franco-German military alliance which he thought might free the continent from the dominance of the United States. This failed because Adenauer was pulled back into line by Kennedy. Then the General turned to a more autonomous line for France, and this led him to patch up a number of differences with the Soviet Union. But all the time, he relied on military force as the basis of this independence. I suspect he failed to realise, or if he did realise, he did not care, that his greatest successes in non-alignment, his greatest influence in the world, came at a time when the French so-called *force de frappe* was practically non-existent, a distant project to be realised later, more a dream than anything else.

It was certainly not France's nuclear capability which enabled de Gaulle to follow a more independent policy. Had he looked at smaller countries like Yugoslavia, or at large but weak countries like India, he would have seen successful non-alignment initiatives in a world where, supposedly, only the two blocs counted.

De Gaulle's independent policy did, however, fulfil one very important function. It proved that the calamities forecast by 'Atlanticists', who had been warning for years of what would happen if France shifted even slightly out of the American sphere of influence, were utterly unreal. Nothing happened. Things went on as usual, except that there was perhaps a little more respect for France in many parts of the world.

To a certain extent, de Gaulle's nuclear arms policy was conducted at the expense of conventional defence, though not to the extent that it is today. Moreover, at least in the first period, the policy was one of 'pure deterrence', based on an anti-city strategy, the only one conceivable with the somewhat crude nuclear weapons of the period.

That policy can, of course, be criticised on several counts but, in any case, in France, as elsewhere, it has been superseded. As years went by, new developments took place. First of all, atom bombs became smaller, which makes them more dangerous since an artillery shell only one tenth the size of the Hiroshima bomb is soon perceived by the 'experts' as usable in actual war. And now, there is the development of the so-called neutron bomb, which certain 'experts' are praising as a war-fighting weapon because of its allegedly 'clean' properties (claims which anybody who has studied this weapon knows to be totally false). But this is the most recent development. Even while de Gaulle was still in charge, the French short-range missiles appropriately called Pluton (after the God of the Inferno) were being developed. They will be superseded under Mitterrand by another infernal object called Hades, with a slightly longer range. Plutons are stationed in the area of Belfort, in Alsace, and they have a range of about 100 miles, therefore landing right in the middle of West Germany. Hades can probably reach the German Democratic Republic. But the main point is that Pluton and Hades, and of course the future neutron bomb or neutron helicopter-launched missiles have completely altered the old Gaullist precepts of deterrence.

Strangely enough, as these developments were taking place, some Gaullist experts like General Poirier were criticising the shifts in American nuclear policy from 'mutual assured destruction' to 'flexible response'. And yet it was Poirier himself who envisaged using the Plutons as a first threat and even as a first salvo against a Russian conventional attack, followed eventually, if that 'warning' were not enough, by a French strategic nuclear strike. All this was supposed to happen at a time when the enemy had theoretically still not fired a single nuclear shell or missile. Which goes pretty well towards proving that there is a logic which takes the military mind 'naturally' from the 'pure deterrent' which is not usable, to the battlefield weapon, which could be used, but which would bring about, inevitably, escalation and, almost certainly, general suicide.

As years went by, French policy developed very rapidly from deterrence to nuclear war-fighting in the spirit of the Schlesinger doctrine. When Giscard and his Chief of Staff General Méry took over, the French bomb was no longer intended solely as a deterrent. It had become a battlefield weapon just like the American weapons. In 1981, Mitterrand and his Defence Minister Hernu continued the same developments, increasing both the nuclear strategic forces and the tactical ones (Hades and plans for the neutron bomb). But there had, meanwhile, been huge changes inside the French Left.

The Birth of the Peace Movements

The entire Gaullist nuclear policy had been powerfully resisted by the Left, ever since 1960. This struggle was quasi-general, although there was no definite policy at the time inside the French Socialist Party (PS). The more leftist federations of that party cooperated with the communists and the new left, progressive Christians, pacifists and even some unions of the CFDT (the former Catholic trade union). The major organising force was, of course, the Communist Party (PCF) and its fellow-travelling mass organisation, the *Mouvement de la Paix* (MDP). The MDP was started immediately after the war by Charles Tillon, who had been Minister of Armaments in one of the first de Gaulle cabinets after having led the partisans during the war. Tillon, who was a very original communist, very broad-minded and democratic, wanted the MDP to be completely independent. That, of course, was one of the reasons why he was expelled from the party and the MDP taken over. But ever since, there have been people inside the MDP, Catholic priests, military officers, journalists and professors, who have struggled for a peace movement independent of the political parties. They remain within the MDP because they see that it is the only mass peace movement in France, and they believe they can not only get across to the masses, but also influence the PCF itself, especially at a time like the present when the party has actually given up its opposition to French nuclear weapons. Despite their efforts, however, the PCF has more or less succeeded in making the movement toe the party line.

But the MDP did not totally monopolise the peace movement. In part because of an urgently-felt need in France, and in part at the call of the British CND and of the newly-formed International Confederation for Disarmament and Peace, led at the time by Canon Collins and the late Peggy Duff, a new independent peace movement, based on the principles of non-alignment, was created in 1962, the *Mouvement contre l'Armement atomique* (MCAA). In 1968, with the help of the new-left socialist party, the *Parti Socialiste Unifié* (PSU), this became the *Mouvement pour le Désarmement, la Paix et la Liberté* (MDPL).

Another independent movement was created, also in 1962, the *Ligue contre la Force de Frappe* (LCFF), led by former socialist minister Jules Moch, and a former communist MP, Maurice Kriegel-Valrimont. The *Ligue* and the MDPL cooperated closely, but owing to lack of organisation and to political difficulties encountered by both Kriegel and Moch, the *Ligue* dwindled away after a few years. Both the *Ligue* and the MDPL cooperated with the Communist Party itself, with the communist-led trade union, the CGT, and the communist-led MDP, with some left-wing federations of the Socialist Party, with some unions from the CFDT and with many smaller organisations. An umbrella organisation, the *Comité contre la Force de Frappe* (CCFF) was founded in 1962 and there were some large demonstrations, based on a quite acceptable political line. It was probably the first time that the Communist Party and its associated groups took up a position against all nuclear weapons, including the French, but also the Russian ones. The prospects at the time seemed excellent for a development along the lines of CND or other European movements. The MDPL, for instance, rapidly acquired 10,000 members, and groups sprang up all over France. However, things started to change rapidly, and not for the better.

Decline of Peace Activism

First, the '1968 revolution' made most young and militant members of the peace movement simply forget foreign and military problems and devote themselves to bringing about the great changes they believed to be close at hand. When the 'revolution' simply petered out, these young men and women were left out on a limb — and seldom became active again. Second, the only foreign policy issue which seemed at the time to be 'in the picture' was the struggle against the American war in Vietnam. This took up much of the remaining energy. Thirdly, a new development was taking place behind the scenes: Mitterrand's efforts to reconcile the Socialist and Communist Parties and to prepare the 'common programme of government' of 1972. Now, thanks to our efforts in the MDPL and to the Jules Moch *Ligue*, anti-nuclear-weapons ideas had begun to make headway inside the Socialist Party. I recall meetings against French nuclear armaments, where Mitterrand was in the audience and came to offer us congratulations after the meeting. There is therefore nothing astonishing about the fact that the CPG in 1972 declared its hostility towards nuclear weapons and called for the abolition of the French nuclear arsenal.

This had on the peace movements as such a double effect. It was encouraging, but it also acted like an anaesthetic. It meant we did not have to fight any more. We had won the battle. All we had to do was wait for the electoral victory of the left. As a result, the efforts of our members and sympathisers and certainly also those of the communists and their friends became much weaker. But at least there was a clear policy we could rely on. However, after a few years, something utterly unexpected happened. All of a sudden (at least as seen from the outside) the PS and the PCF made a complete volte-face in 1977, and decided to support French nuclear weapons. Within my organisation, we had noticed that something curious was taking place months before it happened. The MDPL held the secretariat of a committee which had been founded to protest against French nuclear tests in Polynesia. One day the socialists on that committee simply did not turn up. That was towards the end of 1976 or the beginning of 1977. When they failed to show up to meetings, the communists said: 'Well, if the socialists don't come, there's little use holding the meeting. Let's cancel this session and wait for the next one.' Next time the socialists were absent yet again, and the communists, who must have known what was going on, said: 'Perhaps we'd better just scrap the whole thing. If the socialists don't come, there's no use going on with it.' And that was (more or less) that.

Taken at face value, the reasons for this curious change could be easily brushed aside. The 'nuclear left' of the Socialist Party, around Jean-Pierre Chevènement and the CERES (*Centre d'Etudes, de Recherches, et d'Education Socialiste*), has always been in favour of the *force de frappe*, for the quite weird reason that French nuclear weapons could act as a deterrent not only against the Soviet Union, but also against American or West German attempts to topple a socialist regime in France. Such attempts, they believe, could be of an economic nature, or else take the form of American support for French rightist civilian or military elements. CERES ideas of a nuclear deterrent against such pressures seem even more ludicrous, if possible, than the idea of using French nuclear weapons against the Soviet Union. But this example typifies the lack of political and strategic thinking on this issue in France, even at the highest levels.

Moreover, I know from friends in the Socialist Party that there was practically no discussion of strategic issues in the gatherings where the decision to retain the nuclear weapons was taken. Party members who tried to raise objections were simply laughed out of court. The real reasons had nothing to do with strategy. They were inner political or had to do with non-military foreign relations. One main reason was the feeling that when the socialists came to power, they would have to make friends with the army, an army which had become increasingly attached to its nuclear toys, the more so since de Gaulle had taken away its colonial ones. The 'nuclear but democratic-minded officer' was a much-pampered specimen in those times. Another reason was the desire not to antagonise the Americans by a stand against nuclear arms. Mitterrand's pro-American policy was already in the making, and the idea that by supporting American foreign and military policy one could appease American hostility towards a French socialist regime with communist participation was natural for 'politicians' who believe that 'policies' are the result of sympathy, hostility or even whims rather than of more permanent or structural factors. Poor old Marx and Engels, and traditional political thinkers like Clausewitz, Riche-lieu, Machiavelli and others! They have clearly been dead for a long time.

As for the change within the PCF, some of the same factors came into play, especially the idea of fostering good will among the nuclear officers and NCOs, but also the idea that the PCF, by supporting the *force de frappe*, would enhance its patriotic credentials. But it had also been evident for some years that PCF hostility towards French nuclear weapons had been on the wane. This development paralleled changes in the Soviet Union, where de Gaulle's more or less non-aligned foreign policy after 1962 had led the Russians to consider the French bomb with a completely fresh mind. And since Pompidou and, to a lesser extent, Giscard had maintained the same broad policy options, the Russians continued for many years (until 1982) to adopt a more or less benevolent approach to the *force de frappe*. This certainly contributed to the evolution of the PCF.

Ironically, this quasi-simultaneous volte-face of the French Socia-list and Communist Parties took place at a time when their relations with each other were at their lowest ebb. By the same token, this double denial of their 1972 position facilitated governmental co-operation when the splits and chasms were patched up in the spring of 1981.

Starting All Over Again

For the peace movement — whether it was the communist-led MDP or our independent movements — the volte-face was tragic. It left us with one small political party, the PSU, supporting our anti-nuclear aims, against the totality of the right and centre parties and the major left parties. The MDP nearly disappeared. Instead it became even more what it had always tended to become (save for a few fellow-travellers): an empty framework which could be filled in at times and used by party members and communist union members for large demonstrations. Many of those who had persisted in trying to work with the communists left the movement, utterly disillusioned. For how could one reasonably attack the American missiles, including Pershing and Cruise, and even Soviet missiles, including the SS20, but support the French strategic weapons and the Pluton?

For the independent movements, it was the beginning of a long, long march. At first we were only intent on surviving. Then in 1980 came the END Appeal,[2] and with it new hope. Many prominent Frenchmen signed the appeal, but only two MPs, neither of whom was a socialist or a communist. Three prominent socialists, who were not MPs, did originally sign, but two took back their signatures after May 1981. They found it too problematic to antagonise Mitterrand and his Defence Minister, Charles Hernu.

Then, at the end of 1981, the MDPL and a number of other organisations, women's movements, ecologists, the PSU (some twenty or thirty groups in all),[3] created an umbrella organisation, the *Comité pour le Désarmement nucléaire en Europe* (CODENE), on the same political lines as END in Britain. Things have started to move, but many years have been lost. CODENE organised a large demonstration on 5 June 1982, which brought some 30,000 people onto the streets of Paris against the visit of Reagan to Versailles. A so-called 'leftist' anarchist group, to a large extent infiltrated by the police, exploded several bombs the night before the demonstration and shattered, among other things, all the windows in the World Bank. The aim was to frighten people off from participating in the demonstration. Some of the young thugs in this anarchist group tried to infiltrate the demonstration and generate violence. They were easily controlled by the marshals, but this was all that was required to trigger Mitterrand's police into attacking the demonstrators with tear gas in the Place de la Bastille, driving away a part of the crowd.

By comparison, the far larger demonstration organised by the Communist Party and its affiliates on 20 June 1982 (an estimated 160,000 people) was perfectly quiet with no police intervention. But politically, it was rather lame if not pointless, all for 'mothers, children, peace on earth'. There was practically no mention of Pershings or SS20s, and nothing at all about French nuclear weapons. Moreover the press (including the so-called left-wing press) played down the CODENE demonstration and gave full coverage to the PCF one. As long as 'peace' is 'communist', it is mentionable in the media, but not if it is independent or non-aligned.

What is strange is that with so much opposition and sabotage from above, French public opinion is far less pro-nuclear than the media would have us believe. In June 1977, an opinion poll by the polling institute SOFRES, published in the large circulation family Catholic weekly, *Le Pélerin*, showed that more than 50 per cent of French people were against French atomic weapons, and only 38 per cent in favour. The percentage against reached 60 per cent among the left-wing electorate. In November 1982 a second poll, conducted by another respected polling institute, Louis Harris, and published by another large circulation Catholic weekly, *La Vie*, showed a decrease in antagonism towards the *force de frappe*: 40 per cent of respondents being against the bomb and 52 per cent in favour of developing it. But those answers concerned peace-time conditions.

In the event of a war, the same poll shows that 65 per cent are in favour of alternative means of defence (including 17 per cent for non-violent resistance) and only 18 per cent in favour of the *force de frappe*. So it appears that, even among the ranks of the 'pro-nuclear', there is a clear majority in favour of the bomb as 'pure deterrent' (never to be used). Of course, the difference between the high degree of opposition to nuclear weapons and the difficulty of getting a movement on its feet reflects the feeling of disillusionment and despair of a large part of the population: 'What can we possibly do against the entire right-wing and the socialist and communist leaderships combined?'

Now an explanation for the attitude of that left-wing leadership is of course necessary. Certain factors have already been mentioned. But one of them should not be underestimated: the lack of up-to-date knowledge and facts in government and official circles. There are in France no institutes comparable in size and activities to the Bradford University School of Peace Studies, the numerous Peace and Conflict Research Foundations in the Federal Republic, the Groningen Institute in the Netherlands, the Institute of Policy Studies and the Centre for Defence Information in Washington or SIPRI in Sweden (to mention only the better known). Consequently, on matters like the balance of forces, nuclear and conventional, the possibility of non-nuclear defence against conventional attack, or the neutron bomb, the French government and the press rely on NATO or American official sources or on Pentagon-inspired documents like the West German white book.

Furthermore, the French military use, as elsewhere, American figures and calculations in order to press for more money and more arms. All this may sound strange, but it is only one more example of the amateurishness of the 'left-wing' government and of the press. Taken together with Mitterrand's desire to support American strategy in order to have Washington tolerate a French socialist government with four communist ministers, it goes a long way towards explaining one of the weirdest foreign and military policies of any socialist government on the face of the earth.

But I should like to conclude by arguing that none of this is immutable. The situation in France is the result of a combination of structures and accidents. The structures derive from history and from deep-rooted features of the French character, including nationalism and chauvinism. But other aspects of the current situation derive more from what I would call historical accidents. Let me review those which are most important.

First, there is the hold of the Communist Party on the old peace movement, which has prevented so many non-communists from seeing peace activism as an acceptable cause. The domination of the PCF was to some extent a freak consequence of the Cold War and has nothing to do with the potential for peace politics in France. With time, this stranglehold can be broken. By the same token, the complete lack of interest in peace activism on the part of the old SFIO (*Section Française de l'Internationale Ouvrière*) derives from two separate historical accidents. First, the fact that the peace movement within the SFIO during the inter-war period was dominated by pacifists. They were opposed to armed resistance and militarism and advocated reconciliation with Germany. This was fine during Weimar, but after the seizure of power by Hitler, these people allowed themselves to be manipulated, first by the Nazis and then by Vichy. As a result 'pacifism' became, and to some extent still is, a dirty word within the socialist movement in France. Secondly, there was the fact that, after 1948, 'peace' was what the communists did. As such, in the context of the Cold War, it could only be bad.

Another major historical accident was the fate of 'non-alignment' in post-war France. When a small number of us began to advocate the cause of non-alignment in 1947-48 and to demand support for countries like Yugoslavia, there was very little popular support for this position because it was not based on a major great-power role for France. When de Gaulle returned to power in 1958, he gradually 'took over' some of the principles which we had been advocating ten years previously. He rejected the word 'non-alignment' or 'neutralist', but he accepted the idea and eventually showed that it was not only feasible but also respectable. However, he did this by combining it with militarism and right-wing politics, and in so doing completely changed the whole nature of the notion of non-alignment.

Then, of course, there is the Gaullian structure imposed on France by the Fifth Republic: the 'Daddy will do it for you' syndrome, which the French first became familiar with under Pétain. De Gaulle was very successful in persuading large numbers of French people that 'it's better if Daddy does it for us', and this presidential ethos has permeated many aspects of the political life of contemporary France. In this sense, Mitterrand has stepped directly into de Gaulle's shoes, making it as difficult for a socialist MP or even a party member to oppose the President as it formerly was for a Gaullist to contradict the General. Visiting delegations of British and German socialists have expressed their amazement at the fact that there is now as little internal opposition in the PS as there is in the PCF.

Finally, there is the failure of my own party, the PSU, which has often been characterised as a laboratory of ideas. This is quite true. Many of the 'progressive' ideas which are current in the French left today were more or less invented in the PSU: ideas about regionalism, ecology, decentralisation and especially *autogestion* (self-management). The party's impact on ideology has been enormous. But its capacity for actually implementing changes in French political life has been destroyed by an extreme-leftist image imposed by its Trotskyite elements and others of the same ilk, originally under the leadership of Michel Rocard. After Rocard left the PSU and joined the PS, he quickly became one of its right-wing leaders. But when he was with us, he was instrumental in killing the PSU's chances of influencing events. For instance, the PSU could have joined the Union of the Left in 1972 and signed the Common Programme of Government with the socialists and communists. But under the influence of Rocard and others, it refused. As a result, the tiny fraction of left-wing radicals which did sign has probably had more influence on French politics than the PSU. That too is a historical accident.

There are many such examples of fortuitous circumstances, and it is for this reason that I think it is dangerous to reduce the situation to some definitive characteristics of the French spirit. For then you tend to solidify them and believe that things will not change. The Marxist view that Gaullism is the necessary result of advanced capitalism is regrettable for, if it were true, we should probably be in for Gaullism for another century! Gaullism also was, to some extent, a historical accident.

All this is not to say that these historical accidents, added together, do not constitute a formidable set of obstacles to a non-aligned peace movement. But because they are accidents, no matter how serious and long-term their consequences have been, it is possible that things will

change. They will not change overnight, but change they will
—eventually.

Notes

1. Claude Bourdet is speaking here as a leading member of the French Resistance during the Second World War. He served on the national council of the Resistance, edited the underground journal, *Combat*, and was arrested and deported by the Gestapo in 1944.

2. The European Nuclear Disarmament (END) Appeal, calling for a nuclear-free zone in all Europe, was launched by the Bertrand Russell Peace Foundation in 1980, and attracted signatures from all European countries and worldwide.

3. For a detailed account of the creation and composition of CODENE, see Chapter Eight.

8 PEACE ORGANISATIONS IN FRANCE TODAY
Christian Mellon

Weaknesses of the French Peace Movement

It is well known that organisations working for peace and disarmament are weaker in France than anywhere else in western Europe. The reasons for this relative weakness are many and varied. Some of them relate to particular circumstances and conditions which are liable to change; others are a more permanent feature of French political life.

The first reason why the peace movement has specific problems in France is the fact that France was not directly involved in the December 1979 NATO decision to site new land-based missiles on European soil. Her apparent aloofness from the NATO modernisation decision has led to a total absence of debate on the Cruise and Pershing issue inside France, leaving French public opinion relatively un-touched by the present wave of protest against the so-called euro-missiles. All peace movements, if they are to become popular, broad-based movements, need a specific topic or event to focus on, where the issues are both concrete and comparatively urgent. Neither ideology nor ethical principles alone will suffice to mobilise mass support. The remarkable growth of recent European peace movements is very largely due to the NATO decision on Cruise and Pershing. Having withdrawn from the NATO military command structure in 1966, France was not a party to that decision, and none of these missiles is to be deployed on French territory. French people therefore find it very hard to grasp what is at stake, their overwhelming impression being that they are only indirectly concerned, if at all, and that they have no means of affecting the decision-makers in this matter anyway. Of course, better-informed people are well aware that the euromissiles issue is one that concerns France very directly. The way President Mitterrand and the socialist government have officially endorsed the decision to deploy Cruise and Pershing, from the moment Mitterrand publicly approved Chancellor Schmidt's position on the euromissiles issue within a few days of taking office in May 1981 (the German press, in honour of the occasion, even coined that eloquent neologism:

Schmitterrand), shows only too clearly that France cannot remain in isolation from anything that pertains to the defence of Europe. Furthermore, it is perfectly apparent that, whatever her claims to an 'independent' defence policy, France would not be spared in a 'limited nuclear war' in Europe, whether or not her own nuclear weapons constituted priority targets for the Soviets.

But a mass peace movement cannot be generated by vague feelings of anxiety, however well founded: it has to have comparatively short-term objectives. The deployment of the new NATO missiles does not constitute, for the French, a specific issue on which they feel there is some chance of their being able to exert pressure in order to get things changed. They know that the relevant decisions are not taken in Paris. And whether people feel directly or only indirectly involved does make a difference to the way public opinion reacts. French people cannot be expected to take to the streets *en masse* against a decision in which they believe the French government has had no formal say, and against weapons which are not going to be sited on French territory in any case. Cruise missiles are simply none of their business.

The famous French *force de frappe* is of course very much their business, and the second question we should consider is why there has been so little opposition to French nuclear weapons themselves. This question involves an assessment not only of the existence of the 'independent' French nuclear deterrent, but also of the uniqueness of its political nature. Whatever opposition there may have been to the building up of the French nuclear arsenal in the early days (we had our Easter marches in the nineteen-sixties, and there were a number of scientists and philosophers, and even at one point a few bishops, in our ranks), and however regularly the protests against nuclear testing in the Pacific made themselves heard up until the decision to switch to underground testing in 1974 (there was the case of the former General de Bollardière, who sailed into the Mururoa testing zone in 1973 with four other French anti-nuclear protesters in order to prevent a scheduled test explosion), successive governments have been skilful enough to carry out nuclear defence programmes without opening the question to public, or even parliamentary, debate. The French have therefore gradually become accustomed to a *fait accompli*, and there have been no spectacular decisions which might have served to crystallise latent opposition. Moreover, the official jargon of 'deterrence', with its stress on 'non-war', and its reluctance to contemplate war-fighting as such, has helped to allay many people's fears.

But the most important single factor resides in that nationalistic ideology which subtends Gaullian political practice, and which de

Gaulle has bequeathed willy-nilly to all his successors, including the socialists. Deep down, the common acceptance of nuclear weapons by the French ('non-opposition' might, in many cases, be a more accurate term than 'acceptance') is in recognition of a political rather than a military fact: the French do not really believe in nuclear weapons as a means of defending their country; on the other hand, they do believe in them as a political symbol, as a means of guaranteeing their national stature and making them independent from both Moscow and Washington. This was quite clearly evidenced by the results of an opinion poll published in 1982 in the Catholic weekly *La Vie*.[1] 52% of French people declared themselves in favour of the modernisation of the nuclear arsenal (27% because it was 'inevitable', and 25% because it was 'indispensable for France's greatness and progress'); on the other hand, only 18% claimed that they would have any confidence in the nuclear strike-force 'if French territory were under direct threat of conflict'.

These factors make it very difficult to muster any serious opposition to defence policies in France, particularly at grass-roots level. The problem is made all the more acute by the lack of political space for the development of any such movement, since the creation of the four-party consensus on the nuclear deterrent. This is the third reason for the weakness of the peace movement, and one which goes even deeper into the political culture of the country than the other two. The difficulties of developing social struggles which are independent of the party-political debate in France are well known. If the four major political forces happen to agree on the suppression of an issue, then it is effectively marginalised by its absence from the mainstream political discourse. The very principle of the nuclear deterrent, accepted since 1977 by the Left just as much as by the Right, can only be challenged within an extremely narrow political space composed of the ecologists, the minority *Parti socialiste unifié*, and the traditional peace movements. So the political landscape of France is very different from that of most other European countries. Not only do all four of the parliamentary parties support in their different ways the maintenance of a French nuclear capability, but all four of them would also resist any idea of the anti-nuclear movement being given access to the media, or of giving support to its cause in any way.

However it is not just across the political spectrum that there is no support forthcoming. Neither the trade union movement, nor the new associative tendencies, nor the professional organisations, nor the religious and cultural bodies in France are capable of generating a mass movement (even supposing they wanted to) if the political parties are opposed to it. This is the crucial difference between France on the one hand, and Britain, Holland or West Germany on the other. The commitment of the Christian churches, for example, has been decisive in Holland and West Germany. In France, the Catholic church has taken a firm line in the past on the arms trade issue, strongly criticising the fact that by the 1970s France had become the third biggest supplier of conventional arms in the world, but on the nuclear weapons issue there have been only rare isolated protests by individual bishops. The French branch of the Pax Christi organisation has adopted a very cautious position, and most of its leaders in fact support nuclear weapons as a deterrent. The recent publication of the American bishops' Pastoral Letter has started a new process of reflection among French catholic bishops. At the same time the French branch of 'Justice et Paix' (an official commission of the Catholic Church) has issued a few pages on French nuclear deterrent policy which are unusually critical of the official views. The French Reformed Church has taken no official stand, although its members are generally more open to ideas on nuclear disarmament.

As for the trade union movement in France, there is again no comparison with the situation in Britain, for example. One problem is that, of the two main labour unions, the CGT and the CFDT, the CGT is close, to say the least, to the Communist Party. This meant that as long as the Communist Party was against nuclear weapons, they could go along with that; but since the Communist Party has started supporting nuclear weapons, the CGT has not done anything to contradict party policy. The CFDT position is somewhat more complicated. With its leanings towards the May 1968 ideas of workers' control, decentralisation, and democratic socialism, the CFDT certainly has something in common with the nuclear disarmers, and most of those people in the nuclear disarmament movement who belong to a union in fact belong to the CFDT. On the other hand, the CFDT in France has been deeply involved for the last two years in supporting the Polish Solidarnosc movement, and has in fact distinguished itself among west-European trade unions by the strength of its commitment to the struggle in Poland. So CFDT leaders have been very ambiguous about associating themselves with the peace movement in Europe, not least because of its frequent presentation in the French press as a bunch of 'pacifists' (always a pejorative term) who are letting themselves be 'manipulated by Moscow'. The impression that the European peace movement failed to give its full support to Solidarnosc when it was needed, for example, is very difficult to dispel among the left-wing intelligentsia in Paris. For the time being, therefore, we can expect potential sympathisers within the CFDT to be fairly reluctant to commit themselves too bluntly to the idea of nuclear disarmament for France. Nevertheless, since September 1983 the CFDT has entered into a kind of alliance with CODENE and has shown itself to be very keen on opening up a general political dialogue around the missiles issue.

So we have a country where neither the mainstream political focus nor the social, cultural and religious institutions offer any basis for the development of the nuclear disarmament movement, whereas in most European countries such movements enjoy the support of a significant group or party to the left of the political spectrum. In France, on the contrary, the socialist government prides itself on having ensured continuity in this sphere between its own policies and those of the previous government, and has shown its good faith by implementing one or two of the decisions which Giscard d'Estaing had not yet taken: going ahead with the seventh nuclear submarine; supporting the NATO decision on Cruise and Pershing. Even within the Socialist Party, it has often been the more left-wing elements, members of the CERES for instance like Jean-Pierre Chevènement, who have been most instrumental in bringing the party's policy round to one which favours nuclear weapons. As for the Communist Party, now also represented in the government, it too has continued to support nuclear deterrence policy since 1977.

The *Mouvement de la Paix* and CODENE

The position of the French Communist Party creates yet another layer of difficulty for the nuclear disarmament movements. On the one hand, as we have seen, the Communist Party effectively opposes those who seek to criticise the present government's defence policy; on the other hand, it controls the *Mouvement de la Paix* (the French section of the World Peace Council), which it supports through its press and organisational structure. The result is that journalists and ill-informed public opinion alike automatically assimilate any movement that mentions 'peace' to a pro-Communist position, even if it happens to be a movement that the Communist Party is in fact opposed to. Now this is not peculiar to France; it is a phenomenon which occurs in other European countries too. The difference is that the Communist Party in France still accounts for over 15% of the electorate, and it represents a genuine political force in French society. In addition, it keeps to a very pro-Moscow line. The accusation of fellow-travelling is therefore much harder to refute than in those countries of western Europe where the Communist Parties are either very weak, or have, as in Italy, distinctly eurocommunist tendencies. For many years, there have been a number of non-Communist activists trying to work within the *Mouvement de la Paix*. In 1977, when the Communist Party rallied in favour of the nuclear deterrent, the *Mouvement de la Paix* stopped criticising French nuclear weapons, and this provoked a certain amount of internal disagreement. In October 1981, the *Mouvement de la Paix* organised a peace demonstration at Pantin, making itself out to be the French equivalent of the European peace movement. In fact, their criticism was aimed almost exclusively at the NATO-controlled euromissiles, and the existence of French nuclear weapons was totally ignored. In December of the same year there was a fresh crisis when the *Mouvement de la Paix* refused to condemn the imposition of martial law in Poland under General Jaruselski.

This was the point at which it became imperative to create some kind of organisation which would be able to coordinate the many different groups working for peace and disarmament from a genuinely non-aligned point of view, which were interested in linking the issue of French nuclear weapons to the wider objective of a nuclear-free Europe. And so the *Comité pour le Désarmement Nucléaire en Europe* (CODENE)[2] was formed, not a movement exactly, but an umbrella organisation of some twenty-five mainly small and very varied movements which came to a common agreement on certain precise objectives, without in any way giving up their own identity and specific aims. The common objectives are as follows:

— to support the European nuclear disarmament movement in its campaign against the installation of the new NATO missiles, Cruise and Pershing.

— to insist on the dismantling of the SS20s on the part of the Soviet Union.

— to halt the modernisation of French nuclear weapons with a view to dismantling them within the framework of a denuclearised and non-aligned Europe.

Since its creation in February 1982, CODENE has maintained existing links and forged new ones with the rest of the non-aligned European peace movements. It has played an active part in the coordination of joint European activities, and in the European Nuclear

Disarmament Conferences in Brussels in July 1982 and in Berlin in May 1983. There is no getting away from the fact, even so, that as a movement, it is extremely small and weak, for the reasons outlined above.

There is also no denying that, in contrast, the Communist-led organisation is capable of mobilising very large numbers of people and staging spectacular demonstrations. Its tactics have been to take the theme of peace and disarmament as a means of widespread mass mobilisation. With this in mind, it organised a major peace demonstration in Paris on 20 June 1982 (approximately 160,000 people), on the basis of an appeal signed by a hundred 'big names', and published as the *Appel des Cent*. But the success of this demonstration should not be allowed to hide the fact that it refused to raise the issue of French nuclear weapons at all. The June 1982 demonstration was repeated on 19 June 1983 with a mass 'picnic for peace' — a festival of music and speech-making — in a Paris park. Again, it was sponsored by the *Appel des Cent* and attracted a crowd of some 300,000. Some people welcome their efforts, reasoning that even if they only make very vague statements about 'peace', and the disarmament sought after always seems to be somebody else's, it is better than nothing to see hundreds of thousands of demonstrators out on the streets in France on an issue of this kind. Others would argue to the contrary that such initiatives have a neutralising effect on large numbers of potential peace activists, diverting them from the non-aligned, unilateralist movements like CODENE in which they would be much more effective.

Composition of CODENE

CODENE is made up of some twenty-five different national organisations of varying degrees of importance and size.

First there is a medley of organisations which have their own justifications and spheres of influence outside the peace movement, and whose espousal of the cause of nuclear disarmament springs naturally from their own proper concerns. There is only one significant political organisation, the *Parti socialiste unifié* (PSU),[3] providing the inspiration and experience of a long-term non-parliamentary opposition group. Recently the general secretary of the PSU, Huguette Bouchardeau, has become a member of the government, in charge of environmental affairs. This does not seem to have influenced, up to now, the anti-nuclear stand of the party. Several ecology groups are affiliated, whose work in this area is often already well established, and which can sometimes offer both national and international networks: the *Réseau des Amis de la Terre* (RAT)[4] is one of these, as is the French branch of *Ecoropa*.[5] A number of ecology groups have recently created a party called *Verts – Parti Ecologiste*[6] which is a member of CODENE, as is another grouping simply called *Les Verts*. The *Service Civil International*,[7] an already well-established international body which organises voluntary service schemes for young people, deserves special mention as furnishing the headquarters of the umbrella organisation CODENE. There is only one important Christian group affiliated to date, and that is the *Mouvement Rural de la Jeunesse Chrétienne*. But there are several organisations whose main concern is the fight against militarism in general, such as the *Mouvement des Objecteurs de Conscience* (MOC),[8] and a support group for soldiers doing their military service, *Information pour les Droits du Soldat*, which provides conscripts with information on their legal rights, and campaigns for increased democracy in the military.

Then there are the peace movements themselves, which require some explanation. The *Mouvement pour le Désarmement, la Paix et la Liberté* (MDPL)[9] began life at the beginning of the 1960s under the name of *Mouvement contre l'Armement Atomique*. It successfully organised several 'Easter marches' around that time, but without ever achieving the scale of CND. It changed its name in 1968, widening its campaign to include the struggle against imperialism in general and against all forms of militarism. Claude Bourdet is the best known of its spokesmen, and his organisation has played a key role in the setting-up of CODENE. The MDPL also publishes its own journal, *Alerte*.

At the beginning of the 1970s there was a spate of small 'non-violent' organisations. Up until then, the 'non-violent' tendency had been represented by the *Mouvement International de la Réconciliation* (MIR)[10] and the *Communauté de l'Arche*, a Gandhian community founded in the late 1940s by Lanza del Vasto. In 1974, a number of the new 'non-violent' groups created a Federation, the *Mouvement pour une Alternative Non-Violente* (MAN),[11] with two essential aims: to link non-violence with a *political* project to transform society in the direction of a 'workers' control' type of socialism, *le socialisme autogestionnaire*; and to develop research on a non-violent popular defence strategy as an alternative to military defence. The *Mouvement pour une Alternative Non-violente* gives its support to a variety of social and political causes, developing its own brand of non-violent campaign tactics as it does so. It plays an important part in the movement against militarism, specifically in terms of conscientious objection and civil disobedience, and has also been active in the successful Larzac resistance campaign. It is currently campaigning for the creation of an Institute for research into the non-violent resolution of conflicts. One of its most famous figures is the former General de Bollardière, who left the army because of his objection to the use of torture in Algeria, and who has been committed to an ideal of total non-violence since 1970. MAN produces a monthly magazine called *Non-violence politique*, as well as numerous pamphlets on conscientious objection, civil disobedience, nuclear weapons, non-violent defence, and similar subjects.

In the last couple of years a number of new groups have sprung up around this theme of non-violence, for example the *Artisans de Paix*,[12] whose tactics are to make an impact on public opinion through the public fasts and vigils they organise. Some of these more recent groups are specifically women's organisations, like *Résistance Internationale des Femmes à la Guerre* (RIFG) and *Femmes pour la Paix*,[13] both of which belong to CODENE. A quarterly journal, *Alternatives non-violentes*, without being tied to any particular movement, provides useful material and outlets for the whole range of peace organisations.

Finally, in a category of its own, is the Larzac movement,[14] initiated by local farmers and peasants, and swelling to an enormous popular campaign of national dimensions over a ten-year period (1971-1981). This totally non-violent 'peasants' revolt', and the sustained campaign which grew out of it, have been exemplary in the history of protest in France; and they succeeded in putting a stop to plans for the extension of a military training-ground in the Massif Central in south-west France. A separate book would be needed to go into all the details of that campaign.[15] Suffice it to say that the measure of support given to the Larzac campaign by the population at large has demonstrated that a mass peace movement is not an impossibility in France, contrary to the expectations of the pessimists, provided that it has some definite and attainable goal. In the event, the Larzac protesters attracted the physical support of over 100,000 people in some of their popular demonstrations, and gained the sympathy of a much larger section of French public opinion. During the summer of 1981, after the decisive victory of their campaign following the election of Mitterrand (who cancelled the plans to extend the military training-ground), they held a major international event in celebration of their success: the *Rencontres internationales pour la Paix*. It was at that event that the Larzac Appeal (*Appel du Larzac*) was launched, calling for the formation of a broad-based federation of movements against nuclear weapons, and triggering off the process which led to the formation of CODENE. Even more importantly, the Larzac was chosen as the venue for the launching of a French 'nuclear freeze' campaign in August 1983.[16] The Larzac remains an area of immense symbolic value for the French peace movements. A Centre for Information and Education continues to operate there, run by a small group of about a dozen volunteers from among the 'non-violent' campaigners. The *paysans du Larzac* still bring out their monthly journal, *Gardarem Lo Larzac*. And the Larzac protest has found a place within the CODENE structure, without in any way surrendering its autonomy.

Possible Developments in the Future

Despite the variety and vitality of the different strands of the nuclear disarmament movement in France, it is easy to understand why such a movement should have difficulty in making its voice heard. We have seen how solidly the political culture, recent history, and present international position of the country combine to make the debate appear irrelevant to the average French person. But the fact that such formidable barriers exist for the time being to prevent the emergence of a mass peace movement in France should not lead to the assumption that the French are enthusiastic supporters of the nuclear deterrent. Far from it. We have seen that it is more a case of their being resigned to a *fait accompli*, and committed to the political value of the deterrent rather than to its effectiveness as a means of defence. This is why it is misleading to talk in terms of a 'general consensus' on defence policy in France. A consensus there certainly is among the political class, and this has remained unbroken since 1977. But there is no reason to assume that this consensus exists among the population at large.

On the contrary, recent polls have given clear indications that ordinary people are in fact more sceptical than their party leaders or members of parliament are about the official nuclear weapons posture. Back in 1977, for example, at the very moment of the famous U-turn by the Communist Party, when readers of *L'Humanité* learned overnight that they had to start saying exactly the opposite of what they had been saying the day before about the bomb, a poll[17] was published showing that 66% of communist voters were against nuclear weapons. And in 1980 the weekly magazine *Le Point* published a poll[18] showing that 72% of French people were opposed 'in principle' to any use of a nuclear weapon; 65% thought that 'if the President *threatened* to use nuclear weapons' his decision would be condemned by the country at large. This poses something of a problem, as the scenario considered — if French territory were directly threatened by an imminent invasion — is precisely the one in which, according to official nuclear deterrence doctrine, the President ought to threaten the use of strategic nuclear weapons. Another finding of the same poll seriously damages the very credibility of the French deterrence posture: 49% said they believed President Giscard would in no circumstances press the button, and only 24% believed that he would. The figure is unlikely to be higher today with President Mitterrand. Yet another, international poll,[19] conducted after the massive demonstrations of Autumn 1981, highlighted the fact that French public opinion is not really very different from that of most west-European countries: 50% pronounced themselves 'in sympathy' with the peace demonstrations, as compared with 52% in Great Britain and 59% in West Germany. The only significant difference was with the Dutch figure of 79%.

It is obvious that the real difference between French and other public opinion is not to be found in feelings about nuclear weapons in general. The main difference is one of information. French people simply never think about the problem; they feel less informed, less concerned. The most significant figure in all the polls that have been quoted is the frequency of the answer: 'Don't know'. In this respect the national samples are distinct: in other west-European countries the 'Don't knows' would be 4% or 5%, possibly 10%; in France they are very often 20%, 25% or 30%. These figures illustrate the fact that the French citizen is one of the least well-informed in western Europe on matters of defence. It is quite likely that most French people would not know the difference between a strategic and a tactical nuclear weapon, let alone between a massive retaliation and a flexible response doctrine. Only very small circles of specialists can even understand the terms of the defence debate.

The future of the peace movement in France depends very much therefore on the question of information.[20] The priority is not to get hundreds of thousands of people out onto the streets chanting about peace and disarmament, it is to *de*specialise defence issues, and to open up a widespread public debate on the problems of defence. France is a country where there has been no discussion involving the general public on defence matters since the Algerian War. People are out of touch and easily taken in by the media.

The deterrence doctrine has also been largely responsible for 'demobilising' the French population: it is after all a system which relies on the technical collaboration of some 20,000 engineers and military personnel and the political will of a single man, the President of the Republic. This explains the lack of 'defence-mindedness' deplored by many military and political figures. However, it is clear that this state of ignorance and indifference is beginning to worry those in the establishment who realise that, even from their own point of view, it is unwise to keep the general public out of the debates and away from the information about defence indefinitely. An agreement signed in September 1982 between the Minister of Education and the Minister of Defence aims to remedy this situation by improving the relations between the army and the schools. Paradoxically, this kind of initiative could have positive side-effects for the peace movement, by enlarging the circle of concerned communities, and by obliging professionals of all sorts of different categories to make up their minds which way they stand.

One thing is absolutely clear: that if the government tries to explain to the French people what the realities of nuclear warfare are, it will not be able to avoid a debate on civil defence, though this is a debate which has been scrupulously avoided so far. Not only has there been no programme to protect the population in the event of a nuclear attack, but the very possibility of such a programme has never been seriously and publicly discussed, giving no stimulus to public awareness. A French *Protect and Survive*[21] would doubtless have the same effect on public opinion as the British one did.

Politically, perhaps the most serious and specific threat to the development of a broad-based, non-aligned pressure group working effectively for nuclear disarmament in France comes, as we have already seen, from the existence of a French Communist Party intent on monopolising the words 'peace' and 'disarmament' at the same time as supporting the nuclear defence politics of the present government. In these circumstances, it is clear that a prior condition for the growth of the movement against French nuclear weapons is its capacity to convince the media and public opinion that it has nothing in common with the peace initiatives of the Communist Party, the *Mouvement de la Paix* and the *Appel des Cent*. If we cannot take the protest out of the hands of the Communist Party, we shall never be in the business of exerting real pressure on the government to change its defence policy.

Two clear lines to take which would highlight the autonomy of the non-aligned peace movement are as follows: firstly an unremitting critique of the government's present nuclear defence policies; and secondly, unambiguous support for those movements which have sprung up inside the Eastern bloc to protest against the militarism of their own governments. It is worth noting in this respect that one of the main reasons why many intellectuals in France are suspicious, and sometimes downright hostile on the disarmament question is precisely because their perception of the peace movements in Europe is that they are not taking seriously enough the problem of human rights in the Eastern bloc. What we have to do is to show that the reverse is also true: that the very fact that there are nuclear weapons in Europe makes it impossible for the peoples of the Eastern bloc to free themselves from their own masters; and that even if one makes human rights in eastern Europe a primary objective, our own struggle for a nuclear-free Europe fits in with that objective instead of contradicting it. This is why CODENE has developed regular links with Charter 77 in Czechoslovakia. On 20 June 1983, members of CODENE and of Charter 77 issued a common communiqué in Prague, which is probably the first text ever to be signed by both a Western peace movement and an Eastern human rights group.

Finally, we should not forget the importance, for the future of the peace movement in France, of developments taking place on the international scene. Anything which may occur to shatter the myth of 'independence' which is so dear to the French is bound to bring the defence debate to life again. Already, Mr Andropov's proposals on taking into account both British and French nuclear weapons in estimating the balance of nuclear capabilities in Europe have made it clear that France cannot continue to determine her policies in splendid Gaullian isolation, even if she would like to. The notion of a 'collective European security' arrangement, with France playing a vital role, is one which keeps coming to the fore with increasing regularity. None of these proposals can be identified with the aims of the peace movements, of course, but they do serve to stimulate thought and discussion on defence matters, which in itself is a golden opportunity to organisations seeking to express alternative views. When President Mitterrand approves the deployment of Pershing 2 missiles in West Germany in the name of balance, the French begin to wonder about the validity of their doctrine of *dissuasion du faible au fort*, according to which a lesser power can successfully deter a stronger adversary if it possesses a *sufficient* deterrent, and which they have always been told renders 'balance' unnecessary. When a socialist member of parliament like Yves Le Drian makes a statement before the National Assembly[22] to the effect that France ought to think about extending its nuclear protection as far as Hamburg, Rome, and Brussels to make up for any weak spots that might appear in the American umbrella, the Gaullist myth is well and truly exploded. When the French realise that their nuclear weapons constitute a major obstacle to Soviet-American agreements on arms control in Europe, they might just begin to reconsider their passive acceptance of these weapons. And is France, and a socialist France at that, really going to become the country responsible for the breakdown of possible negotiations on the denuclearisation of Europe?

Such questions are due to be aired in discussions of France's future defence policy. If the peace movement makes the most of the opportunity, it will get the chance to make its voice heard and enlarge its constituency. To achieve this, it will also have to get to grips with another question which has not yet been adequately tackled within its own ranks, and that is the question of alternative defence policies. How are we to defend ourselves without nuclear weapons if we are attacked? Some members of CODENE are in favour of a popular armed militia, some favour non-violent civil resistance, others have been unwilling to face the problem. And yet we know from experience that one of the biggest weaknesses of the nuclear disarmament movement is its failure to satisfy the man in the street when he asks the same question. This is one weakness that it lies within our power to remedy.

Notes

1. *La Vie*, 18-24 November 1982.

2. CODENE, 23 rue Notre Dame de Lorette, 75009 Paris.

3. PSU, 9 rue Borromée, 75015 Paris.

4. Réseau des Amis de la Terre, 72 rue du Château d'Eau, 75010 Paris.

5. ECOROPA (Ecologica Europa), 107 rue de la Course, 33000 Bordeaux.

6. Les Verts — Parti Ecologiste, Cité Fleurie, 65 Bd Arago, 75013 Paris.

7. Service Civil International, 129 rue du Fg Poissonière, 75009 Paris.

8. Mouvement des Objecteurs de Conscience, c/o CCSC, 8 Villa du Parc Montsouris, 75014 Paris.

9. Mouvement pour le Désarmement, la Paix et la Liberté, B.P. 2135, 34026 Montpellier.

10. Mouvement International de la Réconciliation, 99 Bd Beaumarchais, 75003, Paris. This is the French branch of the International Fellowship of Reconciliation (IFOR).

11. Mouvement pour une Alternative Non-Violente, 20 rue du Dévidet, 45200 Montargis.

12. Artisans de Paix, 15 quai des Pêcheurs, Strasbourg.

13. Résistance Internationale des Femmes à la Guerre, B.P. 52, 94210 La Varenne; Femmes pour la Paix, c/o Solange Fernex, 68480 Biederthal.

14. Le *Cun* du Larzac, St Martin, 12100 Millau.

15. A booklet in English has recently been published by R. Rawlinson, *Larzac – a victory for non-violence* (Quaker Peace and Service, Friends House, Euston Road, London NW1 2BJ).

16. See Vladimir Fišera's personal account of the August 1983 Larzac meeting in Chapter Ten.

17. SOFRES Poll in *Le Pélerin*, June 1977.

18. *Le Point*, 9 June 1980.

19. *Le Nouvel Observateur*, 20 November 1981.

20. The aim of public education and information has been taken up since the beginning of the 1980s by three groups which are now coordinating their efforts:

Défense et Paix, 23 rue Notre Dame de Lorette, 75009 Paris

La Forge, 10 rue de Paris, Longpont-sur-Orge, 91310 Montlhéry

Le *Cun* du Larzac, St Martin, 12100 Millau.

21. *Protect and Survive*, prepared for the Home Office by the Central Office of Information 1976, reprinted 1980.

22. *Journal Officiel*, Assemblée Nationale, 2nd Session of 12 November 1982, p.7085.

9 ECOLOGISTS AND THE BOMB
Tony Chafer[1]

The subject of this chapter is the attitude of the French antinuclear movement, and more generally of the ecology movement, to the issue of nuclear weapons. Unlike its British counterpart, the antinuclear movement in France has always been more predominantly concerned with the campaign against nuclear power and has given a far lower priority to the nuclear weapons issue. Indeed to the average French person *le nucléaire* implies the nuclear energy debate first and foremost, and is not immediately associated with the question of nuclear weapons. In this chapter I shall seek to examine the reasons for this difference in priorities and shall suggest that, with the decline of the movement against nuclear power in France and the election of a socialist government committed to an ambitious nuclear weapons programme, there are now grounds for thinking that French ecologists may, in future, attach greater importance to the nuclear weapons issue.

The National Context

As one would expect, ecology movements in different countries share the same basic ideology: opposition to economic growth and nuclear power, decentralisation of power away from technocratic and bureaucratic elites to the people, and the promotion of world solidarity through an end to exploitation of the Third World by the so-called developed countries. As one would expect, they are also opposed to nuclear weapons. However, the ways in which these themes are articulated and expressed in different countries depend on the national political context. Attitudes on specific issues, and the exact form that dissent from the established order takes, are determined inevitably by history and the national political context. It is no more possible to understand the French ecology movement and its stand on different issues than it is to understand any other political movement in isolation. In particular, an examination of the national political scene may help us to understand why the movement against nuclear power in France has traditionally been stronger than that against nuclear weapons.

At first sight, the ecologists' position regarding nuclear weapons appears straightforward. In Britain and Germany, the ecology movements express their opposition to nuclear weapons in the form of support for unilateral nuclear disarmament. According to the principal French reference book on political ecology, the position of the French ecologists is equally clear: 'We propose ... the unilateral nuclear disarmament of France.'[2] The reality however is more complex. Brice Lalonde, who was the French ecologists' presidential candidate in the 1981 elections and is the national leader of the French contingent of Friends of the Earth (*Amis de la Terre*), recently made it clear that his opposition to nuclear weapons is very different from what the British Campaign for Nuclear Disarmament (CND) calls 'unilateral disarmament':

> I think CND is right when it says that the best system of defence is not necessarily to imitate the enemy. But total unilateral nuclear disarmament is not credible in my opinion. It is a purely moral position, and like any moral position it is well-meaning but it forgets one thing: the appearance of weakness is a cause of war. Scientific ecology, as opposed to moral ecology, requires us to think in terms of systems, and recognises that, in order to change a system, it is better to do it by degrees rather than taking an axe to it. Because destabilising a fragile system is risky.[3]

For Lalonde, disarmament is clearly intended to be part of a phased, negotiated process and is to take place in return for real concessions from other nuclear powers. He specifically rejects unilateral nuclear disarmament as understood by CND as not being a credible political option. Indeed, his position is not dissimilar from the traditional 'multilateralist' argument, but his view of 'deterrence' differs in one fundamental respect:

> Like all ecologists, I am horrified by nuclear weapons. However, for an ecologist, there is no sure way of deciding whether or not nuclear deterrence works. All one can say is that, at the present time, there has been no nuclear war against France. But it is likely that deterrence has a limited lifespan and that it will even become counter-productive at a given moment in time. The result of deterrence may ultimately be to weaken the country rather than strengthen it. When everyone has the atom bomb (thanks to French

exports of nuclear technology, for example to Iraq and Pakistan), it will no longer serve any useful purpose. The worst thing is that deterrence tends to disarm civilians: nobody is bothered about defence in France because we possess nuclear weapons and the specialists take care of them. One has the impression that the population at large is totally unconcerned.

When asked whether he believed the French nuclear deterrent to be *necessary* in the present international situation, Lalonde replied that he did not, but that he could see 'no way of abolishing it overnight'.

Nor are such differences of opinion confined to leading figures in the French ecology movement. At a national Congress of the Greens (*les Verts*) in Besançon in May 1983, one of the items discussed was a proposed common platform for the European Greens for the 1984 European Elections.[4] This included a commitment to unilateral nuclear disarmament, which gave rise to a number of objections and proved to be the major obstacle to agreement to the text. The common platform was however eventually accepted by a majority of four to one of the delegates.

It probably seems surprising that some ecologists should have doubts about unilateral nuclear disarmament, particularly given the central role played by French ecologists in the campaign against civil nuclear power and the now well-established and widely accepted links between civil and military nuclear power. However, for French ecologists as for the French antinuclear movement, there has traditionally been a clear distinction between the two. The French sociologist Alain Touraine pointed this out in his 1980 study of the French antinuclear movement, *La Prophétie antinucléaire*. As one of the antinuclear activists he interviewed commented: 'against the threat of war we feel powerless, whereas with nuclear power we feel we have a role to play'.[5] The existence of this distinction was confirmed by Claude Bourdet in a 1981 interview, when he commented that 'many ecologists still do not believe that the nuclear bomb represents an immediate or urgent threat'.[6] A survey of members of the *Rennes-Verte* list, which contested the March 1983 municipal elections in Rennes, further confirmed the existence of this distinction for French ecologists.[7]

It is almost as if the bomb does not exist, or at least is too big to do anything about. Military nuclear power is the State in its most distant form, immune from opposition groups, while civil nuclear power is in the domain of everyday life: it directly affects people and is something on which people can have a direct influence. One of the *Rennes-Verte* activists made a comparison between the weekend demonstration against the proposed nuclear power station at Plogoff in May 1980, which drew 150,000 people, and what would happen if a demonstration were called at the Ile Longue, a military base on the Breton coast: 'Go and see how many tens of people would come to the Ile Longue.'[8] A factor in this feeling of powerlessness with regard to the bomb, and in the somewhat ambivalent position of the French ecologists with regard to unilateral nuclear disarmament, is undoubtedly the relative isolation of those campaigning against the bomb in France. In Britain and Germany, the antinuclear movement has not been alone in its opposition to the bomb. In both these countries it has drawn support from parts of the church and from significant parts of the established left: leading figures and activists in both the British and German trade union movement and in the British Labour Party and German Social Democratic Party have played a central role in the peace movements in these countries. This is not the case in France, where the Communist Party (PCF) is strongly in favour of both nuclear power and the French independent nuclear deterrent and the Socialist Party (PS), while adopting - at least in opposition - a more ambivalent stance on nuclear power, has been an even more enthusiastic supporter in government of the French nuclear deterrent and of the deployment of American Cruise and Pershing missiles in Europe than the previous right-wing administration of Giscard d'Estaing. The largest French trade union, the *Confédération Générale du Travail* (CGT), which is close to the PCF, echoes the communist position on both nuclear power and nuclear weapons, and the second-largest union, the *Confédération Française Démocratique du Travail* (CFDT), while playing a leading part in the campaign against civil nuclear power, has until recently had little to say on the nuclear weapons issue. This may now be changing however with the joint declaration by the CFDT and CODENE against nuclear weapons, issued on 27 September 1983.

However, a feeling of powerlessness with regard to the bomb is not sufficient to explain the apparent ambivalence of some members of the French ecology movement with regard to nuclear weapons and the relative insignificance of the nuclear weapons issue in its campaigning priorities. To understand this, there is a need, once again, to see the French ecologists within their national political context. In particular, it is necessary to examine the political agenda as defined by the existing political parties and the need for the ecologists to define their positions in the context of this agenda and to stake out a distinctive political position in opposition to the existing parties. A recent survey[9] of French ecology movement activists gave an interesting insight into their attitudes and political perspectives. In response to the question 'Which political party do you feel closest to?' — the *Rassemblement pour la République* (RPR - Gaullist); the *Union Démocratique Française* (UDF - Giscardian); the *Parti Socialiste* (PS); the *Parti Communiste Français* (PCF); or the *Parti Socialiste Unifié* (PSU - very small left-wing party, pro-Third World and against nuclear power) — many opted for the PSU but many chose not to answer. More interestingly, in response to the question 'Which party do you feel furthest from?' a high proportion of respondents replied: the PCF. Accordingly, one would expect the ecology movement frequently to define itself in opposition to the PCF and this is in fact the case. The PCF stands for economic growth at all costs, is in favour of nuclear power and has a centralised and hierarchical party structure. The ecologists stand for the opposite of each of these things, which helps to account for the often almost pathological dislike of the PCF among French ecologists. With regard to the majority French peace movement (*Mouvement de la Paix*), this was originally created by the PCF and has always been dominated by it (see Chapter Eight). It is perhaps not surprising, therefore, that the ecologists have adopted the attitude they have to the bomb. Furthermore, an interview with activists from the *Rennes-Verte* list showed that none of them was prepared to envisage a situation which would involve joint action with the PCF. The French ecologists, therefore, although opposed to nuclear weapons, are clearly not prepared to be publicly associated with the PCF on this issue.

The attitude of the ecologists to the PCF can be explained in large part historically. Many active members of the ecology movement served their political apprenticeship in the late sixties, and in particular in May 1968. They remember the attitude of the PCF to the May movement and its attacks on the students in particular. To many of them the PCF is as great an enemy, if not a greater one, than the right. It is an attitude which emerges frequently in interviews with French ecologists. The term 'stalinist' is used regularly by Brice Lalonde to describe everything to which he is most opposed. For example, in the May 1983 issue of the French Friends of the Earth members' newsletter *La Baleine* (*The Whale*), in which he explains why he will not attend the Greens' Congress at Besançon, he writes: 'I often feel closer to libertarian socialists (*autogestionnaires*) and to genuine, well-informed liberals, than I do to many so-called 'eco-logists', who are really pathetic totalitarians ... and I want nothing to do with any trouble-makers or stalinists.'[10] His anti-communism and anti-Sovietism are frequently in evidence in interviews he gives: 'Personally, you will never hear me shouting "Better red than dead". I prefer to remain green.'[11] Soviet ecological disasters, such as the pollution of Lake Baikal, are mentioned and it is clear that the Soviet system represents everything to which French ecologists feel most passionately opposed. In a recent series of interviews with French ecologists, several actually mentioned that peace movements only existed in the West and were not permitted in the East.[12] It is thus probably not too far-fetched to suggest that some French ecologists see the bomb as an ultimate defence against the Soviet threat, and therefore of their right to be 'green' rather than 'red'.

The ecology movements in France, Germany and Britain were generally created by a generation which is now in its thirties. As a movement in revolt against society and as a generation in revolt against their parents, they chose to express their dissent from the established order through their activity in the antinuclear and political ecology movements. These movements are frequently predominantly middle-class and have in common the rejection of a materialist, consumer society which their parents have helped create for them. However, the national political context against which their political views are formed has a significant influence on the form this dissent takes. We have already seen that many French ecologists are influenced in their political views by the existence of a strong Communist Party in France and by its behaviour particularly in 1968. Another important event in the recent French collective memory is that of Munich in 1938. For confirmation of this one has only to read editorials in some French 'New Left' reviews, which are otherwise generally sensitive to green politics, on the European peace movement.[13] It is clear that for this generation, which is also the generation of many ecology activists, the desire to avoid another Munich and to struggle against attitudes of appeasement is very strong. The contrast with the situation in Germany could not be greater. Here, war is almost a taboo subject. As Alfred Grosser put it: '1945 is the point of reference for the new generation of Germans, while for the French it is a question of avoiding 1938 and another Munich, of struggling against appeasement and humiliation.'[14] In this context, the possession of an independent French nuclear deterrent is, for present French generations, a kind of assertion of strength and national identity. Germany, on the other hand, could not assert its independence through possession of a nuclear deterrent, having been banned from manufacturing such weapons. Indeed German peace campaigners perceive the greatest threat to the nation as the danger that, in any new confrontation in

Europe, Germany will be at the centre of the battlefield. Many of the new generation of Germans therefore assert their national identity through the peace movement, which also has underlying it an anti-American element. A strong German national identity implies a reduction of American domination in Germany, and the rejection of American missiles. The final dream is of a reunified German nation, which is only possible in a Germany free of American missiles in the West and of Soviet missiles in the East. Therefore, while the French new generations' affirmation of their national identity may imply support for the French independent deterrent, for the German new generations 'the affirmation of a national identity can only take a pacifist form'.[15]

Other than what are often strategic as well as principled reasons for a lack of action on the issue of nuclear arms amongst ecologists, one also sometimes detects traces of a 'Gaullist hangover'. The French nuclear strike force is officially independent of NATO and therefore especially of America, which was of course de Gaulle's principal aim. This notion of independence from America, on every level, is to be seen right across the political spectrum and could be perceived in a reply to a question to *Rennes-Verte* activists concerning the installation of American missiles in Autumn 1983. More than one person replied that, among other reasons, they were against the installation as it would increase American influence in European affairs. Not a sufficient basis for generalisations perhaps, but an indication nevertheless of a still existent heritage. This rejection of American weapons would not necessarily extend to French weapons. However, as we shall see, the socialist government's support for the deployment of American missiles may help to arouse opposition that would have been less concerned had it been simply a question of modernising the French nuclear deterrent.

Mitterrand and the Ecologists

France under President Giscard d'Estaing had pursued the most ambitious civil nuclear programme in the world. Between 1974 and 1981, new nuclear power stations were ordered at the rate of five or six a year and the President identified himself closely with this programme. The period of his presidency was marked by frequent demonstrations on the sites of projected nuclear power stations, which reached their peak in 1977 with the demonstration on the site of France's first planned commercial fast-breeder reactor, *Superphénix*, at Creys-Malville.[16]

The coming to power of a socialist president, François Mitterrand, in 1981 gave rise to some hopes in the antinuclear movement for modifications in French nuclear policy. Between the presidential and parliamentary elections of 1981, the projects to build a new nuclear power station at Plogoff in Brittany and a military camp in the Larzac had been cancelled.[17] The PS in opposition had supported the 1979 petition against the government's nuclear power programme, organised mainly by the ecologists, and it had produced a comprehensive alternative energy plan[18] which was in many respects close to the ideas of the antinuclear movement. Furthermore, a number of other promises — the slowing down of the nuclear programme, the abandoning of the extension to the La Hague reprocessing plant and of the commercial fast-breeder reactor programme, and the terminating of reprocessing agreements with foreign governments — had been made during the election in response to pressure from the ecologists. It now seems that the cancellation of the Larzac military camp and of the Plogoff nuclear power station was largely symbolic as the other promises have since been broken. A slowing down of the nuclear programme has taken place, but this is largely due to economic pressures on the government and the slower-than-expected growth in energy demand. The slowdown would have been unavoidable whoever had won the 1981 elecions and in no sense represents a significant policy change. With a few exceptions, at the Cap de la Hague reprocessing plant near Cherbourg, at Chooz near the Belgian border, and at Golfech in south-west France, the antinuclear movement is now disillusioned and demobilised. After several years of mostly fruitless campaigning against nuclear power, the victory of the socialists represented, for many antinuclear activists, the final chance, if not to win their battle, then at least to gain a more sympathetic hearing. Although at times a large and vocal movement, the French antinuclear movement has been unable to have any significant impact on the government's nuclear programme. In the face of this, and of increasing public acceptance of nuclear power,[19] it is not surprising that the movement is demoralised and in decline.

However, whereas the election of François Mitterrand seems to have marked the end of the campaign against nuclear power as a mass movement, there are reasons for thinking that his election may have the opposite effect on the French campaign against nuclear weapons. While France pursued an ambitious pro-nuclear policy for energy, it is logical that ecologists should have developed a vigorous antinuclear campaign, based at first mainly on the risks, for the environment and for the population, of such a policy and later more on the type of centralised and technocratic society implicit in such a policy. However, the situation has now changed. On the one hand, the antinuclear movement has, for its interlocutor, a socialist government. It was often alongside socialists that ecologists found themselves campaigning against the previous government's nuclear programme. Ecologists therefore sometimes find themselves in a somewhat ambivalent position as to what attitude or tactics to adopt with a government of the left, with which, in some other areas such as social policy, they are probably in sympathy. They also find themselves confronted with a *fait accompli* in respect of nuclear energy. Even if France were to order no new nuclear power stations, she would still be dependent on nuclear energy for over half her electricity supplies well into the twenty-first century. Nuclear waste is clearly an increasing problem and the antinuclear movement has a role to play here in informing the public and in exerting pressure on government to find more satisfactory ways of dealing with the waste problem. However, this is at present unlikely to form the basis for a mass campaign on the scale of the antinuclear movement in the seventies, although this could change if a major accident were to occur, for example, during transport of such waste. For these reasons, and those outlined earlier, it is unlikely that the campaign against nuclear power will, in the immediate future, be as important as it has been in the past.

On the other hand, Mitterrand's policy on nuclear weapons does appear to mark a major break from that of the previous administration. Like his predecessors, he refuses to have the French deterrent counted with the West's nuclear force in arms negotiations with the Soviet Union. However, unlike his predecessor, he is an enthusiastic and outspoken supporter of the deployment of American Cruise and Pershing missiles in Europe,[20] even to the extent of making a speech in front of the Bundestag during the German election campaign which was taken to support the position of the right-wing candidate Helmut Kohl on missile deployment.[21] As we have already seen, French ecologists are not immune from the Gaullist heritage and it is therefore possible that, while development of the French deterrent would be accepted, support for new American missiles in Europe will arouse opposition from ecologists.

At the same time, the Defence Minister, Charles Hernu, nicknamed *HERNUcléaire* by the antinuclear movement, has pushed through the re-equipment of the strategic land-based missiles with improved warheads and has continued support for research and testing of the neutron bomb.[22] Furthermore, the budget which he presented in

October 1982 gave 'absolute priority' to nuclear weapons, on which spending was to be increased by 25 per cent in 1983, compared to an increase of under 10 per cent for conventional forces. Spending on nuclear weapons in 1983 is to represent 32 per cent of the total defence budget.[23] France's seventh nuclear submarine has been ordered and production of the Hades tactical missiles has been announced. Meanwhile, French nuclear tests in the Pacific have continued unabated.[24] It is clear from this and from the socialist five-year defence plan for 1984-88 that the government intends to develop an 'essentially nuclear-based defence of France'.[25] It is also clear that, without rejoining NATO, France intends to be more closely involved in the coordinated western defence system against eastern Europe.[26]

While it is still too early to assess the precise influence such policies might have on the French antinuclear movement, there are already signs of an increasing interest, within the movement, in the nuclear weapons issue. In part, this is the result of the well-publicised activities of the European peace movement. Although these activities are generally covered in an extremely partial way by the French media, the very fact of their being covered has served to increase awareness of the nuclear weapons issue. Secondly, the recent increase in co-operation between the Greens in different west-European countries is undoubtedly significant. The achievements of the German Greens have impressed many French ecologists. As has been mentioned, at the Greens' Congress at Besançon in May 1983 a proposal for a common platform for the Greens throughout western Europe raised some objections because it contained a commitment to unilateral nuclear disarmament. However, the text was eventually carried and the size of the majority by which it was carried may well have been influenced by the comment of one speaker in the debate that 'the German Greens would never accept a text which did not include a commitment to unilateral nuclear disarmament'. This cooperation was further promoted by the recent visit, in April 1983, of Petra Kelly, leader of the German Greens, to sections of the French ecology movement.

Nevertheless, it is still true that in 1983, the 'Year of the American missiles', France has proved remarkably immune from demonstrations against their deployment. Of course, part of the reason for this is geographical. Whereas American missiles are actually going to be stationed in Britain and Germany, none will be stationed on French soil. As Y. Cochet, leader of the *Rennes-Verte* list for the 1983 municipal elections in Rennes admitted: 'the problem is psychologically less present in people's minds'.[27]

Another development which has recently attracted considerable interest among ecologists and which may significantly affect their attitude towards nuclear weapons is an article published in the October 1982 issue of *Sciences et Vie*.[28] This article was reproduced in the Newsletter of the antinuclear movement in the Rhône-Alpes region, *Super-Pholix*, and has furnished the movement with a new argument for their opposition to the fast-breeder reactor under construction at Creys-Malville. In essence, the article says that previous justifications given for the fast-breeder reactor, such as the future world shortage of uranium for conventional nuclear reactors,[29] have been shown to be invalid. The only reason, claim the article's authors Michel Genestout and Yves Lenoir, why the government has continued with the fast-breeder programme, despite its election promises, is that 'the military need fast-breeder reactors'. The point they make is that this type of reactor produces a plutonium of a particular quality which is highly suitable for use in nuclear weapons. Plutonium for French nuclear weapons has until now been produced in the nuclear reactors built specially for this purpose at Marcoule in south-east France. However, these reactors are now nearing the end of their useful life and one has already been closed down. No new reactors are either planned or under construction to replace them and provide the military with the plutonium they need. Given the enormously increased French requirements for plutonium resulting from the socialist government's ambitious nuclear weapons programme, the authors conclude that the fast-breeder reactor under construction at Creys-Malville is intended to be the main supplier of France's weapons-grade plutonium in the future. The authors go on to give a number of other reasons why they believe this solution has been chosen, which include the fact that part of the cost of producing weapons-grade plutonium can, in this way, be 'lost' in the civil nuclear programme.[30] Electricity consumers are therefore in effect paying part of the cost of French nuclear weapons. Another major advantage of the fast-breeder reactor is that it is capable of producing plutonium of the correct isotope for the neutron bomb, on which development work is, as has already been mentioned, continuing. This issue of the link between nuclear power and nuclear weapons has been taken up by ecologists in the region around Creys-Malville and is now arousing widespread interest throughout the movement.

Future Prospects

There are already clear signs that French ecologists are increasingly interested in the nuclear weapons issue. One of the leaders of the Ecology Party, Solange Fernex, took part in the international 'Fast for Life' starting on 6 August 1983.[31] This hunger strike was intended to draw public attention to the nuclear arms race and appealed to governments to call a halt to it. In addition, the Ecology Party is one of the French signatories of the international movement which demands an immediate freeze on all nuclear weapons testing and construction.[32] With CODENE (see Chapter Eight), the French branch of the European non-aligned peace movement, now providing ecologists with an alternative to working with the communist-dominated *Mouvement de la Paix*, it is possible that ecologists feel the door is now open for them to take a more active part in the peace movement. As public awareness of the nuclear weapons issue increases, as public opinion becomes better informed and as the socialist government goes ahead with its huge nuclear weapons programme, many French ecologists are beginning to think that the movement should play a greater role in the campaign against nuclear weapons.

As Brice Lalonde points out, the movement is discussing the issue as well as the problem of alternative defence systems:

> There is a debate among political ecologists about how to introduce another system of defence and what sort of system should be adopted: armed or unarmed civil defence. Ecologists have no majority position on this. Our criticism of the defence system is similar to our criticism of the health system: we are badly served by specialists, or supposed specialists, with their barbarous and extreme techniques. On this we are agreed. But there is disagreement about the timetable, how it can be achieved, and what is the most suitable substitute for the present system. As far as an alternative defence system is concerned, nuclear weapons must be got rid of by stages. We must start with the weapons that are not particularly useful and which can be traded off within the context of multilateral negotiations: the Plateau d'Albion missiles and the nuclear bombers. We must get rid of nuclear submarines last of all. They are mobile and impossible to detect at the moment, so they are not vulnerable to a first strike.[33]

He also makes a distinction between types of nuclear weaponry when he observes that 'the movement for nuclear disarmament in France may well become more important if the socialists persist with their plans for tactical nuclear weapons'. There are degrees of unacceptability.

The Ecology Party also has a commission on defence. A discussion document written by the chairman of this commission states that western Europe should leave NATO, that the aim must be the creation of a neutral nuclear-free zone in western Europe, even if no concessions are forthcoming from the other side, and that the first priority must be the unilateral nuclear disarmament of France, together with a proposal for: 'an alternative defence system, capable of avoiding both a nuclear holocaust in Europe and a conventional military confrontation which, in the present state of vulnerability and civil nuclearisation of Europe, would have the same result'.[34]

With increased debate of the issue goes an increased awareness of its significance. While the development of nuclear power, both civil and military, was perceived by the majority as part of a technological modernisation and as essential to France's greatness in the world, it was largely accepted by public opinion. However, in a future situation of international tension, when the French nuclear deterrent might be clearly perceived as neither national nor independent, this state of affairs could easily change. This is especially possible because only 34 per cent of French people are in favour of the deployment of Pershing 2 missiles in Europe, while 44 per cent are against, even if the Soviet Union retains its SS20s. These figures become 32 per cent and 51 per cent respectively for the 18-34 age group.[35] Public opinion is clearly ahead of the politicians in its lack of enthusiasm for the deployment of new American missiles and, in a tense international climate, it is a gap that could grow if the nuclear deterrent came to be perceived by public opinion more as a real threat of mass annihilation than as a symbol of French greatness.

In conclusion, it is true that up to now French ecologists have directed their energies largely into other spheres. This situation may be changing however. A questionnaire recently carried out among ecology movement activists shows that many of them now attach a high priority to the nuclear arms issue.[36] Furthermore, the work of CODENE, which is the French interlocutor of the European peace movement, the increase in cooperation with the European Green movement, and perhaps also the growing realisation that nuclear fall-out is not obliged to pass through customs, are all likely to have a significant effect on the French ecology movement's stand on this issue in the future.

Notes

1. The author wishes to acknowledge the contribution to this chapter of Brendan Prendiville, who researched and wrote the sections on Rennes as a research student at Rennes University.

2. *Ecologie: Le Pouvoir de vivre* (Aujourd'hui L'Ecologie, 1982), p. 238.

3. Speaking in an interview in Paris with the author on 9 February 1983.

4. The proposal for a common platform was drafted by representatives of the Green movement from France, Germany, Britain, Ireland, Belgium and Sweden at a meeting in Brussels on 26-27 March 1983.

5. A. Touraine et al., *La Prophétie antinucléaire* (Seuil, 1980), pp. 98-9. This book was recently translated into English under the title *Antinuclear Protest: the Opposition to Nuclear Energy in France (Cambridge University Press, 1983)*.

6. C. Bourdet, interview with V. C. Fišera, *Newsletter of the Association for the Study of Modern and Contemporary France*, No.6, July-August 1981, p.5.

7. This survey took place during May 1983 and was based on personal interviews and a written questionnaire.

8. Interview with Gérard Paget, leading member of the *Rennes-Verte* list and member of the Rennes Friends of the Earth group, 23 May 1983.

9. This survey of ecologists, which was made possible by a French government grant, was undertaken by Tony Chafer in various towns throughout France during the election campaign for the 1983 municipal elections and at the Greens' national congress in Besançon in May 1983.

10. See also his interview with Tony Chafer in the *Newsletter of the Association for the Study of Modern and Contemporary France*, No.14, May-June 1983, pp.16-18.

11. Interview with *Le Matin,* 6 May 1982, p.2.

12. These interviews were taken during the survey mentioned in note 9. Brice Lalonde also says in the *Le Matin* interview already cited: 'We must recognise that the ecology movement has only been able to flourish in the West.'

13. See for example the editorial of the first issue of *Intervention,* No.1, November-December 1982, pp.2-3. This review is associated with New Left elements within the PS and in particular with supporters of Michel Rocard, who used to be in the PSU. This current has traditionally been relatively sympathetic to ecologists' themes and ideas.

14. Quoted by A.-M. Le Gloannec in 'Allemagne: l'identité nationale passe par le pacifisme', *Libération,* 21 January 1983, p.2.

15. Ibid., p.3.

16. For a more detailed history of the antinuclear movement in France, see Tony

Chafer, 'The Anti-Nuclear Movement and the Rise of Political Ecology', in P. Cerny ed., *Social Movements and Protest in France* (Frances Pinter, 1982), pp.202-220.

17. The campaigns against the plan to build a huge new nuclear power station at Plogoff on the west coast of Brittany and against the extension of the military camp on the Larzac plateau in the Massif Central had become symbols of, and rallying-points for, the whole antinuclear and ecology movement in France.

18. Parti Socialiste, *Energie: l'autre politique* (Club Socialiste du Livre, 1981).

19. See opinion poll in *Le Figaro* 6 October 1981. In October 1981, 62% of those polled declared themselves in favour of the development of nuclear power stations, with 37% against. An equivalent poll in November 1978 had shown 47% for and 42% against.

20. 'Mitterrand et Thatcher disent NON à Andropov', *Libération*, 6 May 1983.

21. *Le Matin*, 21 January 1983.

22. BBC Radio 4 News on 27 June 1983 announced that in an interview with a German magazine Charles Hernu had stated that France had recently successfully tested a neutron bomb in the Pacific.

23. *Le Monde*, 8 October 1982 and *La Nouvelle République*, 8 October 1982.

24. *Guardian*, 22 April 1983. The latest French nuclear tests on the Mururoa atoll in the Pacific have been strongly condemned by Australia, which has said it will end uranium exports to France unless the tests stop. By the end of 1982 France had conducted 113 nuclear tests, over a third of them atmospheric, and the rate of testing reached an all-time peak in 1980-81. For further information on nuclear test figures, and on the 1979 Mururoa accident and subsequent damage to the atoll, see *SIPRI Yearbook 1983*, pp.98-100; and *SIPRI Yearbook 1982*, p.429.

25. *Guardian*, 22 April 1983.

26. *Guardian*, 21 and 22 April 1983. It is also symptomatic of this closer relationship between France and NATO that the NATO foreign ministers were invited to meet in Paris in June 1983 for the first time since France left NATO in 1966.

27. Interview with Y. Cochet, 30 May 1983.

28. For a summary of the main points of this article, see W. Patterson, 'Pay your electricity bill and buy a bomb', *Guardian*, 16 December 1982, p.18.

29. A major plank in the pro-fast-breeder lobby's argument has always been that uranium will eventually begin to run short. The claimed advantage of the fast-breeder in this respect is that it produces plutonium at the same time as producing electricity. This plutonium, after reprocessing, can then be re-used as fuel, thus lengthening the life of world uranium stocks. These claims have been challenged by the antinuclear lobby mainly on the grounds that the reprocessing facilities, on which the whole fuel cycle of the fast-breeder depends, are far from perfected.

30. The advantages of this are not lost on the military as a similar point was made by General Thiry at a meeting of the Foreign Affairs Commission of the Radical Party in January 1978, when he said: 'France knows how to manufacture atomic bombs of

different types and power. She will be able to manufacture large quantities of them when fast-breeders supply the necessary plutonium.' This meeting was reported in *Le Monde*, 19 January 1978.

31. Solange Fernex was the head of the French ecology list, *Europe-Ecologie*, for the 1979 European elections. The idea of the 'Fast for Life' was launched in San Francisco but there are participants from many other countries, including Japan and Canada.

32. The 'Freeze Movement' was launched in the USA and is intended as a first step in stopping the nuclear arms race, opening the way ultimately to agreed reductions in nuclear arms.

33. From Brice Lalonde's interview with the author on 9 February 1983.

34. This document was prepared by Jean Brière, a member of the Ecology Party, Rhône-Alpes region, and also a member of the Party's national executive.

35. A. Fontaine, 'Quelles armes contre la guerre?' *Le Monde*, 18 June 1983, p.1.

36. In the questionnaire (see Note 9) ecologists were asked to place various issues in order of priority and nuclear disarmament was frequently identified as *a*, if not *the*, major issue for ecologists. The full results of this survey will be published by Tony Chafer in 1984.

10 THE NEW LEFT AND DEFENCE: OUT OF THE GHETTO?

Vladimir Claude Fišera[1]

There is a verse of the *Internationale*, that anthem of the entire revolutionary left, written by the French *Communard* Eugène Pottier in June 1871, a verse which is among the lesser known and lesser sung ones, and which goes: 'Paix entre nous, guerre aux tyrans; Appliquons la grève aux armées; Crosse en l'air et rompons les rangs'.[2] This indicates symbolically the real dimension of the dilemma facing the French New Left —the radical left outside the 'reformist' socialist and communist parties — when confronted with the issue of defence.

It establishes immediately the radical exteriority of the non-establishment left (*la Gauche non-respectueuse*) as regards the institutions of the state, which are always seen as a class tool, an instrument of both exploitation and domination. Armies will always be led by 'tyrants' and the revolutionary left, the left which wants radical change, will want to dispose of these wicked instruments as it disposes of those who are using them. The international unity of the human race is the aim of the revolution. It is synonymous with universal peace as the left does not recognise any endogenous human drive, be it collective or individual, towards aggression and destruction. Men are good by nature, an exploitative and authoritarian social system being the only cause of thanatophilic tendencies. At what moment in the evolution towards peace might a pacifist line be adopted? Should one use peaceful means of collective struggle in order to achieve such a peaceful end? If nothing human is inherently bad, at what stage do human institutions and human military science get out of hand and mere instruments, from being neutral, become perverse *per se*? Pottier fought against the foreign and the native 'pro-bourgeois' troops with a weapon in one hand as he was writing the peace verse of the *Internationale* with the other. The Paris Commune, even its Proudhonian wing — which was to become the matrix of French predominantly collectivist and anti-capitalist anarchism — seized bourgeois arms and used the bourgeois art of war. The revolution, like all successive revolutions which followed, armed itself and merely 'massified' the army, the state and the nation itself, thus taking its

233

place consciously in French history, in the 'manifest destiny' of the French people/nation, as the inheritor of the soldiers of Year Two of the first French revolution, the barefoot volunteers of Valmy in 1792. The working people, to paraphrase Stalin, lifted up again the flag of independence and of the republic which had been abandoned by a treacherous bourgeoisie and aristocracy.

By so doing, up to a point, the left had changed, in character and/or form, the institutions and the values it had occupied, just as a soldier-crab occupies an empty shell. The enemy, they thought, was made up solely of foreign class fiends and mercenaries. Henceforth, most of the radical left, except for the individualist anarchists and some radical Christian Socialists, was to accept *just* wars such as the Resistance, conscription at any time ('on te donne un fusil, prend-le!' —'if you're handed a gun, take it!' — would be the Trotskyist/Maoist/PSU slogan in the wake of 1968), and the defence of national independence. This attitude was not devoid of a mostly subconscious 'Franco-centric' conception of culture and politics which Marx lucidly denounced in the French Proudhonians (he was less lucid about his own German national pride). This led to certain left-wing intellectuals (Claude Bourdet and Jean-Pierre Vigier, for example) flirting with the idea of France as the 'progressive great power', an idea which they shared as late as 1979 with left-wing Gaullists, oppositionists and former Resistants in their joint committee against 'Germano-American Europe'. As *Tumulte* rightly put it, the independent French peace movement is lagging behind the rest of Europe because of 'an undeniable cultural chauvinism *vis-à-vis* Northern Europe'.[3] Some on the French New Left itself decry this 'nordic moralism'.[4]

Marxism in its French vulgate version, by courtesy of Jules Guesde and later French translations of Soviet ideological outpourings, considers that violence is a secondary by-product of capitalism, the harbinger of war and revolution. The latter will have to be inaugurated by violence, be it only as the last mass-inflicted leg up or *coup d'épaule* as Michel Rocard, then the PSU (*Parti Socialiste Unifié*) candidate for the presidency, put it to rapturous crowds in 1969.

The New Left Approach

The anarchists themselves, following Bakunin, would globally concur with the above, the only internal difference inside the pro-violence revolutionary left being one of tactics (does one use, split or neutralise the army?) and of methods, from the putsch to the mass uprising via the general strike and the use of militias. The latter are generally favoured as a means of what the *Mouvement pour une Alternative Non-Violente* (MAN) calls today *transarmament*[5] before the revolution changes people's minds, although some would prefer an army under workers' popular control and others a straight transition to popular non-violent defence. In any case, the revolution of the people will defend itself and nobody, I stress nobody, not even among the pacifists who see capitalism as a product of war rather than the reverse, the individualist anarchists or the radical Christians, propagates a line of accommodation to enemy domination. Nobody, at least in France, says 'better red than dead'. The constant peaceful guerrilla based on civil disobedience which is waged by the French conscientious objectors against the 'liberal democratic' or 'democratic socialist' state is a witness of that resolution and of its certain relentless escalation if it were confronted with a fascist or other totalitarian native or occupation regime. The unified *Mouvement des Objecteurs de Conscience* (MOC) declares in its statement of aims that conscientious objection is not 'limited to an individual refusal to carry weapons' but aims at a 'collective, social and political dimension'. The MOC sees itself as a 'committed part of the struggle against militarisation and the arms trade, for disarmament and the research and acquisition of other forms of defence'.[6]

It is in the camp of radical political dissent in France that one finds some of the most implacable enemies of the Soviet system which even the orthodox Trotskyists call 'totalitarian',[7] as Trotsky did in 1940 in his last book. Nobody among the *contestataires* is in favour of exporting the revolution by force as Tukhachevsky proposed in 1920 during the Soviet-Polish war. This was not so clear until the late 1970s among French Leninists (Communist-oppositionists, Trotskyists and Mao- ists), but the belated awakening to the horrors of the Gulag, Soviet military interventions and the Sino-Vietnamese conflict of March 1979 led people to conclude that 'red' states armed to the teeth with nuclear bombs were not red after all, otherwise one would have to conclude: 'le socialisme, c'est aussi la guerre' ('socialism also means war').[8] The PCF (*Parti Communiste Français*) stands alone in con- doning this behaviour with its East Berlin and Moscow imported concept of 'real socialism'. The radical Left which is now totally involved in the anti-missile struggle has evolved with French public opinion as a whole in this rejection of the Soviet model.[9] Only some Trotskyists see the USSR as a transitional, if degenerated, workers' state but even they ascribe to it militaristic attributes. In fact, the real reason why they remain on that half-way house position is their overriding strategic priority of a take-over bid of the 'workers' masses' influenced by the PCF. These are considerations of purely French internal politics which they share with the Maoist PCML (*Parti Communiste Marxiste-Léniniste*) and some anarchists, and which have little to do with the USSR or 'the present danger'. All in all, this 'nebula' of French *contestation* has indeed lost its Mecca,[10] and if it has its doubts about its own French fatherland — which it is ready to fight for only in the case of a defensive war — it has no surrogate revolutionary or proletarian fatherland to the East. Its conception of internationalism, like its conception of French patriotism, is based — with the exception of the pro-Chinese PCML — on a relationship, *to* and *among* peoples/masses/movements rather than institutions/states. This 'populism' might be a utopianism but it is certainly a refusal to accept the rules of the game, be they the strategic or the diplomatic ones. This enlarges the field of international relations to the North-South dimension (anti-imperialism, third worldism, new economic order) and leads to the quest for a dialogue with dissidents in the pseudo-Socialist countries, especially in Poland. Only in France, the same political milieu (the inheritors of May 1968) can be seen as the basis of the pro-Solidarnosc, pro-Salvador, pro-Afghanistan *and* pro-nuclear freeze activism. This is epitomised in the work of local and regional CFDT (*Confédération Française Démocratique du Travail*) organisations,[11] of the PSU,[12] of the MAN,[13] of the radical *Confédération Nationale des Syndicats de Travailleurs Paysans* and of the Larzac farmers who fought victoriously from 1973 to 1981 against the extension of a local military camp.[14]

The Strident Minorities and the Silent Majority

Similarly, most of this conglomerate of radical tendencies does reject both American and Soviet missiles. It is also against the NATO connection and, again with the exception of the Maoists, opposed not only to the modernisation of the *force de frappe* but also to the French deterrent itself. This, as has been explained in the preceding chapters, is a position which distinguishes these radicals quite fundamentally from the national consensus, shared by the 'Big Four' political parties — including, since 1977, the PCF and, since 1978, the PS (*Parti Socialiste*) — and a majority of French public opinion. Thus they *all*, PSU, Trotskyists, Maoists, libertarians, pacifists, ecologists, radical Christians, feminists, communist oppositionists and trade union 'basists', take with a pinch of salt the myth of national unity/national interest and are not afraid to be in a minority. This is a function and a consequence of their radicalism itself which perceives itself as 'leading the way' (vanguardism, 'one step ahead of the masses'), as a protest against the establishment, and against the consensus of bourgeois/ professional politics as represented by the 'Gang of Four'. It also sees itself as being the mouthpiece of the real, non-institutionalised France (*la France 'sauvage'*), of the workers (*l'avant-garde ouvrière*), of the young, of women and also of the Christian community which has now become a minority among other radical minorities or oppressed groups. This leads to the politics of 'witnessing', with a tinge of utopian prophetism, and to the choice of direct action and rank-and-file, extra-parliamentary —although not violent — activities.

Terrorism of the Left is minuscule indeed (confined to *Action Directe*, marginal anarchists and ecologists, and some socialist nationalists from the ethnic minorities) and has not intervened on the peace scene yet except by way of a few references to the militaristic fascisation of the French, US and Soviet states, references which do not isolate the nuclear aspect at all and confuse the army, the police, the civil service and the employers in one great indistinct Leviathan. Besides, the terrorists do not proselytise, while all the others believe in mass action and open politics as the one main avenue for social change. Popular mobilisation (so lacking since 1977 in France generally[15]), together with militant activism — rather than representative parliamentary democracy on the one hand, or terrorist violence on the other — are the fundamental prerequisites for self-management and workers' control as the majority of the New Left see it. The nuclear-military-technological complex represents for them the ultimate *hétérogestion*, to use this antonym of *autogestion* coined by the French radical sociologist Yvon Bourdet. All these organisations, even the Leninist ones (*Ligue Communiste Révolutionnaire, Parti Communiste Marxiste-Léniniste, Lutte Ouvrière*), stress their grass-roots approach, especially as their institutional presence is quasi-inexistent. The stronger they become in the political institutions (in March 1983 the PSU increased the number of its local councillors to over 800 and saw its national secretary, Huguette Bouchardeau, become the Secretary of State for the Environment and Quality of Life) the weaker their extremism might become. For instance among the four conditions laid down at the PSU congress of December 1981 for a participation in government, two had to do with defence: 'a new foreign policy independent from the Americans' and 'a limitation of the arms race', the other two dealing with new workers' rights and work sharing.[16] And yet, the PSU joined the government without obtaining any guarantees on these matters even if the demands were couched in vague terms. This happened despite the traditional distrust that the PSU, like all the extreme left, feels towards institutional political power, especially state power.

However, after May 1981, to various degrees, these groups had to give some sort of critical support to the left-wing government, especially in a situation of lack of popular mobilisation and of frontal attempts at destabilisation conducted by the right-wing opposition.[17] Thus for the forces of *political* radicalism (as opposed to those which are religious or do not define themselves as being left-wing) the question of the bomb cannot be, any more than any other *single* issue, the one cause of the break with the socialist government. Unlike single-issue campaigners, who come into politics through what is, for them, a central issue, political movements go from the general to the particular and in this particular case will all want to persuade peace campaigners that if they want a *lasting* peace they will have to go beyond defence, beyond international relations and even beyond the new international economic order and fight for a *social* revolution. Of course, they agree with peace campaigners that the threat of war is real — while public opinion at large does not — and that negotiations between the superpowers will not solve the problem. However, they are less inclined than the 'peaceniks' to fear the possible nuclear apocalypse and do not conceive of militarism as a new mode of production or of exterminism as the main tendency of great-power industrial-military complexes.

For these radical parties, the fundamental question is that of the nature of the *social* regime in power in the different countries: a truly Socialist France in which the workers would be in command would be the 'best guarantee of the preservation of the interests of our people in the event of a world war'.[18] In these circumstances, some of them, especially those which are traditional parties in their mode of organisation and in their ambitions, and/or which give a priority to work among the working class, will want to keep their contacts with the PCF-dominated *Mouvement de la Paix* (MDP), not because of its particular line on the missiles — to which they are likely to prefer the CODENE line — but because of the weight it represents. For instance, the *Jeunesse Ouvrière Chrétienne* (JOC)[19] and the PSU,[20] which were not associated with the MDP demonstration of 25 October 1981 because the movement was 'extremely weak' and also 'boycotted by the other European peace movements', did take part in, or at least supported, the most recent and much more successful MDP 'picnic for peace' on 19 June 1983. The LCR (*Ligue Communiste Révolution-*

naire), most Trotskyist and pacifist national organisations and the Maoist PCML did the same, which led to the first 'historic' handshake between Georges Marchais and Alain Krivine. The former also desperately needs to get out of his own ghetto. Similarly, while the PSU was the only real party to launch the CODENE (with the help of the MAN, the *Mouvement pour le Désarmement, la Paix et la Liberté* (MDPL), the *Service Civil International* and *'les Larzac'*) in late 1981,[21] many more had joined the movement by the time of the June 1983 Larzac appeal: among others, the *Verts – Parti Ecologiste*, and the official Pablists or *Alliance Marxiste Révolutionnaire*.

However, while it is relatively simple to sign the vague PCF-organised *Appel des Cent* (with slogans such as: 'I love Peace — I love Life' and 'Negotiate'), it is much more difficult politically, unless one is already heavily involved with CODENE, to sign the CODENE or Larzac nuclear freeze declarations. Even if in the Larzac text the critique of the French deterrent is cosmetically reduced to the freeze, this text still stresses the non-aligned, independent, anti-bloc, pan-European dimension, opposed to the two superpowers. The emphasis is on real disarmament *and* on the 'liberation' of the subject peoples in Europe and in the world. CODENE's link with the new European independent peace movements, the total absence of a plea to the French government to negotiate, all this precludes any support from the pro-NATO left (leaders of the PS, *Fédération de l'Education Nationale, Force Ouvrière*, and, in part, of the CFDT), or the pro-Soviet left (PCF, *Confédération Générale du Travail*). It also excludes those who still think that the West (code name 'imperialism') is the main danger (PCF oppositionists, LCR and other orthodox Trotskyists except the *Parti Communiste Internationaliste* and *Lutte Ouvrière*) as well as those who believe the main threat comes from the East (PCML, although this may change now that China has praised the Western peace movement and decided to attend the international antinuclear conference at Hiroshima in August 1983).[22] Finally, the CODENE line also excludes all those who believe in the French independent deterrent in the perspective of France as a Socialist — and non-aligned — Great Power (PCF oppositionists, left-wing Gaullists, the *Centre d'Etudes, de Recherches, et d'Education Socialiste* (CERES), PCML, former Maoists) and those who believe that non-alignment without first a socialist revolution is an illusion (all orthodox Trotskyists).

This will necessarily restrict the number of different organisations and ideological currents supporting CODENE to the *autogestionnaires*, the ecologists, the anarchists, to the political wing of the *non-*

violent movement, to the feminists and to those pacifists who accept coexistence with those who consider that a 'popular defence' will include conventional defensive weapons, and that neither demi-litarisation of society nor even unilateral nuclear disarmament can be achieved at once but only in stages. The latter more realistic attitude has been taken, not only by the PSU, which dropped all references to militarisation (developed in 1980) in the final drafts of all the conflicting motions proposed at its last congress in June 1983, but also by the MDPL which accepts conventional defence and which conceded at its last congress in January 1983 that there should be no contradiction between multilateral and unilateral disarmament so long as there are first selective, partial steps taken, backed by a European popular movement.[23]

Out of the Ghetto?

The New Left in France has not developed a political sub-culture of its own, an autonomous 'alternative scene' as is the case in West Germany or the Netherlands. Hence its relative ideological ossification since it is not challenged nationally by alternative social movements which produce their own ideologies. The ecologists are in decline and are incapable even of leading CODENE; so are the feminists. Moreover, the peace movement itself has not acquired an independent dynamic: too few of its members join CODENE on an individual basis as direct members with no other affiliations. Those who could have acted as catalysts reaching beyond the New Left ghetto, progressive non-aligned intellectuals, progressive Christians or Rocardian socialists, have been found wanting. Their late discovery of the Soviet anti-model made them accept the Atlanticist line of the 'present' overriding Soviet danger and the rupture of nuclear balance: *Esprit, Libération, Le Monde, Faire/Intervention* have campaigned systematically against 1930s neutralism or *les 'munichois'*. The *Le Monde* cartoonist Jean Plantu and the ex-Maoist libertarian new philosopher André Glucks-mann can at the same time attack the *Appel des Cent* and refuse to support CODENE while sharing muted but real sympathy with grass-roots French and West German anti-Great-Power peace move-ments.[24] But for them the struggle for human rights means *primarily* helping to roll back the USSR rather than resisting French militari-sation.

This is starting to change as both peace movements clearly show (witness the 19 June 1983 and 6-7 August 1983 mass successes) that they are reaching beyond the PCF and the New Left ghettoes. The Larzac rally in particular, organised by the Larzac Farmers, the *Artisans de la Paix* and CODENE, was a much greater success than either the organisers or the media expected. *Le Monde*, for the first time ever, mentioned the French independent peace movement on its front page, and *Libération* and *Le Matin* both started evaluating positively this same movement. It was evident to me as a participant observer that the 15,000 to 20,000-strong audience represented a potentially powerful movement. First because of its largely 'partyless' composition. The PSU and the MAN were the only 'political' organisations present. Their presence was central to the event and yet unobtrusive. The great majority of the public belonged to the 1968 generation on the one hand —often 'returnees' to political action via life-style politics of which peace, ecology, human rights and third-worldism are the main components — and to the under twenty-year olds who share this political culture, albeit in the absence of any past party-political allegiance. The resolution which was carried focused on the refusal of the French deterrent and on the support of East German dissidents as much as on the refusal of SS20s and Cruise. However, the rally rejected extreme positions such as the immediate scrapping of the French deterrent and tried to see the Vincennes *Mouvement des Cent* rally as a first step in the right direction, as a separate but non-contradictory movement to their own. The resolution clearly inserted the freeze movement into a global alternative approach to wider issues of defence, foreign policy, energy and employment. It applauded Solidarnosc and Charter 77[25] and, with Huguette Bouchardeau and the pro-PCF Euro-MP E. Maffre-Baugé, refused above all the division into military blocs. Significantly the actions proposed were varied and of a local, individual, decentralised nature, addressing themselves to 'personal witnessing' as much as to a collective organised action. The rally ended with a Larzac farmer attacking nuclear tests and recalling his own visit to Hiroshima, before returning to the Larzac struggle of the 1970s and reading the 1983 Larzac oath: 'I pledge myself to act against the nuclear arms race which is growing in both western and eastern Europe and in which my country, France, is taking part, regardless of the reasons presently invoked to justify it.'

All the opinion polls demonstrate that the consensus on the nuclear bomb is a conditional one: French public opinion supports the bomb because it is *French*, because it is not to be used (which excludes both euromissiles and the French tactical nuclear weaponry), because supporters do not believe that war is a real 'present danger', and because so far they have confidence in French great-power foreign policy. But this is changing: the question of world peace as the number one preoccupation of the French has jumped from between 3% to 5% in 1982 to 24% in 1983.[26] The world role of France is seen as declining[27] and the confidence in French foreign policy plummeted from 46% to 33% between December 1982 and March 1983.[28] Consequently the confidence in NATO dropped from 74% in 1981 to 63% in 1983[29] and the sacred cow of the support for the French deterrent which was at 52% in 1973, 53% in 1976, jumping to its peak of 72% in 1981 — *purely* because of the *ralliement* of the PS and PCF — is now down again to 67% in 1982 and 66% in 1983.[30] There never was a majority belief that the deterrent could *win* a war for France: only 37% believed it in 1982: they are only 18% in 1983.[31] Since 1981, there has always been at least a relative majority against all euromissiles, with those in favour never going above the 35% mark and being made up of right-wing voters. Left-wing voters, young people, women, public and private sector low- and middle-ranking employees, city-dwellers, and workers too — to a lesser degree — have always been, to the extent of 60% or above, against Cruise and Pershing even if the SS20 were to stay. The same cross section is, by the same margin, in favour of a neutral France.[32] However, even if those in favour of conventional and non-violent resistance in the event of an invasion of France have steadily increased from 20% in 1980 to 32% in 1981 and 37% in 1983 (including 17% in favour of non-violent resistance),[33] there is still a popular majority (especially among workers) against unilateral acts of disarmament by France.[34] Nevertheless, the key point here is that there never was more than the 35% core (right-wing) pro-bomb constituency in favour of the modernisation or *perfectionnement* of the French deterrent. Since 1981, this figure has been falling and there are now only about 20% who favour it, while the same number (but growing and composed of a majority of left-wing voters) is in favour of its reduction and about 40% in favour of its 'maintenance'.[35] This puts the 'Big Four' political parties in a minority and explains why the image-conscious CODENE and the PSU have switched to the 'Freeze', as opposed to wholesale immediate French nuclear disarmament, while the PCF-led *Appel des Cent* remains silent on the question of *French* nuclear weaponry.

So the tendency is shifting slowly towards CODENE and even the ambiguous *Appel des Cent*, whose demonstrations are very strongly welcomed by public opinion as shown in the polls.

This shows that France, in this matter as in others, has its own rhythm and that its peace movement has not peaked yet: the Polish crisis and the popular support for the national deterrent manipulated by the dominant parties have not caused its decline as has been the case elsewhere in Europe.[36] The new sophistication of CODENE and of the PSU and MDPL in refusing to provoke public opinion with a demand for blanket French unilateral disarmament might again show the revenge of civil society against the state and its ideological apparatuses, including the traditional political parties themselves, a revolt of the popular element against political and international series and 'serialisation'.[37] It will certainly revive anti-militarism and the civil rights movement and help to create a united 'left-wing alternative' in which disarmament and international anti-bloc non-alignment will figure predominantly.[38] As the Political Bureau of the PSU put it, the peace campaign is not just 'one more campaign': it can touch many people, especially young people, far beyond 'the militant sphere', as it is a theme which concerns them particularly.[39]

The role of the political New Left is crucial here. In a peace movement which by its very nature can merely draw a 'spectacular panorama of Europe in a nuclear fire', the politicised militants alone can, as Howard Barker put it, 'assign the blame', since: 'It's madness if yer don't. Cos that's how we go on, blame this, blame that, get it wrong sometimes, of course, but never say we're barmy, or we will be...'[40]

Notes

1. The author wishes to express his thanks for the assistance given by Ms Chantal Fisera-Rameau, Ms Paule Opériol, Ms Jeanne Brunschwig and Mr Eric Cahm in the preparation of this chapter.

2. 'Peace among us, death to the tyrants; Let us apply the strike weapon to the armies; Let us mutiny and break ranks.' This was quoted recently by the foremost French libertarian peace campaigner Bernard Thomas in *Le Canard Enchaîné*, 23 February 1983 ('Courte et bonne'), where he inherited the cloak of the late Morvan Lebesque who was, with Louis Lecoin, Claude Bourdet and Lanza del Vasto, one of the very few living links between the old (i.e. pre-Fifth Republic) French radical left and its orphaned grandchildren of May 1968.

3. *Tumulte*, No.13, December 1981, 'Pour l'Europe dénucléarisée', p.29.

4. See Luc Rosenzweig, 'Le néo-pacifisme: la conscience malheureuse des nationalismes européens', *Libération*, 18-19 June 1983, p.4.

5. The theme seems to have gained currency following an international conference devoted to it in Munich back in 1967, under the leadership of Theodor Ebert. See Christian Mellon, 'La Paix: objet de recherches et d'études' in *Non-Violence Politique*, April 1983, p.5.

6. In *La Voix Protestante*, 15 April 1983, p.32. This extreme politicisation of

French dissent in 1968, which weakened the MCAA-MDPL as its militants left to join political groups, led in turn to a politicisation after 1968 of the single issue campaigns themselves — including the CFDT — which allowed disaffected *gauchistes* to drift back into them later (see my interviews with Claude Bourdet in *Journal of Area Studies* no.4, 1981, p.23 and in *ASMCF Newsletter*, no.6, 1981, p.5).

7. Ernest Mandel (in 'Menace de guerre et luttes pour le socialisme', *Critique Communiste*, No.12, Paris, October 1982, p.24) writes about the 'totalitarian and counter-revolutionary dictatorship of the Soviet bureaucracy which is in great part responsible for the survival of imperialism on the world scale (and thus, indirectly, for the very existence of the nuclear threat)'.

8. Ironical headline and articles in that most representative but now defunct common mouthpiece of the non-aligned radical, post-1968 Left, *Maintenant* (no.1, 12 March 1979), the successor to *Politique Hebdo*.

9. The image of the USSR became negative in French public opinion in 1974, and has deteriorated dramatically since. The USSR was seen as a military threat by 40% of the French in 1978. This figure jumped to 47% in 1981 and to 63% in 1982 (see *Le Monde* 13 November 1982, p.9, and opinion polls in *Le Figaro*, 3 November 1981 and *Paris Match*, 5 February 1982). However the main threats to peace for the French are an inter-Arab conflict (*le Quotidien de Paris*, 10 November 1981), Iran or Libya (*VSD*, 12 November 1981), *not* the USSR or the USA. This explains in part the relative lack of a fear of immediate nuclear holocaust and the consequent limited impact of the anti-missiles campaign.

10. See Alain Joxe, 'Défense et non alignement' in *Critique Socialiste*, no.41, 1981 and 'Castoriadis devant la guerre' in *Critique Socialiste*, no.43, 1982.

11. Regional (e.g.Midi Pyrénées) and branch (e.g.public employees) organisations of the CFDT took part in the Larzac *Rassemblement* for the nuclear freeze on 6-7 August 1983 (see text of the appeal in *Autogestion-l'Alternative* , 16 June 1983, p.11.

12. For example, the common statement published by local Afghanistan, Poland and Salvador Solidarity committees, the local PSU and thirty-odd local associations, unions, New Left and solidarity organisations in the Essonne department on 8 June 1983 on the theme of the struggle against the missiles, the blocs and for the liberation of all oppressed peoples in (*Autogestion-l'Alternative*,23 June 1983, p.3).

13. See MAN, 'Pour une défense populaire non violente', p.4, supplement to *Non Violence Politique*, no.49, 1982.

14. *Gardarem Lo Larzac*, 'mensuel d'information du Larzac', no.84, June 1983, editorial on the 'Rassemblement' by A. Desjardin; see also Daniel Garcia 'Non violence sur le Larzac' in *Le Monde*, 12 September 1982, the 1981 Larzac appeal against the nuclear threat in *Le Monde*, 25 August 1981 and an article by Yves Poulain, 'Larzac: l'été de la cardanelle' in *Témoignage Chrétien*, 31 August 1981, p.32.

15. See V. C. Fišera, 'French Left in Power: one year later', *Labour Leader*, June 1983, pp.6-7; and V. C. Fišera and Peter Jenkins, 'The Unified Socialist Party (PSU) since 1968', in D.S. Bell ed., *Contemporary French Political Parties* (London, Croom Helm, 1982), pp.108-119.

16. *Tribune Socialiste*, 6 January 1982, p.3. See also PSU, *Pour une France non alignée*, Paris, Syros, 1981.

17. See V. C. Fišera, 'The French New Left and the Left Wing Regime' in S. Williams ed., *Socialism in France* (London, Frances Pinter, 1983), pp.155-164.

18. Marc André, member of the Political Bureau of the Maoist PCRml (now part of the unified PCML), 'URSS et USA accumulent les préparatifs de guerre' in *Que Faire Aujourd'hui*, no.4, 1980, p.40. See also E. Mandel, 'Menace de guerre et luttes pour le socialisme', *Critique Communiste*, No.12, October 1982.

19. Jean Klein, 'Les chrétiens, les armes nucléaires et la paix' in *Stratégique*, No.17, 1983, p.27.

20. See the letter of the PSU Political Bureau of 23 November 1981 in Internal Supplement, *Tribune Socialiste*, 2 December 1981, p.1.

21. List of the first thirteen signatories and appeal in *Tumulte*, no.13, December 1981, p.29.

22. Pierre Burnand, 'Des usines polonaises aux montagnes afghanes', editorial in *L'Humanité Rouge*, 7 January 1982, p.3.

23. *Alerte Atomique*, No.85-86, 1982, Claude Bourdet, 'Le MDPL et le désarmement' in *Témoignage Chrétien*, 9 November 1981, p.38 and Bernard Ravenel 'Congrès du MDPL' in *Autogestion-l'Alternative*, 15 March 1983, p.4. Conversely, the anarchist *Union des Travailleurs Communistes Libertaires* , which sees militarism and exploitation as near synonyms, seems to find CODENE too moderate and ends up by 'tailing' the even more moderate *Appel des Cent* demonstrations (see 'L'armée, le dos au changement' in *Lutter*, no.3, 1982, p.30).

24. See J. Plantu in *Non-Violence Politique*, February 1983, pp.10-11 and André Glucksmann who 'as always asks the most interesting taboo question, being a poet, a near innocent, a writer philosopher' in *Le Figaro Magazine* 11 June 1983, p.80.

25. See the CODENE-Charter 77 joint statement reprinted in *Tribune Internationale*, No.6, 1983, p.26.

26. 5% among the 14-20 age group in 1982, see Louis Harris France, *Les 14-20 ans et la politique* (Paris, Louis Harris, 1982); 3% overall, see BVA poll in *Paris Match*, 12 November 1982, p.54; for 1983 see IFOP poll in *le Nouvel Economiste*, 28 February 1983, p.45.

27. See SOFRES poll in *Le Figaro Magazine*, 4 June 1983, p.84: the number of those who consider that the world role of France is declining grew from 54% in May to 58% in June 1983.

28. Louis Harris France polls in *Le Matin*, 19 January, 17 February and 16 March 1983. This decline is *exclusively* due to the shift in the attitudes of left-wing voters, PCF and PS supporters. F. Mitterrand's wholesale support for the Cruise missiles and NATO at his speech to the *Bundestag* on 10 January 1983 is a main factor here. However, 9% of these 13% of disappointed left-wing voters took refuge among the 'don't knows'. This is a constant feature in the French attitudes to defence in general which are marked

by the highest percentage of 'undecided' and 'uninformed' in Europe.

29. Louis Harris polls in *L'Express*, 9 July 1981 p.65 and *Institut de Géopolitique* poll quoted in *Le Monde*, 18 June 1983, p.7.

30. See *L'Express*, 9 July 1981 and SOFRES-Ministry of Defence poll in *Le Quotidien de Paris*, 25 November 1982, p.6 and SOFRES poll in *L'Expansion*, 6 May 1983, p.102.

31. Louis Harris Poll in *Ça m'intéresse*, September 1982 quoted in *Le Matin* on 28 September 1982 in a tiny corner of p.3 and more prominently in *Rouge* on 5 November 1982, p.13; poll quoted by Walter Schwarz, 'Mitterrand's Nuclear Stand Angers Peace Groups' in *The Guardian*, 13 January 1983.

32. Polls quoted in *Le Figaro*, 23 November 1981, *VSD* , 12 November 1981, BVA polls in *Le Nouvel Observateur*, 21 November 1981, p.57 and in *Paris Match*, 5 February 1982, p.81 and Louis Harris poll quoted in *L'Humanité*, 15 June 1983.

33. SOFRES poll in *Actuel*, January 1981 quoted in *Le Matin*, 3 January 1981. A contemporary poll in *Le Point* showed back in 1980 that the French approved of the French deterrent but were hostile to the President using it or even threatening to do so (quoted by P. Hassner 'Defence, Human Rights and Détente. A Dialogue with Viveret' in *Esprit*, July 1981 reprinted in *Telos*, 5, 1982, p.112); for 1981, see *Quotidien*, 10 November 1981; for 1983, see *The Guardian*, 13 January 1983.

34. See polls quoted supra and *Que Faire Aujourd'hui*, No.4, 1980 — survey by François Nolet, 'Les risques de guerre: ce qu'on en pense dans un quartier', pp.26-7.

35. See, for example, Ministry of Defence poll in *Quotidien de Paris*, 25 November 1982 and contrast with previous polls.

36. See E.P. Thompson, 'Peace and the East' in *New Society*, 2 June 1983, p.350 and 'The Might Will Return' in *New Statesman*, 24 June 1983, pp.8-10.

37. See V. C. Fisera, editorial, 'The Significance of the French Elections' in *Journal of Area Studies* (Portsmouth Polytechnic), no.4, Autumn 1981, pp.1-2.

38. The first signs of it in the centre of the political left scene is the petition *Pour une alternative de gauche* signed by Communist and CGT oppositionists, some CFDT leaders, all the tendencies of the PSU, former *Politique Hebdo*, journalists and 'gauchistes' in the 1968 tradition such as Jean-Pierre Vigier and former *Tumulte* and OCT militants (text in *Le Monde*, 24 June 1983).

39. 'Au Bureau Politique du 21 mars' in *Autogestion-l'Alternative*, 31 March 1983, p.10.

40. Howard Barker, *No End of Blame, scenes of overcoming* (London, John Calder, n.d.), p.55.

POSTFACE:
FRANCE AND THE EUROPEAN PEACE MOVEMENT
E P Thompson

I would like to raise some political and cultural issues which have not been fully explored in the preceding chapters.

The crisis in Europe at the end of 1979 was not just about nuclear weapons. It was also about the growing militarisation and confrontation between the two blocs. The Afghanistan invasion was one of the events which precipitated the sense of crisis at that time. In a sense, we have in the present study been narrowing our view, perhaps too much, to nuclear strategies. I wish to suggest that one of the problems we face when we relate France, the western peace movements, and Europe as a whole, is not so much one of *nationalism* (because a country that has just gone through the Falklands war ought not to be too self-righteous about nationalism), but of a certain slippage of *internationalism*. There seems to be something off-phase in the political and cultural life of France in relation to other western European nations. There is a curious sense of separatism, which we loosely describe as 'Gaullist traditions', in the political and cultural life of France, so that the very heartbeat of internationalism in Europe has been slowed down. We cannot have an internationalist Europe without an internationalist France. France has been for so long at the centre of internationalist traditions. And yet now France, more than any other major western European nation, is somehow 'displaced'.

Some of the reasons for this have already been discussed. There is this whole trick done with logical mirrors by which France is in effect within the western military bloc, but is technically not integrated into NATO. And therefore the very important consequence follows that France was not involved in the NATO modernisation decision. Now this NATO modernisation decision was the precipitant in the recipient countries, and also in Scandinavia, for the development of a west-European international peace movement of resistance to that decision. But because it did not involve the placing of Cruise or Pershing on French territory, nor even France's formal assent to this decision, that enforced the separatism of the French position.

Along with this, there is the fuzzy political notion of a certain 'independence' attached to the *force de frappe*. Now while this both reflects and reinforces a certain nationalism in French political life, we must not forget the element of nationalism in the western peace movement. It has been precisely the growing resentment at client status within NATO to the hegemony of the United States which has been one element in transforming those peace movements into large popular national forces. This is of course particularly clear in West Germany, but it is present also in Britain, in Holland, and in Italy. It is not, therefore, a question of 'nationalism' in France and 'internationalism' in other nations. Rather, it is one of nationalist feelings of resistance to clientcy *vis-à-vis* the USA being co-opted by the peace movements in the other nations, whereas in France they have been co-opted by the military.

There has also been, for complex intellectual reasons, a certain history of cultural separatism, an intellectual separatism, in France over the last twenty years. They have even had a Gaullist PCF, not to mention a separatist marxist-structuralist theory at one stage, and a certain self-isolation in other areas of theory. And this has prevented various kinds of direct and rapid intellectual, theoretical, political dialogue.

One of the most important consequences of this, which has not been brought out sufficiently, is that the issue of human rights occupies a different space — I wouldn't say a larger space, but a different space — in the political and intellectual life of France, from the one it occupies now in Italy, Germany, Holland or Britain. I myself regard this as largely a legacy of the long posthumous Stalinism of that particular intellectual group most closely attached to the French Communist Party. The final discovery of the Gulag came extraordinarily late, was passionate, was for a period of two or three years obsessional — at the expense of any other kind of analysis and concern — and led into a human rights movement in which there are very many former communist personalities who are still in a state of shock. This has to some degree captured the internationalist tradition in France.

The western peace movement, from what I see of the French press (thinking of *Le Monde* or *Libération* for example), is constantly being misrecognised and misrepresented in Parisian discourse. The arguments and positions of a non-aligned peace movement which is *also* a movement for human rights scarcely have a presence in that area of the French press. The peace movement is assumed to be, without examination, either pacifist or philo-soviet. It is assumed to be a movement at odds with — or indifferent to — the issue of human rights. This is strengthened by the *true* traditions of Parisian internationalism: for example by the large number of very able *émigrés* from the East in Paris, and by the energies put into human rights activity and dialogue. But the human rights activity has been placed within the parameters of a Cold War dialogue, rather than within the parameters of recreating a Europe in peace and in freedom. This alternative perspective has not been effectively raised in France. As a result we have a really serious intellectual blockage, in which I have been astonished to see former communists, intellectuals, colleagues, historians — good historians — all of them blocked into positions of *either* human rights *or* peace movements, but not both forces together.

Take the example of France and the trade union and human rights issue in Poland. Poland and France have very close relations, but recently it is a Cold War type of relationship that has been established. And we in Britain have had very little help from France in trying to promote a different kind of dialogue in which the forces making for trade union rights and democracy in Poland would relate to the labour and peace forces in the West. In a sense this has been blocked, and is being blocked, partly in Paris itself.

The point I wish to make, then, is that we face a major contradiction. I should like to illustrate this by reference to Claude Bourdet. He is a most remarkable man. He is a man who came through in that central *Combat* group in the French Resistance, and was one of those voices from 1945 to 1947 who tried to find a 'third way' between Stalinism and Atlanticism. From that point on, Bourdet has consistently been a voice of the 'third way' and of a non-aligned peace movement in Europe, and indeed is now the most distinguished figure in western Europe in that non-aligned peace movement. I first met Claude Bourdet more than twenty-five years ago. It was always through him that relations between the French peace movement and CND, in its first years, were maintained. Later, through the International Confederation for Disarmament and Peace, Claude Bourdet was always 'Mr Non-aligned-Peace'. He has been for almost forty years 'Mr Non-aligned-Peace', not only in France but throughout Europe. And the contradiction is this: the ideas of the 'third way' originated in France and yet now seem so little understood in France. The rebirth of the 'third way', of the arguments of the 'third way', has not fully taken place. When the END appeal was launched in April 1980 (and Claude Bourdet had a part in the revision and drafting of it), we had a very distinguished group of signatories from France, collected partly by his efforts. And yet it seems that that group has not yet been able to impose its intellectual presence in the way it should. People in Paris now, for well over a year, have been reading what is, I think, a third-rate book by Cornélius Castoriadis *Devant la Guerre*. Castoriadis also used to be a leading voice of a certain 'third way'. But by concentrating exclusively on the 'Soviet menace', he has helped swing the balance among Parisian intellectuals in favour of Cold War discourse. And yet if you look at the signatories, at the French signatories to the END appeal, you see people of, to my mind, enormous intellectual distinction, like Pierre Bourdieu, whose input into a transcontinental discourse is so greatly needed.

This brings me back to the complexity of the main point I wanted to make: that the END appeal was not just an appeal against nuclear weapons. It was an appeal to break down the two blocs. And it had built into it clear statements about the relationship between peace and human rights, and about the necessity for exchanges between individuals and movements, East and West. And it is that argument which we should try and help our friends in France to break open at an intellectual level and at a political and theoretical level, so that the misrecognition of the western peace movement which is going on wholesale in *Le Monde*, *Libération*, and other respected journals can be ended.

There is also an important question of time-scale. Admiral Sanguinetti believes that many people in France look forward to the breaking up of the two blocs and to the creation of a collective European security system. Claude Bourdet also envisages this as a further general perspective. I am asking whether this is not an *immediate* perspective. Whether we are not *now* in a political situation when the blocs will either confront each other, or break up in extremely dangerous and destabilising ways. Can the peace movement monitor and stabilise the break-up? We have two governments in southern Europe now that are moving out of NATO, or at least were elected on a plank of moving out of NATO: Greece and Spain. We have a Polish situation, to which I think the western peace movement's response has been inadequate, in which one solution would be a central European relaxation of military tension, allowing for more Polish autonomy.

The reason I return to this problem once again is that, if we are talking about a strategy to break down both blocs, and a transcontinental internationalism, this cannot be done without the French. Simply because of France's history, and France's place, and also France's intellectual position. There is a debate to be conducted, and it is being conducted. East-European dissidents are sometimes in a position in which they play to a theatre which is either in Paris, or in London, or in New York. One such group of east-European intellectuals is now saying:

We want to have a dialogue with the western peace movement. We want to work with the western peace movement if it pledges itself to honour the Helsinki agreements. We want to ask the western peace movement to have nothing to do with 'official' peace committees if these do not support the right of other groups in our countries to work for peace and to communicate with the West.

They want this dialogue. There are some very distinguished dissidents and oppositionists in eastern Europe who really do want this dialogue.

Some of the dialogue of these constructive oppositionists who are wanting to talk to us goes direct to Paris. More intellectual dialogue between Poland and the West goes through Paris than through any other capital. And the advice they tend to be getting back from Paris is: 'Avoid the peace movement. Have nothing to do with the peace movement.' We in the European peace movement have got to attend to this situation, we must spring this trap, we must conduct a debate in Paris itself with the intellectuals concerned.

There is further cause for urgency. For the last three years, World Peace Council elements and non-aligned peace movements have managed to co-exist in Europe. This is fine as long as it is not at the loss of principle. I do not want to force engagements. It is better very often to withdraw from engagements, and let discussion continue and enlarge, and let it get into more and more places. But we may be facing a situation in which disengagement becomes no longer possible. One issue is that of the KGB's crackdown on independent peace groups in Russia. Our information is that, whatever murky cold-war fishing is going on in these waters, these independent peace groups are made up of *bona fide* Soviet citizens trying to communicate on peace issues with the West. There is no way a peace movement in the West can avoid this issue. Our opponents are going to see to it. This is an issue that is going to go on and on. Either we stop the KGB from harrassing these people, or every speech from Mrs Thatcher, Mr Reagan, or any of our opponents, is going to start off by saying: 'Look, they can't even have a peace movement in Russia.'

This is not a diversion from France. These matters go directly into our relationship with the French movement. We *must* know the position of the French movement on these questions, and a debate which touches on these sensitive issues may indeed actually transform the situation in France, because French intellectual opinion is so very sensitive to the contradictions of the human rights *versus* peace issue.

And when France begins to speak directly to this question, we in the European peace movement shall have much to gain.

BIBLIOGRAPHY

BOOKS

Ailleret,C. *L'Aventure atomique française* (Paris, Grasset, 1968)

Arnal,F. & Auban,A. *Contre la CED* (Paris, SFIO, 1953)

Aron,R. *Le Grand Débat. Initiation à la Stratégie atomique* (Paris, Calmann-Lévy, 1963)

Aron,R. *Paix et Guerre entre les Nations* (Paris, Calmann-Lévy, 1962)

Aron,R. *Peace and War: a theory of international relations* (London, Weidenfeld & Nicolson, 1966)

Artaud,D. *La Question des dettes interalliées et la reconstruction de l'Europe 1917-1929* (Lille, Université de Lille III, 1968)

Association française pour la communauté atlantique *La participation de la France à la défense de l'Europe dans le cadre de l'Alliance atlantique* (Paris, AFCA, 1975)

Bacon,J. *Les Saigneurs de la Guerre* (Paris, Presses d'Aujourd'hui, 1981)

Bahu-Leyser,D. *De Gaulle, les Français et l'Europe* (Paris, PUF, 1981)

Bariéty,J. *Les Relations franco-alllemandes après la première guerre mondiale* (Paris, Ed. Pedone, 1977)

Baudouin,R., Stak,M. & Vignemont,S. *Armée-Nation* (Paris, PUF, 1975)

Beaufre,A. *Introduction à la Stratégie* (Paris, Armand Colin, 1963)

Beaufre,A. *Dissuasion et Stratégie* (Paris, Armand Colin, 1964)

Beaufre,A. *NATO and Europe* (New York, Vintage, 1966)

Beaufre,A. *L'OTAN et l'Europe* (Paris, Calmann-Lévy, 1966)

Beaufre,A. *Stratégie de l'Action* (Paris, Colin, 1966)

Beaufre,A. *Stratégie pour Demain* (Paris, Plon, 1972)

Bell,D.S.(ed.) *Contemporary French Political Parties* (London, Croom Helm, 1982)

Berg,E. *Non-alignement et nouvel ordre mondial* (Paris, PUF, 1980)

Bergot,E. *La Guerre des appelés en Algérie, 1956-1962* (Paris, Presses de la Cité, 1981)

Bertram,C.(ed.) *The Future of Strategic Deterrence* (London, IISS, 1981)

Bertrand,M. *Pour une doctrine militaire française* (Paris, Gallimard, 1965)

Bilis,M. *Socialistes et Pacifistes, 1933-39* (Paris, Syros, 1979)

Bosc,P. *Les Notables en question* (Montpellier, Presses du Languedoc, 1977)

Bourdet,C. *Le Schisme yougoslave* (Paris, Minuit, 1955)

Bourdet,C. *L'Aventure incertaine* (Paris, Stock, 1975)

Bourdet,C. *L'Europe truquée: supranationalité - pacte atlantique - force de frappe* (Paris, Seghers, 1977)

Bouthoul,G. *Les Guerres. Eléments de Polémologie* (Paris, Payot, 1951)

Bouthoul,G. *Le Phénomène guerre* (Paris, Payot, 1982)

Bressand,A.(ed.) *Ramsès 1981* (Paris, IFRI, 1981)

Bressand,A.(ed.) *Ramsès 1982* (Paris, IFRI, 1982)

Brigot,A. & David,D. *Le Désir d'Europe. L'introuvable défense commune* (Paris, FEDN, 1980)

Brossat,A. & Potel,J.-Y. *Antimilitarisme et Révolution* (Paris, UGE 10/18, 1976)

Brossolet, Capitaine *Essai sur la non-bataille* (Paris, Belin, 1975)

Buchan,A. *The End of the Post-war Era: a New Balance of World Power* (London, Weidenfeld & Nicolson, 1974)

Buffotot,P. *Le Parti socialiste et la défense ou la recherche de la fonction patriotique* (Paris, Université Paris X, 1981)

Burrows,B. & Edwards,G. *The Defence of Western Europe* (London, Butterworth, 1982)

Cagnat,R., Doly,G. & Fontaine,P. *Euroshima* (Paris, Media, 1979)

Calder,N. *Les Armements modernes* (Paris, 1975)

Carlton,D. & Schaerf,C. (eds.) *The Arms Race in the 1980s* (London, Macmillan, 1982)

Castellan,G. *Histoire de l'Armée* (Paris, PUF, 1948)

Castoriadis,C. *Devant la guerre. I. Les Réalités* (Paris, Fayard, 1981)

Centre des Démocrates Sociaux *L'Autre Solution* (Paris, CDS, 1977)

Cerny,P.G. *The Politics of Grandeur. Ideological Aspects of De Gaulle's Foreign Policy* (Cambridge, CUP, 1980)

Cerny,P.G.(ed.) *Social Movements and Protest in France* (London, Frances Pinter, 1982)

Challener,R.D. *The French Theory of the Nation in Arms, 1866-1939* (New York, Columbia UP, 1955)

Chantebout,B. *L'Organisation de la Défense nationale en France depuis la fin de la seconde guerre mondiale* (Paris, LGDJ, 1967)

Charlot,J.(ed.) *Les Français et De Gaulle* (Paris, IFOP, n.d.)

Charlot,J. *L'UNR:Etude du pouvoir au sein d'un parti politique* (Paris, Colin, 1967)

Charlot,J. *The Gaullist Phenomenon: the Gaullist Movement in the Fifth Republic* (London, Allen and Unwin, 1971)

Chevènement,J.-P. & Messmer,P. *Le Service militaire* (Paris, Balland, 1977)

Close,R. *L'Europe sans défense* (Paris, Arts et Voyages, 1977)

Close,R. *Encore un effort... et nous aurons définitivement perdu la troisième guerre mondiale* (Paris, Belfond, 1982)

Couve de Murville,M. *Une Politique étrangère, 1958-1969* (Paris, Plon, 1971)

Defrasne,J. *Le Pacifisme* (Paris, PUF, 1983)

Delmas,C. et al. *L'Avenir de l'Alliance atlantique* (Paris, Berger-Levrault, 1961)

Delmas,C. *La Stratégie nucléaire* (Paris, PUF, 1963)

Delmas,C. *Armements nucléaires et guerre froide* (Paris, PUF, 1973)

Delmas,C. *Le Désarmement* (Paris, PUF, 1979)

Delmas,C. *La Coexistence pacifique* (Paris, PUF, 1980)

Delmas,C. *L'OTAN* (Paris, 5e édition, PUF, 1981)

Delmas,C. *Le Pacte de Varsovie* (Paris, PUF, 1981)

Delmas,C. *La politique militaire soviétique* (Paris, PUF, 1983)

Deutsch,K. et al. *France, Germany and the Western Alliance* (New York, Scribners, 1967)

Docre,B. & Mars,P. *M. comme Militaire* (Paris, Alain Moreau, 1979)

Doly,G. *Stratégie France-Europe* (Paris, Media, 1977)

Dubos,J.-F. *Ventes d'armes: une politique* (Paris, Gallimard, 1974)

Ducasse,A. et al. *Vie et Mort des Français, 1914-1918* (Paris, Hachette, 1959)

Duroselle,J.-B. *Histoire diplomatique de 1919 à nos jours* (Paris, 8e édition, Dalloz, 1981)

Dutailly,H. *Les problèmes de l'armée de terre française, 1935-39* (Paris, Imp. Nat., 1980)

Duverger,M. *Political Parties* (London, Methuen, 1959)

Duverger,M. *La République et le régime présidentiel* (Paris, Fayard, 1961)

Eden,A. *L'Epreuve de Force* (Paris, Plon, 1965)

Ferrard,S. *Les Matériels de l'armée française* (Paris, Lavauzelle, 1982)

Fontaine,A. *L'Alliance atlantique à l'heure du dégel* (Paris, Calmann-Lévy, 1959)

Fontaine,A. *Un seul lit pour deux rêves. Histoire de la détente, 1962-1981* (Paris, Fayard, 1981)

Fontaine,A. *Histoire de la Guerre froide* (Paris, 2e édition, Seuil, 1983)

Fox,W.T.R. & Schelling,W.R. *European Security and the Atlantic System* (New York, Columbia UP, 1973)

Frailé,R. *La Guerre biologique et chimique: le sort d'une interdiction* (Paris, Economica, 1982)

François-Poncet,A. *Réflexions sur la CED* (Paris, Marx, 1953)

Frankenstein,R. *Le Prix du réarmement français, 1935-39* (Paris, Sorbonne, 1982)

Freedman,L. *Britain and Nuclear Weapons* (London, Macmillan, 1980)

Freymontier,J. *Pied de Guerre* (Paris, Fayard, 1982)

Furniss,E.S. *De Gaulle and the French Army: a Crisis in Civil-Military Relations* (New York, 20th Century Fund, 1964)

Fursdon,E. *The European Defence Community: A History* (London, Macmillan, 1980)

Gallois,P.-M. *Stratégie de l'âge nucléaire* (Paris, Calmann-Lévy, 1960)

Gallois,P.-M. *Paradoxes de la paix* (Paris, Presses de la Cité, 1967)

Gallois,P.-M. *L'Adieu aux armées* (Paris, Albin Michel, 1976)

Gallois,P.-M. *Le Renoncement: de la France défendue à l'Europe protégée* (Paris, Plon, 1977)

Galtung,J. *The European Community: a superpower in the making* (Oslo/London, 1973)

Gaulle,C. de *Le Fil de l'épée* (Paris, Berger-Levrault, 1932)

Gaulle,C. de *Vers l'Armée de Métier* (Paris, Berger-Levrault, 1934)

Gaulle,C. de *La France et son armée* (Paris, Plon, 1938)

Gaulle,C. de *Mémoires de Guerre* (Paris, Plon, 1959)

Gaulle,C. de *Discours et Messages* (Paris, Plon, 1970)

Giesbert,F.-O. *François Mitterrand ou la tentation de l'histoire* (Paris, Seuil, 1977)

Gilpin,R. *France in the Age of the Scientific State* (Princeton, Princeton UP, 1968)

Girardet,R. *La Société militaire française dans la société contemporaine* (Paris, Plon, 1953)

Girardet,R. *La crise militaire française, 1945-62* (Paris, Colin, 1964)

Girardet,R. *Problèmes contemporains de défense nationale* (Paris, Dalloz, 1974)

Goldberg,H. *The Life of Jaurès* (Madison, UWP, 1962)

Goldblat,J. *Agreements for Arms Control: a critical survey* (London, Taylor & Francis, 1982)

Goldschmidt,B. *Les Rivalités atomiques, 1939-66* (Paris, Fayard, 1967)

Gombin,R. *Les Socialistes et la guerre* (Paris, Mouton, 1970)

Gorce,P.-M. de la *La République et son armée* (Paris, Fayard, 1963)

Grosser,A. *Les Occidentaux: les pays d'Europe et les Etats-Unis depuis la guerre* (Paris, 2e édition, Seuil, 1983)

Grosser,A. *The Western Alliance* (London, Macmillan, 1980)

Grosser,A. *La Quatrième République et sa politique étrangère* (Paris, Colin, 1964)

Guérin,D. & Gengenbach,R. *L'Armée en France* (Paris, Filipacchi, 1974)

Haenel,H. *La Défense nationale* (Paris, PUF, 1982)

Hagen,L.S.(ed.) *The Crisis in Western Security* (London, Croom Helm, 1982)

Hamon,L. *La Stratégie contre la guerre* (Paris, Grasset, 1966)

Hamon,L. *Le Sanctuaire désenclavé* (Paris, FEDN, 1982)

Harrison,M. *The Reluctant Ally: France and Atlantic Security* (Baltimore, Johns Hopkins UP, 1981)

Hernu,C. *Soldat-Citoyen: essai sur la défense et la sécurité de la France* (Paris, Flammarion, 1975)

Hernu,C. *Chroniques d'attente* (Paris, Tema, 1977)

Hernu,C. *Nous... les grands* (Lyon, Boursier, 1980)

Hoffmann,S. *In Search of France* (Cambridge, Mass., Harvard U.P., 1963)

Hoffmann,S. *Primacy or World Order* (New York, McGraw-Hill, 1978)

Hoffmann,S. *La nouvelle guerre froide* (Paris, Berger-Levrault, 1983)
Huntington,S.P. *The Common Defense: Strategic Programs in National Politics* (New York, Columbia UP, 1961)
Huntzinger,J. *Europes* (Paris, Ramsay, 1977)
Imbert,A. *L'UEO* (Paris, LGDJ, 1968)
Janowitz,M. *The Professional Soldier* (Chicago, Chicago UP, 1960)
Jaurès,J. *L'Armée nouvelle* (Paris, L'Humanité, 1915)
Johnson,R.W. *The Long March of the French Left* (London, Macmillan, 1980)
Joxe,A.(ed.) *Demain la guerre?* (Paris, Editions ouvrières, 1981)
Kaiser,K. et al. *La Sécurité de l'occident: bilan et orientations* (Paris, IFRI, 1981)
Kaldor,M. *The Disintegrating West* (Harmondsworth, Penguin Books, 1979)
Kaldor,M. *The Baroque Arsenal* (London, André Deutsch, 1982)
Kaldor,M. & Smith,D. *Disarming Europe* (London, Merlin, 1982)
Katzenstein,P.J.(ed.) *Between Power and Plenty: Foreign Economic Policies of Advanced Industrial States* (Madison, UWP, 1978)
Klein,J. *L'Entreprise du désarmement* (Paris, Cujas, 1964)
Kohl,W. *French Nuclear Diplomacy* (Princeton, Princeton UP, 1971)
Kolodziej,E. *French International Policy under De Gaulle and Pompidou* (Ithaca, NY, Cornell UP, 1974)
Kriegel,A. *Les Communistes français* (Paris, Seuil, 1970)
Krop,P. *Les Socialistes et l'armée* (Paris, PUF, 1983)
Kuisel,R. *Capitalism and the State in Modern France* (Cambridge, CUP, 1981)
Kulski,W. *De Gaulle and the World: the Foreign Policy of the Fifth Republic* (Syracuse, NY, Syracuse UP, 1966)
Labayle-Couhat,J. *Les Flottes de Combat* (Paris, Editions maritimes, 1981)
Lacroix,P.(ed.) *Eviter la guerre* (Paris, Maspéro, 1983)
Larminat,J. de *L'Armée européenne* (Paris, Berger-Levrault, 1952)
Launay,B. de *Le Poker nucléaire* (Paris, Syros, 1983)
Lavau,G. *A Quoi sert le PCF?* (Paris, Fayard, 1981)
Leebaert,D. *European Security: Prospects for the 1980s* (Lexington, Heath, 1979)
Lefever,E. *Les Armes nucléaires dans le monde* (Paris, Economica, 1981)
Lellouche,P. *La Science et le désarmement* (Paris, IFRI, 1981)
Lellouche,P.(ed.) *La Sécurité de l'Europe dans les années 1980* (Paris, IFRI, 1981)
Lellouche,P.(ed.) *Pacifisme et dissuasion: la contestation pacifiste et l'avenir de la sécurité de l'Europe* (Paris, IFRI, 1983)
Lerner,D. & Aron,R. *La Querelle de la CED* (Paris, Colin, 1956)
Lutz,D.S. *La Guerre mondiale malgré nous?* (Paris, Maspéro, 1983)
Malbosc,F. *Civils, si vous saviez* (Paris, Maspéro, 1977)
Mandelbaum,M. *The Nuclear Question: the United States and Nuclear Weapons, 1946-1976* (Cambridge, CUP, 1979)
Manel,M. *L'Europe sans défense?* (Paris, Berger-Levrault, 1982)
Marrane,G. *L'Armée de la France démocratique* (Paris, Editions sociales, 1977)
Martin,M.L. *Warriors to Managers: the French Military Establishment since 1945* (Chapel Hill NC, UNCP, 1981)
Massigli,R. *Une Comédie des erreurs, 1943-56* (Paris, Plon, 1978)
Melandri,P. *L'Alliance atlantique* (Paris, Gallimard, 1979)
Melman,S. *The Permanent War Economy: American Capitalism in Decline* (New York, Simon and Schuster, 1974)
Mendl,W. *Deterrence and Persuasion: French Nuclear Armament in the Context of National Policy* (London, Faber and Faber, 1970)
Merle,M. *Les Problèmes de la sécurité européenne* (Paris, IEP, 1973)
Merle,M. *Forces et enjeux dans les relations internationales* (Paris, Economica, 1981)
Meyer,M. *Le Mal franco-allemand* (Paris, Denoël, 1979)
Meyer-Spiegler,M. *Antimilitarisme et refus du service militaire dans la France contemporaine*

(Paris, FNSP — thesis — 1969)

Mitrani,D. *Où va le service militaire?* (Paris, Tema, 1974)

Moch,J. *La Folie des hommes* (Paris, Laffont, 1954)

Moch,J. *En retard d'une paix* (Paris, Laffont, 1958)

Moch,J. *Non à la force de frappe* (Paris, Laffont, 1963)

Moch,J. *Histoire du réarmement allemand depuis 1950* (Paris, Laffont, 1965)

Moisi,D. *Crises et guerres au XXe siècle: analogies et différences* (Paris, IFRI, 1981)

Monteil,V. *Les Officiers* (Paris, Seuil, 1958)

Morse,E. *Foreign Policy and Interdependence in Gaullist France* (Princeton, Princeton UP, 1973)

Moulin, Club Jean *La Force de frappe et le citoyen* (Paris, Seuil, 1963)

NATO *Documents fondamentaux* (Brussels, Nato, 1981)

Newhouse,J. *De Gaulle and the Anglo-Saxons* (New York, Viking, 1970)

Nobécourt,J. *Une histoire politique de l'armée, 1919-1942* (Paris, Seuil, 1967)

Nugent,N. & Lowe,D. *The Left in France* (London, Macmillan, 1982)

Parti communiste français *Défense nationale: indépendance, paix et désarmement* (Paris, PCF, 1976)

Parti républicain *Le Projet républicain* (Paris, Flammarion, 1978)

Parti socialiste *Energie: l'autre politique* (Paris, Club Socialiste du Livre, 1981)

Parti socialiste *Paix, sécurité et désarmement* (Paris, PS, 1982)

Parti socialiste *Projet socialiste pour la France des années 1980* (Paris, PS, 1980)

Parti socialiste unifié *Pour une France non-alignée* (Paris, Syros, 1981)

Pelletier,R. & Ravet,S. *Le Mouvement des Soldats* (Paris, Maspéro, 1976)

Perrault,G. *Les Parachutistes* (Paris, Seuil, 1961)

Pigasse,J.-P. *Le deuxième pilier. Données et réflexions sur la sécurité européenne* (Paris, FEDN, 1980)

Pigasse,J.-P. *Le Bouclier d'Europe: vers une autonomie militaire de la communauté européenne* (Paris, Seghers, 1982)

Planchais,J. *Une histoire politique de l'armée, 1940-1967* (Paris, Seuil, 1967)

Poirier,L. *Des Stratégies nucléaires* (Paris, Hachette, 1977)

Poirier,L. *Essais de stratégie nucléaire* (Paris, FEDN, 1982)

Prins,G.(ed.) *Defended to Death* (Harmondsworth, Penguin Books, 1983)

Rassemblement pour la République *Propositions pour la France* (Paris, Stock, 1978)

Rawlinson,R. *Larzac – a victory for non-violence* (London, Quaker Peace and Service, 1982)

Renouvin,P. & Duroselle,J.-B. *Introduction à l'Histoire des relations internationales* (Paris, Colin, 1964)

Richard,D. *Le Procès de Draguignan* (Paris, Rocher, 1975)

Riche,D. *La Guerre chimique et biologique: l'horrible visage de la troisième guerre mondiale* (Paris, Belfond, 1982)

Rioux,J.-P. *La France de la Quatrième République* (Paris, Seuil, 2 volumes, 1981-83)

Robrieux,P. *Histoire intérieure du PCF* (Paris, Fayard, 3 volumes, 1981-83)

Rogers,P. *A Guide to Nuclear Weapons* (Bradford, University of Bradford, 1981)

Roqueplo,J.-C. *Le Statut des militaires* (Paris, Documentation française, 1979)

Rose,F. de *La France et la défense de l'Europe* (Paris, Seuil, 1976)

Rose,F. de *Contre la Stratégie des Curiaces* (Paris, Julliard, 1983)

Roucaute,Y. *Le PCF et l'armée* (Paris, PUF, 1983)

Ruehl,L. *Les Neuf et l'OTAN* (London, IAAI, 1974)

Ruehl,L. *La Politique militaire de la Cinquième République* (Paris, FNSP, 1976)

Saaty,T.L. *Mathematical Models of Arms Control and Disarmament* (New York, John Wiley & Sons, 1968)

Sanguinetti, Alexandre *Histoire du Soldat* (Paris, Ramsay, 1979)

Sanguinetti, Antoine *Le Fracas des Armes* (Paris, Hachette, 1975)

Sanguinetti, Antoine *Le Devoir de Parler* (Paris, Fernand Nathan, 1981)

Saul,J. *Mort d'un général* (Paris, Seuil, 1977)

Schell,J. *Le Destin de la Terre* (Paris, Albin Michel, 1982)

Serman,W. *Les Officiers français dans la nation, 1848-1914* (Paris, Aubier, 1982)

Simonnot,P. *Mémoire adressé à Monsieur le premier ministre sur la guerre, l'économie et les autres passions qu'il s'agit de gouverner* (Paris, Seuil, 1981)

Soppelsa,J. *Géographie des armements* (Paris, Masson, 1980)

Stevenson,D. *French war aims against Germany* (Oxford, Oxford UP, 1982)

Sudreau,P. *La Stratégie de l'absurde* (Paris, Plon, 1980)

Talbot,S. *Endgame: the Inside Story of SALT II* (New York, Harper and Row, 1979)

Tebib,R. *L'Armée en France, sa philosophie et ses traditions* (Paris, 1982)

Toulat,J. *Combattants de la non-violence* (Paris, Cerf, 1983)

Touraine,A. *La Prophétie antinucléaire* (Paris, Seuil, 1980)

Union pour la Démocratie Française *Une Doctrine de défense pour la France* (Paris, UDF, 1980)

Union pour la Démocratie Française *La Loi de programmation militaire nécessaire à la France en 1983: propositions de l'UDF* (Paris, UDF, 1983)

Vaisse,M. *Sécurité d'abord. La politique française en matière de désarmement, 1930-34* (Paris, Pedone, 1981)

Valentin,F. *Une politique de défense pour la France* (Paris, Calmann-Lévy, 1980)

Vasto,L. del *Technique de la non-violence* (Paris, Denoël, 1971)

Wall,I. *French Communism in the Era of Stalin* (Westport, Ct., Greenwood Press, 1983)

Whetten,L. *New International Communism* (Lexington, Heath, 1982)

Williams,S.(ed.) *Socialism in France* (London, Frances Pinter, 1983)

Willis,F.R. *The French Paradox* (Stanford, Hoover Press, 1982)

Wright,V. *The Government and Politics of France* (London, Hutchinson, 1978)

Yergin,D. *La Paix saccagée: les origines de la guerre froide et la division de l'Europe* (Paris, Balland, 1980)

Young,R.J. *In Command of France: French Policy-Making and Military Planning* (Cambridge, Ma., Harvard UP, 1978)

Zeldin,T. *France, 1848-1945* (Oxford, Clarendon, 1977)

Zorgbibe,C. *Le Risque de Guerre* (Paris, ERPP, 1981)

Zysman,J. *Political Strategies for Industrial Order: Market, State and Industry in France* (Berkeley, UCP, 1977)

REVIEWS and ARTICLES

We have not attempted to list all the articles referred to in the footnotes to the present volume, or to establish a bibliography of relevant journal articles. These run into their thousands. The following is a list of specialist journals, subdivided into specialist categories.

Defence, Strategic Studies and Foreign Policy Journals

Cahiers d'Etudes Stratégiques (Periodic: Centre interdisciplinaire de recherches sur la paix et d'études stratégiques (CIRPES), GSD-EHESS, 54, Boulevard Raspail, 75006 Paris)

Défense Nationale (Monthly: 1, Place Joffre, 75007 Paris)

Etudes polémologiques (Bi-annual: Institut Français de Polémologie, Hôtel national des Invalides, 75007 Paris)

Politique Etrangère (Quarterly: Institut Français des Relations Internationales, 6, rue Ferrus, 75014 Paris)

Politique Internationale (Quarterly: 11, rue du Bois de Boulogne, 75016 Paris)

Stratégique (Quarterly: Fondation pour les Etudes de Défense Nationale, Hôtel des Invalides, 75007 Paris)

In addition, there are numerous official army, navy and air-force journals published under the aegis of the Ministry of Defence, 14, rue St. Dominique, 75007 Paris.

Specialist Reviews Published by Political Parties

Armée Nouvelle (Quarterly: Conventions pour l'Armée Nouvelle, 25, rue du Louvre, 75001 Paris — PS)

Correspondance Armée-Nation (Occasional: Comité national de liaison défense-armée-nation, PCF, 2, Place du Colonel Fabien, 75019 Paris)

Nouvelle Revue Socialiste (Bi-monthly: 10, rue de Solférino, 75007 Paris Cedex 07 — PS)

Cahiers du Communisme (Monthly: PCF, 2, Place du Colonel Fabien, 75019 Paris Cedex 19)

International Journals and Reviews

Adelphi Papers (UK)
Armed Forces and Society (USA)
Atlantic Community Quarterly (USA)
Etudes internationales (Canada)
Europa-Archiv (West Germany)
Foreign Affairs (USA)
International Affairs (UK)
International Organisation (USA)
International Security (USA)
Jane's Weapon Systems (UK)
The Military Balance (UK)
Military Review (USA)
NATO's Fifteen Nations
Orbis (USA)
Review of International Studies (USA)
Revue internationale de défense
Revue de l'OTAN
SIPRI Yearbook (Sweden)
Strategic Review (USA)
Survival (UK)
World Military and Social Expenditures (USA)
The World Today (UK)

Recent Special Issues on Defence by French Journals

Après-Demain (180, 235, 236)
Esprit (10/1975, 2/1983)
La Nef (1953, 1961)
Revue d'Economie politique (1982)
Revue française de sociologie (1961)
Politique Aujourd'hui (2/1983)
Projet (79, 104, 167)
Les Temps modernes (435)
Tribune internationale PSU (5/1983)

Journals and Publications Issued by Peace Organisations

Alerte atomique (Bi-monthly: Mouvement pour le Désarmement, la Paix et la Liberté, BP2135, 34026 Montpellier)
Alternatives non-violentes (Quarterly: Mouvement pour une Alternative Non-Violente, Craintilleux, 42210 Montrond)
Bulletin du CODENE (Quarterly: CODENE, 10, rue de Paris, Longpont-sur-Orge, 91310 Montlhéry)
Cahiers du Forum (Periodic: Forum pour l'Indépendance et la Paix (FIP), 23, rue Bréa, 75006 Paris)
Cahiers de la Réconciliation (Monthly: Mouvement international de la Réconciliation, 99, Bd. Beaumarchais, 75003 Paris)
Le Calumet (Bi-monthly: Comité jeunesse pour la paix, 35, rue de Clichy, 75009 Paris)
Combat pour la Paix (Bi-monthly: Mouvement de la Paix, 35, rue de Clichy, 75009 Paris)
Disarmament Campaigns (Monthly: Postbus 18747, 2502 ES, The Hague, Netherlands)
END Journal (Bi-monthly: END, 227, Seven Sisters Road, London N4)
Gardarem Lo Larzac (Monthly: Paysans du Larzac, Potensac, 12100 Millau)
Le Journal des Objecteurs (Periodic: Mouvement des Objecteurs de Conscience, c/o CCSC, 8, Villa du Parc Montsouris, 75014 Paris)
Le Journal de la Paix (Monthly: Pax Christi France, 44, rue de la Santé, 75014 Paris)
Non-Violence politique (Monthly: MAN, 20, rue du Dévidet, 45200 Montargis)
Pacific Bulletin (Bi-monthly: Pacific Concerns Resource Center, P.O.Box 27692, Honolulu, Hawaii 96827)
Paix et Liberté (Quarterly: Ligue Internationale des Femmes pour la Paix et la Liberté, 24, Quai Louis Blériot, 75016 Paris)
Union Pacifiste (Monthly: Union pacifiste de France, 4, rue Lazare-Hoche, 92100 Boulogne)

INDEX